THE BAWDY CHRONICLES

"Ah, Yes, I Remember it Well"

A MEMOIR
BY
BILL BORDY

RoseDog❧Books

PITTSBURGH, PENNSYLVANIA 15222

For more information or to order additional books,
please contact:
RoseDog Books
701 Smithfield Street
Pittsburgh, Pennsylvania 15222
U.S.A.
1-800-834-1803
www.rosedogbookstore.com

ACKNOWLEDGMENTS

A Special Thanks to:

Clarence Schotter
Who started it all by compiling the history of the Schotter Family

Herb Teison
Who wrote a funny history of the Teitelbaum Family

Cordell Ley "Butch" Carmalt
My nephew, who wanted to know more about his family

HOMESTEAD, PENNSYLVANIA

THE BEGINNING - FLYING

PREFACE

The first thing I can actually remember is flying through the air, bouncing off the electric wire, breaking through my mother's clothes line, and landing in her clothes basket. My left leg didn't quite make it into the basket; it was broken way up near my crotch. That was the summer of 1934, when I was three and a half years old. There is still a scar there, where the bone protruded. To this day, while I'm sleeping, I relive that sensation of flying. Although, in my dreams, I always save myself by "swimming," in the air.

THE BORDY FAMILY - SUMMER OF 1934

BILL, PEARL, RUTH, ED, SAM, KATE, MARTHA, MARIE, MAMA & PAPA

Our house was located at 117 East Seventh Avenue, in Homestead, Pennsylvania, a suburb of Pittsburgh. It was an old two story building, with a cement yard, that was located one block north of the cat houses, and two blocks north of the railroad tracks. On the other side of the tracks was the U.S. Steel Mill, and The Mesta Machine Corporation. Then, came the Monongahela River. In those days, kids used to swim in it, despite the turds that floated there, and the waste from The Mill.

The front of our house had been transformed into the Sam Bordy Shoe Repair Shop. My father believed in living in the same place where he worked. That way, he not only saved money on rent, but he could always have fresh

1

meals brought to him, whenever he wanted. And, he could keep an eye on his growing family.

How did I come to be flying that day? Well, I'll tell you. Our house had a second story porch, where I had been placed to play, although my brother Sam told me, years later, that I had somehow crawled through his bedroom window, out onto the porch, of my own volition. In any case, I was alone that day, I know not why. Usually, my six year old sister, Pearl, and my eight year old sister, Ruth, would be playing there; this was their playroom. They must have been elsewhere, probably with the neighbors' kids. They really didn't like playing with their little brother, in any case.

On that porch, the girls had a tea set, and a small wooden table, with chairs. That's where they had their little tea parties. Somehow, the legs got broken off the table, and the top was leaning against the railing. I was playing on the floor, when I heard the sound of a train passing, and tooting. So, I wobbled to the railing to watch it pass. It was too difficult to observe from where I was, so I climbed up onto the edge of the table top. It slid, I fell, and I flew. Whee!

My fifteen year old sister, Katy, was in the yard below, helping my mother hang up clothes, when I came crashing to her feet. Mama panicked, so Katy carried me into Papa's shop to find out what to do. He didn't think there was anything wrong with me, but after Katy showed him the jutting bone in my thigh, off to the hospital we went.

It must have been on a Monday, because my mother always washed clothes on Mondays. All her life, her set routine was that she'd wash clothes on Monday, iron on Tuesday and Wednesday, shop on Thursday, then clean house on Friday so it would be presentable for the week-end, "just in case we have company."

Saturday mornings, she would make bread and rolls for the week-end meals, by mixing and kneading her dough, then setting it aside for an hour or so to "rise." She'd grease up her bread pans and cupcake tins for her three sectioned "cloverleaf" dinner rolls. Then, into the oven they'd go. I usually talked her into saving some of the dough to make us some *fank. Fank*, pronounced "funk," is a Hungarian fried bread, or doughnut, which I *loved.* She would take a wad of the dough, stretch it thin, then drop it in deep fat to fry. After it was done, she'd sprinkle it with sugar or salt. I liked both sugar and salt. She'd put on the sugar, I'd add the salt. Yummy!

Usually, the entire family would make it to her boiled chuck and dumpling dinner, on Sundays. Everyone raved about what a good cook she was. She boiled the hell out of the chuck, added potatoes, carrots, some celery and an onion, then let it simmer until everyone came home from church, or from wherever. When everyone was ready to sit down and eat, she would drop tablespoons of gunk, she made out of cream of wheat, into the broth to make "dumplings." Mama called it her "Gum Boat Soup." That was the first course, along with her cloverleaf rolls.

2

"Oh, Mama, this is sooo good!" all would coo. It was so good that most doused the broth with ketchup, to give it some flavor.

The next course was the chuck, potatoes and carrots, spread out on a platter. More ketchup, or mustard, or horse radish! That was our Hungarian/German boiled dinner. The main course was always followed with thin, red Jello gelatin, usually with bananas, and sometimes put over chocolate cake. On special holidays, we had vanilla ice cream on top of that, too. That was my favorite.

Sunday afternoons, she took it easy. That was her "day of rest," although, often, she would get on a streetcar to visit her friends, or wait at home to be visited by them. Not too many people had telephones in those days, so it would become a great game to see who would get to whose house first. So often, she would be trying to visit the Landels, at the same time they were trying to visit her. No matter, occasionally they did meet, and sit in the "untouchable, guest only, Living Room," and speak German for hours, or was it Hungarian? Both sounded the same to me.

I don't remember Papa driving Mama and me the hospital, but I do remember waking up there, with my leg in a caste, suspended from above the bed.

What stands out in my mind, about my stay in the hospital, was not the pain or discomfort; it was big, fat gum drops. I discovered gum drops, and love them to this day, especially the red ones and black ones. It was my fifteen year old sister Katy who brought them to me, first.

She had recently discovered The Salvation Army, and became an avid member; that's probably where she got the drops. Our family was always getting goodies from them. Not too many years later, she joined "the Army," went to their college and became a Lieutenant, and an ordained minister. She *did* start something with those gum drops.

My orders were, that no one got in to visit me, unless they brought me gum drops. I don't remember my brothers Ed and Sam visiting at all. They were out doing boy things, I guess. Ed was eleven, and I think by that time, he had already gotten into "trouble." I never did find out what that "trouble" was, but eventually, he had to leave regular school, and was went to a trade school, instead.

Sam was thirteen and a half, ten years older than I. Soon he would go to work at the Law and Finance Building, as an elevator operator. He was a pretty good looking kid, and many of the anxious women, who worked there, were captivated. They had to wait until he "grew up," at least until he was sixteen, before they took advantage of him.

My two oldest sisters, Marie and Martha, worked there doing stenographic work, for the various companies in that building. They were two pretty smart girls to start their own business, at the ages of twenty and eighteen.

Marie had graduated from Drake Business School, did free lance work for business men in the Grant building, and called her business, The Grant Secretarial Service. She was beautiful, personable, and was in great demand. Business was so good, that she took a small office in the nearby Law and Finance Building.

Then, Martha went to work with her. She wasn't beautiful like Marie, but she was pretty, "cute," and flirtatious. I don't know if they got work because they were good stenographers, or because of their looks, probably a little of each.

Marie and Martha brought me gum drops, too. They were those tiny, acrid ones, that I didn't like at all, and told them so, too. The next time they came they had better bring me those big ones! They did. After several visits, the store where they bought the drops ran out, so they substituted them with "green leaves," spearmint gum drops, in the shape of leaves. I was quite perturbed, but they insisted I try them, and wow! I think I like green leaves even better than the regular drops.

Because of the Depression, business was bad all over. Many workers had been laid off from the Steel Mill, which affected Papa's business, drastically. The steel workers were the brunt of his business.

He had always dreamed of going to sunny Hollywood, California, where the streets were "paved with gold." So, one day, he and his friend Lajosbacsy, Louis, ventured there, during the height of the Depression; Papa went to Hollywood to mine some of those golden nuggets.

The next thing, I remember, took place on October 28th, 1934. That's the day my baby sister, Sue, arrived. She was delivered by a repulsive lady named Mrs. Pfaff, who carried a big, black satchel. I disliked her, immediately. When she told me that she had brought my mother's new baby, to the house, in that satchel, I disliked her even more.

Mrs. Pfaff had arrived in the early evening, and was still there in the morning, when I got out of bed and went into the bathroom, to pee. That woman was there bathing this ugly, little thing in the bathtub, that she said was my baby sister.

The baby's belly button was bleeding, so I started pounding on Mrs. Pfaff's back, "You mean old lady, you made by baby sister's belly button bleed. Get out of here and go home."

Little did I realize that, she was the woman who brought me into the

4

world, as well as most of my other brothers and sisters.

Around Christmas time, I did a terrible thing. There was a neighborhood boy who had receive a kid's gardening set, as a Christmas present. It included a hoe, a spade, and a rake. His family had invited me over to their house to play. He was so smug and proud of this kit, and wanted to show it off, but wouldn't let anyone touch any of the implements. By accident, his rake brushed my forehead, which gave me a slight scratch. Naturally, I screamed, and cried, and rushed home to Mama. Poor little "Mikey" was scared to death.

The next day, he came by the house with the gardening tools, and by way of an apology, offered to let me play with them. I picked up the rake, like I was going to hit him, and he cowered. I said, "Don't worry, Mikey, I ain't gonna hitcha."

He didn't quite believe me, and he was right. I cold heartedly hit him, hard, on the head, with the prong end of the rake. Revenge was mine. Of course, there was a big to-do about the whole thing. Why was everybody so upset? After all, didn't he hit me with the rake first?

The following two summers, I remember many afternoons, and early evenings, where most, of the brothers and sisters, would hang out in front of the house, along with the neighboring kids. I'd sneak out, to join them.

We had immigrant kids, from all over Europe, in Homestead. Our neighbors were the Mastrillas, the Korpacis, the Carpowitzes, the Francettas, the Manteas, the Hiltons, and many whose names we've forgotten.

A favorite chant in our neighborhood was: "Hunky, Deigo, Sheenie, Wop, you eat spaghetti with the worms on top." We didn't realize that we were being offensive, this was just a fun way we kids greeted each other. After all, all of our parents were "Hunkies," or "Deigos," or "Wops," from all over Europe. We Bordys were Hunkies, and proud of it.

On Sunday evenings, we were often taken to the Hungarian Church. Mama's best friend, Mrs. Albright, and her son Bob, also attended. What amazed me was, that Bob, and all the other kids, spoke Hungarian, as well as English.

On Saturday afternoons, Katy, Martha, and sometimes Marie, would set their hair with "gook" and wave clamps. The green "gook" was actually called Dr. Ellis Wave

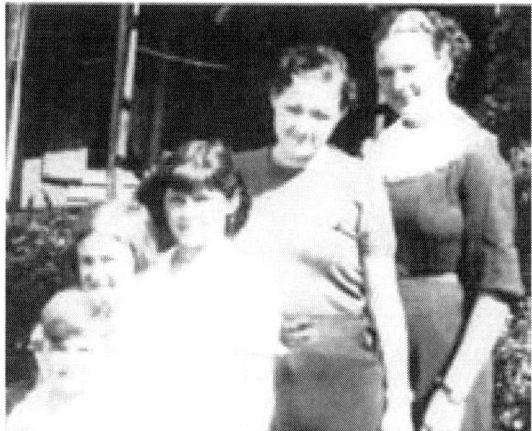

5

Set. They'd gook their hair, comb it through, then add hair clamps, carefully adjusting them to make waves. After the gook dried and hardened, they could comb it out, and have beautiful waves.

The first time I saw this, I begged to have it done, too. Katy would usually comply. This became a weekly ritual, Katy setting my hair. To this day, I still have a wave in my hair, thanks to Dr. Ellis Wave Set, and Katy.

As evening approached, Sam and Ed would come out to the front of the house, to join us. I had seen one of the big, neighborhood boys pick up a little kid, and play "airplane," with him. That meant, he picked up the kid, by his hand and foot, and swung him around in a circle. It looked like fun, so I asked the big kid to play airplane with me, too. He told me to go ask my brothers, which I did.

The first time, Sam and Ed each took a hand and an ankle, then swung me gently, back and forth. No, no, that wasn't what I wanted. I wanted to fly like an airplane. "Swing me 'round," I demanded.

Ed let go, and Sam started "flying" me, gently, at first, then he got carried away. He swung me high, he swung me low. He swung me higher, and higher, then lower and lower, then faster and faster.

At first I giggled and laughed. "Whee. More, more. Faster, faster."

He obliged. Soon, I was screaming to stop, stop. But Sam kept on, and on. Finally, he slowed down, came to a stop, and put me on my reeling feet. After I fell, I recovered, stopped screaming, and began laughing. "Do it, again, Sam. Do it, again." He obliged. I guess he was exhausted after the first "flight," because he barely got me off the ground, the second time.

There were many flights after that. Each week, someone would "fly" me until I got to be too big. None ever compared to that first flight I got from Sam and Ed. Ed would try to fly me by himself, but he wasn't big enough, or strong enough.

As I grew bigger, I began sneaking out of the yard to explore the neighborhood. I had seen some of it when Mama took me shopping with her, but now it was time to discover Seventh Avenue, by myself. One day, I managed to get out of the yard, turn left, and walk down the street.

What I noticed most was the sugary smells of Wolford's Bakery, and a sweet, pungent smell, emanating from Stafford's Fish Market, the next door restaurant. All the Eighth Avenue businesses had their rear entrances on Seventh. Our street was, really, a kind of glorified alley, kept busy with garbage pick-ups, and deliveries.

It was not so busy that I couldn't cross the street, alone, and toddle toward those delicious aromas. When I got to the restaurant, I was in luck. An old man, with a Hunky accent, was sitting there, cleaning and snapping green beans. On the ground, in a crate, in front of him, was a live turtle. Oh, how exciting! I wanted to play with it, but the nice man warned me that I might get bitten. Why was the turtle there? Was it his pet?

No, he was going to kill it, shortly, to make turtle soup. That sweet, delicious smell, wafting from the back door, was turtle soup. The nice man comforted me, when I began to cry, by telling me that he would not kill this turtle, not to worry, he would keep it as a pet. Sure he did! I've, still, never eaten turtle soup.

Around Halloween, the neighborhood kids started to talk about the witch, who lived, way down, at the end of Seventh Avenue. They played all kinds of dirty tricks on her, like soaping her windows, and toilet papering her trees, and putting their feces on her door step. They were really mean.

I was determined to see what a real witch looked like, by paying her a visit myself. On my exploratory trips on Seventh Avenue, I never really roamed more than a few houses from the front door. To make this excursion, I would have to venture, way down, in the other direction, to the end of Seventh Avenue, passing Jack Foster's Garage, and the back entrance to *The Homestead Messenger*. The house was, probably, about three or four blocks away. It would be a long journey for a five year old to make, but I was determined to do it. It took my little legs a long time to get to that house, at the end of Seventh Avenue.

It looked like so many haunted houses, I've seen in the movies, since. It was old and rundown, with a scraggly fence, and overgrown with weeds. Someone peered out from behind the raggedy curtains. Was it the witch?

As I walked right up to the front door, and rang the bell, I thought I'd be frightened. I wasn't. She came to the door, and asked what I wanted. Without thinking, I said, "Sugar Bread." Sugar Bread was a favorite confection, among the Hunky kids. It consisted of a piece of white bread, spread thickly with lard or Crisco, then doused heavily with white sugar. Mama would never make it for us. The closest we ever got to that kind of sweet was scraping the cake, mixing bowl.

The "witch" must have been charmed, because she invited me in and made me Sugar Bread. Yummy, was that delicious! The second one was just as good. She must have charmed me, too, because I stayed all afternoon. I don't remember anything we said or did, but it was a wonderful first adventure, to take by myself. Did my mother find out about my sojourn? Not likely. I was really a pretty sneaky little kid. Was I growing up, a bit? Or was I just adventurous? Probably both.

The Depression was going on, and many of the businessmen Marie and Martha were doing business with, could no longer afford full time secretaries. So, The Grant Secretarial Service was hired by these businesses, to replace them. Each client had the telephone company install phone extensions to Marie's, centrally located, office. There, either she or Martha answered each line, as if she were that businessman's private secretary.

This proved to be quite successful, and soon, other businesses in the building wanted Marie and Martha to work for them, too. How could that be done? Her first clients were on the same floor as them, so running extension wires was no problem. It would be impossible to run extension wires from the other floors, so she put the dilemma to The Bell Telephone Company. Soon, they came up with a solution, and the telephone answering system was born.

The next thing I remember was, that for some reason or other, we were going to be moving from Homestead, to some place, called Carrick. In reality, by Papa being in California, and the Depression being so bad, our house went into foreclosure. This was the Spring or Summer of 1936.

Marie had married (or was about to marry) a fellow named Art Tombs, a widower, with a very small son, named Bobby. They had met through Marie's best friend, Ethel Sloane. She was dating a guy named Bus Brady, and Art was his friend. They started double dating, and Ethel became Ethel Brady, and Marie became Marie Bordy Tombs.

Art had a very good job, as an engineer, in the Mesta Machine Company. The Mesta was a huge conglomerate of buildings, miles long, along the Monongahela River, in West Homestead, which abutted the U.S. Steel Mill, in Homestead.

The Mesta made much of the equipment that the U.S. Steel Company needed to smelt and make its steel. Whether Marie actually loved Art, or married him because the family needed financial help, we'll never know.

Martha was just starting to date her future husband, Martin G. Jogeese, Joe for short. He was a salesman for Philco Radio Corporation, who met Martha and Marie at their place of business, in the Law and Finance Building. Initially, he was interested in Marie.

He loved tall women with big breasts! Somehow, Martha, who was not tall, charmed him, and won him over, even though she only had breasts the size of champagne glasses, just like Marie Antoinette. After awhile, Joe reconsidered and said, that anything that "spilt over," when placed in a champagne glass, was wasted.

They didn't marry until 1938 or 39, but I think that, monetarily, he helped out, too. He was mad about Martha, loved Mama, and would do anything for them. Somehow, by hook or by crook, the family left Homestead, and moved to that strange, far off land, called Carrick.

I REMEMBER MAMA

AND PAPA AND ALL THE REST

PROLOGUE

Mama was born Susan Elischer, on August 28, 1893, somewhere in Europe. She always said that she was German, but somehow, we could never learn exactly where she was born.

I remember asking her, but she would always try to change the subject, or she would answer with some strange sounding name, and the name seemed to change. I tried to have her point it out on the map, but she never seemed to be able to find it. She said the town was too small to be on the map.

Brother Sam insists that she was born in Transyl-vania, which in reality is in Romania. Of course, when she and Papa were born, all of Central Europe was The Austrian/Hungarian Empire, where countries and nationalities overlapped.

Even today, in the Transylvania Mountains, there is a section that is inhabited by Hungarians. Mama, however, did speak perfect Hungarian, perfect German, and a smattering of many other languages.

As a girl of sixteen, she came to America to work as a domestic for the Landel (or Landl) family. Like Mama, they were either Hungarian or German, or both, although they were Jewish, and Mama was Catholic.

According to my sister Martha, when Mama first began working for the Landel's, started dating a rich businessman, who fell madly in love with her, and wanted to marry her, but Fate stepped in.

At the Hungarian Church picnic, "Some Enchanted Evening" (afternoon, actually), happened. Her eyes locked with that excruciatingly, good looking young man, who turned out to be my father. It was really love at first sight, and "bye-bye" to a rich, luxurious life.

She was a tall, buxom girl, with a corseted, hourglass figure. On all the

photos I've seen of her, she always looks so sad. Even as an adult, I seldom remember Mama smiling or laughing. Was it because she had nine kids? No, that wasn't it, she was "sad" even before we came.

Mama had a younger sister, who, during World War II, had written to us. The letter is gone, but the photo remains. On the photo, the sister looks just like a younger, happier version of Mama.

On the back of the photo, she wrote, "*Das bin ich, Kornelia Elischerova*" — "This is I, Kornelia Elischerova." That's Mama's maiden name, with a Russian or Polish ending. Could Mama have been from Poland? Also, on some documents, Mama is called Susanna. We'll never know.

What I remember most about Mama, when I was a kid, was that she always seemed to be whacking me across the face, with her hand, for all the "bad things," that I was doing. I never knew what those "bad things" were, I was just being a kid, and trying to amuse everybody.

Members of the family told me that I had imagined those whacks. After a while, they convinced me that I was wrong. Mama would never "abuse" any of her children. Years later, I saw the 16mm movie, that Joe Jogeese had taken in 1938. Taking movies was his hobby. He shot film of himself and Martha, while they were dating, and now, he was going to come visit, and take movies of the Bordy family.

I remember that day well. Again, I had done something "bad," and was told that I wouldn't be allowed to have my picture taken.

So I said, "Who cares? I don't want any dumb old movies taken of me, anyway!"

I stayed inside and moped, soothing myself by suckling on my own, personal cocoanut. The movie making, in the back yard of our Churchview Avenue house, went fairly well, until they decided, that I should be in the movie, as well.

Martha tried to drag me outside. She got me to giggle, a little, but then I remembered that I was angry. But, they did manage to drag me out.

Mama, without even thinking about it, whacked me across the face. Then sheepishly, she looked at the camera, and smiled broadly, showing her two missing front teeth, that I supposedly knocked out, with a wooden spoon, when I was a baby. Don't get me wrong, Mama was not a child abuser. It was a kind of conditioned reflex, she never even realized that she was whacking me.

Years later, I got a hold of that film, from Martha, and made videos, for the entire family. It's still bitter-sweet to watch.

There were many nice things I remember about Mama, too. We spent much time together, "visiting," while she ironed, or did other chores. On Fridays, we would go grocery shopping. When she did her Saturday baking, I was there, patiently waiting for my *fank,* or ready to lick out the mixing bowls.

And, believe it or not, the most pleasant memory I have of her is, that after she was finished with the Monday laundry, and the last batch of clothes were on the clothes line to dry, she would sit on the front porch glider, and gently rock. I would sit beside her, and lean my face on her cool, fleshy arm.

Then, she would put her arm around me, and we would glide together, back and forth. We didn't speak, we just glided. She smelled of Clorox bleach, but to me, that became one of my favorite smells, and memories, just the two of us, alone together, in a Clorox stupor.

Mama was a born actress. Perhaps, that's where I got my flair for the dramatic. Whenever things got to be "too much," or the "children weren't listening" to her, or she wasn't getting her way, Mama would commence "to die."

She'd stumble up the stairs, gasping and moaning, until she got to her bed. Then, she would cry and wail, "I'm dying. I'm dying. Nobody listens to me. Nobody loves me. Why do I try so hard? No one appreciates everything I do for them."

The girls, usually Ruth and Pearl, or whoever else was around, would run to her bedside and cry, "Don't die, Mama. Don't die. We'll be good and listen to you, Mama. Just, don't die!"

Then, they would become hysterical. I couldn't imagine why the girls kept falling for this ruse. It was used so often. She would keep on gasping, and groaning, and sobbing. "Where's my Billy? Billy," she would call to me, "Where are you?"

I guess, I was the cause of many of these "attacks." She could get all the girls under her spell, but *not* me!

"What do ya' want?" I would snarl.

"Come up and talk to me, I vant to see you," she would beg.

"I'll talk to you when you come downstairs, you ain't foolin' me!" I don't think she ever heard the final part, or she would have had a relapse.

Eventually, she would, miraculously, be "healed." The girls would help her get up, and bring her back down the stairs. Sometimes she would just stay up their, and fall asleep, for a while. Certainly, she needed the rest. Poor soul. I think she really believed that she would die on those occasions. In any case, they were very cathartic for her; she'd awaken very refreshed, and actually, quite cheerful.

Mama did die at a fairly young age. After several bouts of cancer, she died at the Shadyside Hospital on August 27, 1946, the day before her fifty-third birthday.

Papa was born Samu L. Bordy (or Bornemiszay), in Transylvania, on June 1, 1888, and became an American Citizen on April 22, 1918, a few days before his twenty-eighth birthday.

Even though he was born in the Transylvania Mountains, which is actually in Romania, he was Hungarian! His first name Samu is pronounced *Sha*moo. What did the "L" stand for? His standard retort was that the "L" was for *El*-exander. And, with the "L" following so closely to Samu, he became Samuel Alexander Bordy.

Papa was a great story teller, but you never quite knew what was fact or fiction. Everything he said always seemed quite logical to me. He said that our name was actually Bornemiszay, not Bordy. Bornemiszay was a royal name, and that I was in reality a *Baro* or Baron. I was *Baro*Bornemiszay Bela, Bela being my Hungarian "first" name.

He broke the name down from Hungarian to English: "Bor" means "wine," "Nem" means "no," and "Misza" means "more" or, literally, "Wine no more" or "Don't drink wine." He, also, told me that when his father lost his property, he lost his title, and the end of his name, and somehow or other, it became Bordy.

It was generally believed that, when Papa emigrated to America, and went through his indoctrination on Ellis Island, his name was shortened, and Americanized, as was done to so many other emigrants. Not true.

An old photograph has been found of him, at his father's grave. The markings on the headstone read, "Bordy Sandor," Sandor being our grandfather's first name, "first" names always come after the family names, in Hungarian.

One time, I had asked Papa about Count Dracula. Were there really Vampires in Transylvania? He didn't know about Dracula, but he did know about Frankenstein. He related that, when he was a boy, their was a real Doctor Frankenstein, who "lived on top of a big hill," in his village, in the Transylvania Mountains, and that all the local people were afraid of him.

Supposedly, the good doctor injected his patients with a special kind of serum that "made monkeys out of them." In Hungarian, I believe, the same word is used for both ape and monkey. Thus, perhaps, began the Frankenstein legend, and possibly the Werewolf legend, as well.

In reality, the doctor probably had patients with that disease, in which people's adrenal glands are over stimulated, where they grow an excessive amount of hair all over their bodies. Poor Doctor Frankenstein was only trying to "cure" them, with his experiments.

Papa had often talked about his first trip to Hollywood, and how he met Mae West. I always imagined that it was just one of Papa's stories. When I was an adult, I asked him about her.

He related to me that, when he and his friend Lajosbacsy first arrived in Hollywood, after a grueling drive across the United States, in a broken-down Buick, they were anxious to meet Mae. How were they to find her? Well, in the telephone book, naturally. That's where they looked, got her address, at the Ravenswood Apartments, in the heart of Hollywood, and set off to see her. After all, didn't Mae say, "Come up and see me sometime."

Somehow, they got up to her door, and knocked. It was in the thirties, life was less dangerous, and Mae didn't have a "male guardian," at that time.

She opened the door and Papa said, "You say, come up and see me, sometime, so I am up to see you, *mit* my friend Louie."

They were graciously invited in. After all, Papa *was* very handsome. She made them some lemonade, and they spent the entire afternoon, visiting with her, having a delightful time. When it was time to leave, she sent them on their merry way, after giving them each a kiss on the cheek.

In 1976, I was asked to accompany one of my writers, Anna Styles, who was to do an interview with "Miss West," for my theatrical publication, *Drama-Logue.* How did she reach Mae West? Believe it or not, she got her phone number out of the telephone book. Yes, Mae was still listed.

A Mr. Novak, answered the phone, and made the appointment. To get the interview, Anna had to agree to the following two requirements: to bring a good looking man with her, so, naturally, she chose me; and not to mention, or talk about, Raquel Welch. On the set of "Myra Breckenridge," the two "ladies" did not get along.

When Anna and I arrived for the interview, we checked in with the concierge, at the Ravenswood. Yes, Mae was still living in the same apartment she was living in, when my father went to visit her, some forty years earlier. Mae owned the building, which was beautifully kept up. We were asked to wait a few minutes in the lobby, then permitted to take the elevator up to the apartment of *Miss Mae West!*

The elevator door opened, and we walked to the end of the hall, to apartment number six. After knocking on the door, Paul Novak answered. Novak was one of the "Muscle Men" who had been in Mae's Night Club Act. He stayed on to be her "companion and confidant." They lived together for twenty-six years, until she died in 1980. He died, shortly after.

"Please, come in and sit down. Miss West will be with you shortly." Then he exited into another room, her bedroom.

We sat on the lush, white sofa and looked around. It was *déjà vu,* I had been there before! The living room was all in white. It had a small, white grand piano, with a nude statuette of Mae, setting on it. I had even seen that statue before. The artist was very flattering in his rendition. Mae *never,* really, had such a good figure. Did I see that apartment in some magazine? Not really, but I seemed to know where everything was located. I choose to believe that Papa did a very good job in describing it to me, so many years before.

Shortly, Miss West made her "entrance." The first thing I noticed was how tiny, and delicate, she was. She was wearing the coral colored pants-suit she wore in "Myra Breckenridge," as well as the "piled high," blonde wig, with the long strands about her shoulders. Her shoes must have been four inches high. I understand that's how she got her unique walk, by wearing very tight, well-corseted dresses, and her own Carmen Miranda-style shoes.

Her hands were very warm. That was something I didn't expect. She looked me up and down, then sat down. Anna commenced the interview, asking first about her upcoming movie, "Sextette." Mae was anxious to get started on the film.

This movie would "complete the circle." It was based on the first play she wrote and produced called, "Sex." That was the production that got her into so much trouble in the early 30's, when she was arrested, and spent a short time in jail.

Finally, "Sextette" was going to be made into a big, Hollywood movie. At the age of eighty-four, Mae would recreate her role of the most sexy woman in the world, who Tony Curtis, Timothy Dalton, George Hamilton, and Ringo Starr would, soon, pursue.

This turned out to be her last motion picture, and not very successful at that. Who could really believe that such young, good looking men could be enchanted by an eighty-four year old sex-pot. *Quelle damage!*

Anna Styles was a tall, sexy blonde, in her fifties, who was a great admirer of Miss West. She envisioned herself as a newer version of the great sex goddess. She had long, blonde hair, and wore skin tight clothing. One of her greatest joys, in life, was her weekly strut down Hollywood Boulevard, to deliver her column to the *Drama-Logue* office. The men would hoot and howl, from their cars, and honk their horns at her. She just ignored them, and kept on walking. Oh, how she loved it!

During the interview, Anna did manage to get Mae to compliment her on how attractive she was. That made her day.

Mae was a little distracted, and didn't seem to know the answers to most of the questions, posed to her, about her past. She would have Mr. Novak answer the queries, instead. In reality, at that time, Novak probably did know the answers better than she. Mae did seem to me to be "failing," a bit.

Sally Struthers had done an imitation of Mae West, on television, and was quite good. Wouldn't she be a good bet to play Mae in a bio-pic? I asked Mae about the possibility of doing a movie of her life. It was "Sunset Boulevard," all over again.

She said that various projects had been discussed, over the years, but none of them ever came to fruition. She granted that a young actress would play her as a child, and in her teen-age years, then she would step in, and play herself, for the rest of the picture. I kid you not. At the age of eighty three, she actually thought she could pull it off. No wonder the picture never got made.

On November 9, 1912, Samu and "Zsuzsi" were married, shortly after they had met at the Hungarian picnic. Zsuzsi is the Hungarian name for Suzie.

She was nineteen, he was twenty-four. Mama felt as if she were deserting the Landels, but love won out.

There is a beautiful wedding photograph of them. By today's standards it may appear to be a little stilted, but in those days, you had to stay perfectly still, for quite a while, when you had a portrait taken. You can't tell for sure, but they seemed to be happy.

In 1908, Papa had been working for "The Pinkerton Detective Agency," as a strike breaker," in Dayton, Ohio.

No one knows exactly what he did, but we heard that he "busted a few skulls," of the people who wouldn't go back to work at the steel mill. The "Steel Mill Wars," was going on.

The Newlyweds moved to Martin's Ferry, Virginia, to set up housekeeping, so that Papa could continue working for The Pinkertons.

No one was more pleased than Papa, after the birth of Marie. He roudly paraded her around the neighborhood in her baby buggy.

And, when Martha was born, his pride doubled. They were two cute little girls.

The Bordys saved every available penny for Papa's dream. In Budapest, where Papa grew up, he had "learned his trade" as a shoemaker.

"Every man should have a trade so he can take care of his family."

He wanted to have a son so that he could become a shoemaker, like him.

Martha often told the story, that Papa was not just a Shoe Repair Man, but that he was a Shoe *Maker*, in the truest meaning of the words.

"He crafted shoes for the royalty, and the wealthy of Budapest and Vienna. People came from all over Austro-Hungary to have shoes made by him." Rather far fetched, I'm afraid, but that was Martha.

Her "interpretations" of the facts were, always, much more interesting than the real thing. She inherited the art of story telling from Papa, and to her, all things were nicer, or prettier, or more exciting than they actually were. In Martha's world we were actually Viennese, *not* Hungarian! She was a Romantic. Papa was much more plausible than Martha. I actually believed his "stories."

All his life, Papa was a health nut. He squeezed fresh orange juice every day, and ate only, so-called, health foods. He'd stand on his head, daily, to get "all da goot juices going." He coughed a lot, blaming it on the years of living in Homestead, among the smoke stacks of the steel mill. He did not die of respiratory illness. While he and his second wife, Margit, were visiting with brother Sam in Florida, he died of an apparent heart attack, on April 12, 1961, two weeks before his 72nd birthday.

Marie Amelia Bordy was born on September 19, 1913, in a Martins Ferry, Ohio, hospital. The family lived in nearby Wheeling, West Virginia. All went well with the birth. Papa was so proud to have such a beautiful, baby girl.

Marie's beauty was not only a blessing, but perhaps a curse. It opened many doors, with many men, but she was never really happy, with any of them.

She graduated the Drake Business School in 1939, where she studied to be a court reporter. Instead of becoming a reporter, she started her own business, by doing free lance secretarial work, downtown Pittsburgh.

She had her own office in the Grant Building, called The Grant Secretarial Service. Martha joined her shortly after she got started. They expanded, and moved the business to the Law and Finance Building, a few buildings away, and began the first Telephone Answering Service in the United States.

She became Marie Bordy Tombs Carmalt Straker, and had three sons: Emmett Duane, born on May 11, 1943; and "Butch" (Cordell Ley actually) Carmalt, born November 13, 1945; and Jim Straker, whom I have never met, except, when he was a fetus, in Marie's belly. That was when my ship pulled into Port Everglades in 1953, when I was still in the Marine Corps. He was born on July 2, 1953.

16

In 1947, she moved from Pittsburgh to Florida, where she went into the Real Estate business. With her partner, Tom Marino, she built the Carmo Apartments in Redington Beach. Later, with several other partners, her company built the Gateway Shopping Center, in Ft. Lauderdale, Florida. She continued, off and on, in the Realty business, until she died of cancer, on September 1, 1988.

Martha Phyliss Bordy was born on December 28, 1915, in Wheeling, West Virginia. Whether Phyliss is really a part of her name, or not, no one knows. I do know that when she was young, she acquired the affectation of calling herself Marthatha Phylisses.

When I was being sarcastic, I would always called her Martha-tha. It never bothered her. Very few things got her upset. She almost always remained "above it all."

Like Marie, Martha was born in a hospital. Unfortunately, she was born a "blue baby," and was pronounced dead. When the Doctor told the bad news to our father, he raged, and grabbed the Doctor, and screamed, "I don't make no dead babies!" He pushed the Doctor aside, and stormed into the delivery room.

Years later, he told me that they had already thrown her into "the garbage can," and were ready to take her away. He snapped her up in his arms, washed her off, cleared her little mouth, and breathed hard into it, while spanking her on the behind. She started crying, and Papa knew he had saved his funny, little runt of a baby girl. He vowed that he would *never, ever* have any more of his children born in a hospital. He was true to his word; all the rest of us were born at home, in Homestead, with the assistance of our, soon to be, permanent midwife, Mrs. Pfaff.

After several years of courtship, Martha married Martin G. Jogeese, who was called "Joe." They had two daughters, the first was Marilyn, born in May of 1940, the other was Lizabeth who was born, probably in March of 1951, I'm not sure exactly. Marilyn died very young, of a brain hemorrhage, and Liz, who became a drug addict, is "lost" somewhere in Texas. Martha, Joe and Liz, lived for many years in Houston.

After Joe died, Martha slowly deteriorated, losing much of her verve and zest for living. After a short stay in a nursing home, she wasted away, and died in a hospital July 19, 1999, when she was eighty-three. We still don't know what she died of. One can only suppose that, this vibrant woman, died because she got bored in that nursing home, and no longer wanted to live.

Katherine Bordy was born on September 28, 1918, on Twelfth Avenue, in Homestead, Pennsylvania. She was the first one born at home, with Mrs. Pfaff's assist.

Kay, or Kate, or Katy (pronounced Kutty in Hungarian) was completely different from her two sisters. She was never classically beautiful like Marie, nor "cutesy-pooh" like Martha. She was more wholesome looking, more serious, and definitely more religious.

She joined the Salvation Army, at an early age. There were always so many social events going on there, and they, often, gave away toys to the kids, and other "goodies" to the adults, so all the Bordy kids would go to the "Army" for fun, and Sunday school.

I still remember one of the songs we sang as children: *"The Salvation Army has the right to beat the drum. The tambourine, the banjo to make the Devil run. Come boys and girls, and get the Gospel gun, and shoot the old Devil, if you wanna see him run."*

Katy really got involved with The Army, and had her "calling" at an early age. Soon, she was living with Major and Mrs. "Ma" Hayman, where she got her indoctrination into what The Army stood for, and what they were required to do.

The Hayman's had a good looking son called Cecil "Ceese," with whom Katy fell in love. They never did get married, even though everyone thought they would. She left the Haymans, when she went to the Salvation Army Theological College, in New York City, to became an officer and an ordained minister.

Mama went to her graduation. She had traveled there with Mrs. Alster, our next door neighbor. Neither had done much traveling (except for Mama's big trip across the ocean.) It was June 16, 1939, during the New York World's Fair.

Mama often told the story of what happened to them, when they arrived in New York.

They didn't know where their hotel was located, so they decided to splurge, and take a taxi cab. Excitedly, they enjoyed their "tour" of New York City, and after a while, arrived at their hotel.

The next morning, while getting ready to attend the graduation, Mrs. Alster looked out the window, and called to Mama, "Hey, Suzie, look. Isn't that the train station we came in on?"

They had been duped, like so many tourists before them. But Mama, believe it or not, laughed. Nothing was going to upset her that day. She was enjoying the American Dream. After all, wasn't one of her children graduating from college? Only in America! And, besides, she had enjoyed the tour of the city.

After Mama's death, Suzie and I went to live with Captain Katherine Bordy at the Salvation Army, in Tarentum, Pennsylvania. During that time, she met her future husband, Clarence Schotter. They were married on July 25, 1947, at Clarence's parents' home, in West View, Pennsylvania. Their first child, Linna, was born on May 12, 1950. She was the most beautiful baby I had ever seen. Several years later, on March 22, 1955, they had a son, Daniel.

As of this writing, in 2010, Kay and Clarence are still "alive and kicking," in King City, Oregon, where they go for walks, almost every day, holding each other up, and amazing all their friends and family, with their dexterity.

Samuel Bordy, Jr. was born on November 11, 1920, at 408 West Street, in Homestead. At last, Papa had a son! Soon he would be trained to be a shoemaker, and work in the shop that Papa had just built, in the front of the house. He never did work in Papa's Shop.

As a little kid, he and Katy went to the Hungarian Baptist Church Sunday School. Their teacher was a strict, kindly old women called Mrs. Polini. The annual Hungarian picnic was the highlight of the year, and all the Bordys would go. After all, isn't that where Papa and Mama met.

Later on, he and Katy went to Sunday School, and other events, at the Salvation Army. As he got older, he and brother Ed did swim in the Monongahela River, in the summertime. How they never got sick, God only knows. They were Hunkies, and indestructible.

Sam didn't have much of a childhood. He had to grow up fast. The Depression was on, and everyone in the family had to work. After Suzie was born, their was another mouth to feed. From the beginning, he loved that little baby, and became her surrogate father.

He quit school, because Marie got him a job as an elevator operator, in the Law and Finance building. That's where he really grew up fast, and met his first love, Annie.

Several years after serving in the Marine Corps, he moved to Ft. Lauderdale, Florida, where he met his true love, a "Georgia Peach," named Betty Seyden. She was ten years his junior, but they married on September 10, 1949.

Denise, their daughter, was born November 18th, 1950. Her brother Samuel III was born, in Pittsburgh, on May 28th, 1953.

After sixty years of marriage, Betty died on March 24, 2009.

Edward George Bordy was born on August 3, 1923. Eddy had the curliest hair. None of the girls had it, nor did Sam. Papa was doubly proud. Now he had two sons! The only problem was that, this one looked like a girl. People would stop him on the street to admire the pretty girl, with all the pretty curls.

"He is *not* a girl!" my father would shout, "He's a boy!" Soon, Papa stopped showing off his new child.

   It never really bothered Ed. Any other kid would have been traumatically affected by such attention. Once he had his first haircut, he became a boy, and what a boy he became!

Ed always got in trouble, and one time, in his early teens, he was taken to juvenile hall for some misdeed or the other. Sister Pearl told me that he was the "lookout" for a bunch of boys, who were caught stealing tires. Rather than being sent to jail, he was placed in a Trade School, where he learned to be an electrician's helper, at Mine Safety Appliances. Later, he went to work for Hertz-Rent-a-Car, as a mechanic's helper, where he would get his early training as an automobile mechanic. Bingo, that would soon become his love, and his career.

He got into trouble with the law several times. One time, as he was trying to escape from one of his capers, he fell on a broken bottle, and wound up with a glass gash in his ass, the right cheek.

While changing clothes in the men's locker room, at the swimming pool, I'd always recognize Ed, from the rear, by the scar on his ass. He never said hello to me, while in the locker room, and I could never understand why. Finally, I figured it out. His eyes were so bad, that without his glasses, he really couldn't see anybody. It's just as well, because I was very shy about being naked in public, anyway. I would go from bathing suit to under-shorts in two seconds.

He served in the Army, during the Second World War, and moved to California, the day after Easter, in 1947. There, he continued his on-the-job training at Fox Automotive, in Huntington Park.

Several months later, he sent for his sweetheart, Helen Smith. They married and had two daughters: Jayne, born on June 17, 1948; and Faye, born on November 15, 1955.

He also married a German girl, Margot, who died, and a "Polock" named Danuta, who just "disappeared," somewhere.

On Christmas Eve, of 2008, he had a stroke, and is striving to "get back to normal." He's a survivor who has outlasted all his "women," except for

Florina Modina, his Philippina girl friend of twenty some years.

He worked with cars, all his life, into his late seventies, until no one would hire him, anymore. They thought he was too old. He wasn't!

Dorothy June Bordy was born on June 21, 1925. "Dorothy" got written on her birth certificate, so legally that's her name. But her name is, and always has been, Ruth. She was truly the most beautiful baby ever born. Her complexion was a little more olive colored than the rest of the family, which led many in the family to believe that, perhaps it was true, Papa's mother, or grandmother, was a Gypsy. I always believed it, and still do. That's where most of us got our sixth sense. We always brag about our E.S.P., and our Hungarian-Gypsy ability to see the future.

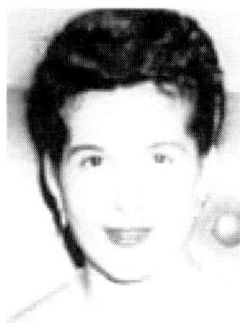

"Blackie" always had an affinity with the sun. She loved, and still loves, basking in it. Every summer, she was the first to get a great tan. Unlike the rest of us, she would continue to get darker. Thus, her nick-name was born. She was called Blackie, partially because she was so dark, and partially, even though she was pretty and feminine, no one could be tougher than she. She was never afraid of any one, or any thing. That holds true today.

When Brother Ed got into trouble with some other kids, Ruth would come out swinging, in his defense. She scared the hell out of the boys. They would, however, call on her to be on their ball teams, because she excelled in all the sports. Or was it because she was so pretty? Maybe a little of each. She preferred being the umpire, where she could "boss" everyone around.

Ruthie went to work at a very early age, and could do almost anything. She worked as a clerk at Isaly's Dairy, a fry cook at Villella's Café, and occasionally, did secretarial work for Marie. During the Second World War, she worked as a welder on L.S.T. landing boats. In her patriotic fervor, she married an airman, Corporal Delwyn Peterson. It didn't last long.

On November 3, 1947, she married Solomon (Sol) Mintz, the manager of a Boardwalk game, in Atlantic City, New Jersey, called Fascination. They had two boys, Bruce, born August 12, 1948, and Bobby, born January 7, 1954.

After Sol's untimely death, in September of 1954, she married bar owner/hotelier Paul Swetkoff, on April 14, 1960, with whom she had a daughter named Sue, on February 22, 1961.

Ruth had cancer of the lungs in 2002, and now in 2010, she is surviving beautifully. She still smokes, but can easily climb the steep stairs to her apartment, each day.

When the sun is shining, she is out basking in it, and reading. And, she can walk faster, and longer, than any other member of the family. Even I have a hard time keeping up with her.

Of course, she plugs into to her "breathing machine," when she needs revitalizing. That brings her around.

Pearl Mae Bordy was born on June 12, 1928. "Pearly Mae," as she was teasingly called, was, and is, a truly unique person, who really marches to her own drummer. As a kid, she was always irritable, angry, and very hard to get along with. Her way was, and is, the only way to do things. Papa had the same stubborn quality. Even when proven wrong, in black and white, he would still insist that he was right.

Over the years, Pearl has mellowed a bit, and at least, is willing to look at the other person's point of view. But, if she doesn't like an individual, the first time she meets him or her, nothing, and I mean *nothing*, will change her mind.

These people, she cuts out of her life, and will have nothing to do with them. How she manages to do this is an art in itself, although, she claims she has no artistic talents. Somehow, she manages to place an invisible shield between herself and the person with whom she wishes to ignore, and in her mind, he or she does not exist. It seems to work. The best part is, that these people do not realize what she has done.

As a child, Pearl was not the most graceful, nor was she athletic. But, that didn't stop her. I remember when she was eleven or twelve, she tried roller skating down Churchview Avenue, to Feld's Ice Cream Parlor, two long blocks away. The wheels never actually rolled on her skates; she just seemed to "walk" on them. Ruth and I went with her to get some ice cream. She managed to clomp, clomp into Feld's for her ice cream cone, then clomp-clomped out the door licking it.

The main entrance to Feld's was kitty corner, on Churchview Avenue and Willett Road. Churchview was level, but immediately outside the door, of the soda shop, the sidewalk, to the left, took a steep dip down Willett Road.

Pearl says that Ruth dared her to skate down that incline. I don't remember it that way. I remember that, instead of going straight down Churchview, as was her intention, she veered left, and rolled uncontrollably down the slope. She couldn't stop herself, so she started screaming.

22

Unfortunately, some man was walking ahead of her on the slope, and didn't hear her yell, until it was too late. She crashed into him, and fell down. He fell on top of her, breaking her arm.

It's probably a good thing that the man was there. If he hadn't been, she would have continued down that steep street, and who knows what would have happened to her?

She was in agony, yelling and screaming at the man who fell on her. He was very apologetic, and stayed with the girls, until help arrived.

I went to the Bowden's house to borrow their son, Bob's, little red wagon, that he used to deliver newspapers. He came with me, and we managed to pull her to the house.

Mama was frantic, while Pearl moaned and groaned in distress. The bone had jutted out of her arm, and she was bleeding. In any emergency, Mama always called Marie, who she thought could fix anything. The only other thing she could think to do, was berate Pearl.

"You dummy. How could you be so dumb, and break your arm? What am I going to do with you? We can't afford doctors," and on and on.

Poor Pearl was in such terrible pain, and Mama gave her no sympathy.

At last, after work, Marie and Art came and took her to Dr. Uptagraph's office, on Sankey Avenue. Luckily, the doctor was still in his office. He's the same doctor, who, had earlier, taken care of my wound, when I gashed the back of my head, falling on a closed off gas pipe.

Pearl has fond memories of Art. Several years after his divorce, when Pearl was probably sixteen, they ran into each other, in front of Dr. Uptagraph's office. He gasped, because he thought she was Marie. Pearl, too, had been growing into a beauty. By that time, Marie had married Dr. Emmett D. Carmalt, the head brain surgeon at Shadyside Hospital. Art never remarried, and several years later, died of a brain tumor.

Pearl married Larry Frazier on July 10, 1954. They met in a Chicago Country Club, where they were both working, he as a bartender, she as a waitress. They moved to Los Angeles, and went into the bar business. Later Larry went to work for Wham-o, the toy manufacturing company, that made the Hula Hoop and the Frisbee. There marriage lasted twenty-five years.

For years, she worked for me, selling advertising for my theatrical newspaper, *Drama-Logue*. After the paper was sold to *Billboard* Publications, in 1998, we both moved to Florida, she to Port Charlotte, and I, to Sarasota.

William James Bordy was born November 2, 1930. That's me. As a kid I was called Billy, by most of the family. Now, I'm just plain Bill, although occasionally, some member of the family will still say Billy. When I talk to myself, I call myself Willy. For some reason, I always preferred that name.

When I lived in England, I tried using my mid-

23

dle name James, and naturally, no one ever called me that. They insisted on calling me Jimmy.

The same thing happened when I decided to use the name, James Martin, as my professional acting name. Everyone called me Jimmy. When Actors' Equity informed me that there was already a James Martin, I said, what the heck, use your real name, and I've been Bill Bordy ever since. Although, once in a great while, I will use my Hungarian name, of Bela Bornemiszay, or, another nickname, Billy Bee.

Billy Bee was a pet name, given to me by an ex-actress friend, who killed herself, diving off the roof of the Traymore Hotel, in Los Angeles. Her name was Carmela. She was Mexican, and was brought to Hollywood to be groomed by Paramount Pictures, to be a Movie Star, along with Diana Lynn, and Gail Russell.

Carmela married the son of a famous radio team. He was an alcoholic, and Carmela became one shortly after. He was a mean drunk, and beat the Hell out of her, breaking every bone in her face. She never regained her looks, and stayed an alcoholic, until life got to be too much for her. So twenty years or so, later, off the roof of the "Trashmore" Hotel she went, crashing into Eighth Street below.

When I met my British friend, Jon Anthony, he thought my last name was "Bawdy," like the Bawdy Houses in England.

To him, I became Bill Bawdy, especially once he learned of my youthful adventures.

It was an apt name, if I do say so myself.

Suzanne Ethel Bordy was born on October 28, 1934. When she was born, she became my property. Sam thought the same thing. I would be four, in a few days, and Sam would be fourteen. From the start, she was a little toughie, cute but tough. Everyone spoiled her.

As we grew up, we did everything together. We were cohorts, and co-conspirators, in every kind of childish prank, usually instigated by her. I would, often, get caught and punished, but Suzie, always, seemed to escape any kind of retribution. She *appeared* to be too "angelic," to get into any trouble. Hah!

24

When Mama died, in 1946, Sue and I went to live with Katy, at the Salvation Army, in Tarentum. From there, she went on to live with Kay, and her new husband, Clarence, in their "Honeymoon" cottage, in West View, Pennsylvania.

Several years later, she, Kay, Clarence and, their new baby, Linna, moved

into their first house, in Wexford, about twenty miles north from where they were living, way out in the sticks.

In 1950, she went to stay with Ruth in Atlantic City, for the summer. That was the year that she "grew up," or so she thought. She was fifteen, going on sixteen, and unfortunately, got involved with a bunch of bar people, who would become her "friends."

She loved playing "grown-up," and found a home in the dark, dank bars of Atlantic City. She was very cleaver about it, and Ruth, being so busy working seven days a week, twelve hours a day during the season, never found out. As she got older, she continued her bar hopping, drinking mostly beer. Boy, could she put it away!

The running joke in the bars was, how long could she stay on her bar stool, drinking ten cent beers, before going to the ladies room? Often, she wouldn't go until she was ready to leave, or when the bar closed.

THE BORDY CLAN - 1925

KATY, MAMA, RUTH, MARIE, MARTHA, PAPA, SAM, ED (SEATED)
- CIRCA 1925

Kay never found out about her drinking habits, for many years. I found out when I came home on leave, from the Marine Corps, in the early '50s, when we went out drinking together. That was when she confessed to me how she got me into trouble, when we were kids.

25

Apologetically, she told me how she would "squeal" to Mama, blaming me for all of our "bad deeds," for which I, naturally, got the spanking, not she. She was so innocent looking, no one dared not believe her.

Suzy lived with Kay and Clarence, until she was in her early twenties Then, she got her own apartment in West View, so she would be closer to her job at the Otto Milk Company, where she made cottage cheese.

Everyone loved Suzie, from when she was a baby, all through her adult life. Her friends reached both ends of the spectrum, from the highest to the lowest. Unfortunately, she only lived twenty-seven years. Her body was found in her car on April 23, 1963, in the West View Park parking lot, just outside one of her favorite bars, with a bullet through her right temple.

CARRICK:

MOVIN' ON UP TO THE SOUTH HILLS

CHAPTER ONE

The Bordy Clan moved to 59 Maytide Street in the summer of 1936. Carrick is a small town, adjacent to the Borough of Brentwood, which abuts Baldwin Township on one end, and Whitehall, on the other. This area of Pittsburgh is called The South Hills, and hilly it is.

Maytide Street is one of the steepest streets in Pittsburgh. It is so precipitous, that the short walk from our house, to the top of the hill, was, and is, very difficult and tiring, especially for an almost six year old.

What a dangerous street it was. Whenever a bus got to the top of Maytide Street, and had to stop for a traffic light, it would rev, and rev, it's engine, trying to keep the bus from drifting backward, down the hill. When the traffic light changed, the buses would, inevitably, drift back about four or five feet, before the driver could shift into gear to reach the summit, and turn onto Brownsville Road. It was terrifying. First time riders would scream. But, after you made the trip several times, you'd get used to it. Except in the winter.

In the winter, it was doubly frightening, and horrific, just trying to drive to the summit. The buses would slip, and slide on the ice, but always, somehow, make it to the top. Again, if it had to wait there for a traffic light to change, you held on for dear life. The rear wheels would spin, and the bus would drift, and slide backward. Then, it would grind, and grunt, and, finally, make it to the top of the hill.

One time. I saw a bus slipping, and sliding, half-way to our house, before the bus driver got the vehicle to growl, and groan forward. I thought, for sure, that bus was going to slide, and roll, right over me! That incident, literally, scared the Devil out of me. Well, for a short time it did, but not for long.

Our house was a nice, two story building, with an attic. There were ten stairs, leading from the street to the first landing, then another five steps to get to the front porch, quite a climb.

All houses had front porches, in those days. How nice they were, especially in the summer time. We had a large side yard, covered with grass, and a small back yard where Mama could have a garden, and grow fresh vegetables.

Even the yard was a hill. At the top, there was a narrow alley, and beyond that, at last, there was an almost level plot of land, where the kids played soft ball. It was there, I got hit in the face with a baseball bat. One of the kids swung at the ball, throwing his bat behind him, hitting me in the face. I didn't want to cry in front of all the big kids, but my nose was broken. Its never been the same.

Our next door neighbor, on the "down-hill" side, was an older widow lady, probably in her sixties, named Mrs. Alster. She was Alsatian who spoke French and German with Mama. They became fairly friendly, and Mama was happy to have such a "refined" lady with whom she could converse.

Mrs. Alster was tiny and slight, very soft spoken, and wore her strait, gray hair pulled back into a bun. She was the friend who accompanied Mama, on her trip, to New York City, for Katy's graduation.

I don't think we even knew who the neighbors, on the other side of the house, were. There was no common area to visit, as there was with Mrs. Alster.

At the summit of Maytide Street, on the "up" side of Brownsville Road, was a large Grocery Store called Donahue's Market. Turning right, on the "down" side of the road, was the soon to be built Murphy's Five and Ten Cent Store. Not too many years later, Mama would slip on their wet floor, having a terrible fall, while she was shopping with Duane, her first grandson.

Two doors further was, what was to become, my favorite place in the world, the Melrose Theater, where the movie program changed three times a week. Going to the Melrose became a ritual for the Bordy kids as soon as we moved to Maytide Street. We would be given our fifteen cents allowance to go to the movies, ten cents for the ticket, and five cents for the candy.

We were expected to stay, and watch the double feature twice, along with the Serials: "Buck Rogers," "The Mole People," "Jungle Jim," and all the rest. We loved sitting there in the dark, watching each movie two times. Mama was rid of us until, at least, five or six in the evening. She loved it. Alone, with no kids!

Beyond the Melrose Movie Theater was the Melrose Bar, an absolutely mystifying place to us kids. Next door to the bar was Vitalie's Drug Store. Then the following block, on Steward Avenue, the First Lutheran Church was located.

We weren't Lutheran, but the church was so convenient that Pearl and I, and later Suzie, would attend Sunday School, there. Sometimes, we would even stay over to attend Reverend John Wannamaker's services.

Like so many ministers, he had a problem son, who was always in trouble. I guess the son turned his life around, because, years later, John Wannamaker, Jr. would become the pastor of his father's church.

Perpendicular, to the Melrose Theater is where Sankey Avenue begins.

28

Why it's called an "Avenue," no one knows. It is only one short city block long that ends at the top of, yet, another hill.

On the left corner, of Sankey Avenue and Brownsville Road, was Hanson's, a very elegant drug store, much nicer than the three other nearby pharmacies.

It had the nicest soda fountain in the area, and many of the women shoppers would come there to get their "pick me up," a small Coca Cola. I think at that time, "Coke" still had a small amount of cocaine in it. No wonder it was so popular with the ladies!

Across the street, on the corner of Sankey Avenue and Brownsville Road, was my favorite "watering hole," Bard's Dairy Store, where you could get your sodas and sundaes cheaper than the Drug Stores. That corner, not too many years later, became the corner that I, and my "gang," would hang out.

Donahue's was very convenient to where we lived, but that steep walk to get there was difficult. Because the store was so close, Mama and I could make more trips to get groceries.

There were no Super Markets, yet, but this was as close to one as you could get, in the thirties and forties. There were no carts for picking up your own groceries. You lined up at the counter, to be waited on. The clerks were

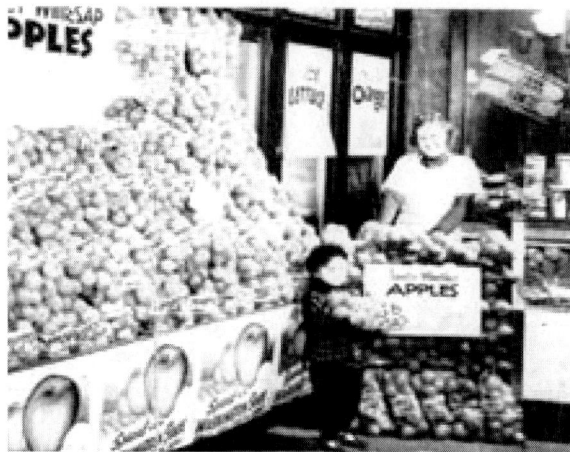

fantastically agile and quick. Mama would read off her shopping list, and wham, bam, these clerks ran, back and forth, and up and down, gathering the items, lickety-split. They gracefully glided in and out, among themselves, obtaining the needed items, never bumping into each other. A trip to the Ballet couldn't have been more impressive.

After they amassed all of the items, they would tear off a piece of wrapping paper and, in a big scrawl, itemize every item they had just retrieved. All items were added up, right then and there. As the clerks spoke the cost of each item, they totaled. They did that quickly, too. Seldom, did they make an error.

There were no fancy cash registers to do the adding for you. All school kids, in those days, learned how to add and make change, without high-tech equipment. They, also, learned how to read and write!

One day, Sam had taken little Suzie shopping, at Donahue's. They had a sale on five pound bags of apples for nineteen cents. A photographer was there to shoot some publicity shots of the store, for a newspaper advertisement. When he saw our little Suzie, he asked Sam if the cute, little girl would model for him, holding the apples. Sam agreed, and the photo was taken.

In that photo, you can see this tough little girl, struggling to hold a five pound bag of apples, in front of a huge display of bagged Washington apples.

Mama tried to get Ed a job there as a stock boy. They informed Mama that they didn't need any more help. But, Mama insisted by volunteering Ed to work, for free.

"You don't have too pay him, nutting. He vill vork for free. Just give him da old vegetables dat you don't sell."

So, Ed "vent to vork" at Donahue's for a while, and Mama had all the vegetables she could ever want. Now, our Sunday soup became vegetable soup. So did our Monday soup, our Tuesday soup, and our Wednesday soup. Ed didn't stay long. Thank God! How much vegetable soup can one eat?

Ed needed money! So, shortly after his sojourn at Donahue's, Ed got a job at the bowling alley as a shoe shine boy. Being very personable, he did quite well. Soon, he owned the three station, elevated shoe-shine stand where he plied his trade. Business was so good that he, actually, hired another boy, to help him.

Ed was called "Dutch." That nick-name stuck with him for many years. Even, our sister Ruth called/calls him that. They were Dutch and Blackie.

In September of 1936, even though I was not quite six, I was enrolled into the Carrick Elementary School, on Carrick Avenue. I don't remember too much about the two years I spent there, except "going to the basement."

If you had to go to the toilet, you raised your hand, and asked the teacher, "May I go to the basement, please?"

The basement was where the toilet facilities were located.

Then, the teacher would ask, "Is it number one or number two?"

If the student answered "number one," the teacher would usually tell him to wait until after class, unless it were a dire emergency. If it were "number two," she would, more readily, grant permission.

One day, just to see if I could, I asked permission to "go to the basement," for number two. I feigned great discomfort, and was given permission to go. What a great feeling! What freedom! I was all alone in the huge hallway, walking slowly down the two flights of cold, marble stairs, to the basement.

When I got there, I saw the janitor, who was sneaking a smoke. I felt a little guilty being there, but figured that as long as I was, I should try to "go." I couldn't. The guilt didn't last long. What a great adventure it had been, to roam those massive halls, alone. Years passed before I found out that "going to the basement" didn't mean that you had to relieve yourself.

It was a pretty long walk to school for a six year old. The direct route was to go to the top of Maytide Street, turn left on Brownsville Road, pass McCann's Bar and Grill, pass the bowling alley, then continue for several more blocks, passing the Birmingham Cemetery. From there, it was a short walk to Carrick Avenue, where a crossing guard got us across Brownsville Road, and to the school.

There was a longer, but less dangerous, way of going to school, by way of back streets. That's the route I seem to remember taking more often. Anyway, it was a long trudge for a small boy. There were no school buses then, and few kids were driven to school. We all walked.

In My second year at Carrick Elementary, a Russian boy had been enrolled. We became friends, and would walk home, together. He lived a little further down the hill, from me.

One day, he invited me to his house to meet his mother. When we met, I was surprised at how old she was. She was even older than my mother! My mother had this terrible German accent, but his mother had no accent at all. She didn't have an accent because she didn't speak English, only Russian. And, *he* spoke Russian! Can you imagine, a seven year old kid speaking Russian as well as English? How amazing!

Why did we Bordy kids only speak English? Because Mama and Papa were going to be good Americans, and speak only "Anglish." Besides, in German or Hungarian, they could talk in front of us, without any of us understanding what they were saying. To this day, I'm still angry that they didn't speak the other languages to us.

All the kids we knew at the Hungarian Church spoke Hungarian and/or German, but we didn't. When you're a child, you pick up other languages by osmosis. I remember Maestro Vasco Mihich, an Italian music teacher, who taught singing in Atlantic City. When I met him in the 1950's, he had a little four year old son who spoke English, Italian, German, and one of the Slavish languages.

The mother was Slavish, the maid was German, and of course, the Maestro was Italian. To me, the boy spoke in English, to the others, he spoke their own language, going back and forth, in all the tongues. To him, it was no problem at all. How I envied him.

31

Marie married Art Tombs. They purchased a beautiful, new house, and decorated it with very modern, elegant furniture. They were living in Brentwood at the bottom of a Hillson Avenue, a mile or so from Maytide Street. What an appropriate name for their street! It was almost as steep as Maytide.

Martha was still dating Joe Jogeese and lived at home. Sam, by now, had quit school and went to work, as an elevator operator, in the Law and Finance Building. That's where Marie and Martha had their secretarial business, so the three of them saw each other quite often.

Katy, Martha, Suzie and all the rest of us, except for Marie, were living on Maytide Street. Ed was working at the bowling alley, Ruth would go to work at Isaly's Dairy, as would Pearl later on. It was located a few doors down from the bowling alley.

Isaly's Dairy was famous for their chipped chop ham, a delicious luncheon meat. They originated the Klondike Ice Cream Bar, which for years, you could only buy in Pittsburgh. They cost five cents and were huge, not like the puny ones that are made today.

Suzie and I always "helped" Mama with her chores. Papa was in California, where he did manage to open a shoe repair shop. He wanted Mama to pack up the kids and move there, but she refused. She was happy in her new surroundings.

To my recollection, Papa never lived with us on Maytide Street. When he came back from California, he had no idea where we were living. He asked around if anybody knew where we were, but nobody seemed to know what had happened to his family. He didn't waste any time, and soon managed to open a new Shoe Repair Shop in Homestead, at 603 Amity Street, with sleeping quarters in the back.

After two years of living on Maytide Street, It was time for the family to move, again. We were looking for a bigger house. Did we lose our lease, or was it just time to move on? I don't know. Anyway, the search was on for a new home. One was found not too far away, on Churchview Avenue, in the Borough of Brentwood.

To get there from Maytide Street was a short walk. All you had to do was walk up Maytide Street, turn right on Brownsville Road, turn left on Sankey Avenue, go to the top of the hill, and turn right on Churchview Avenue. After walking one long block, and passing Waidler Street, which was the summit of yet another steep hill, our new house could be seen, about seven houses down.

CHURCHVIEW AVENUE:

THE PRE-TEEN YEARS

CHAPTER TWO

In the summer of 1938, the Bordy Family moved to a nice, large house at 1916 Churchview Avenue, in the Borough of Brentwood.

Before our move, I remember being in on the negotiations with the landlord. Sam and Mama managed to get this big three story house, with a large front porch, and a foyer, and a beautiful grand staircase, for forty five dollars a month.

I was aghast at the high figure. Where were we going to get forty five dollars a month?

Some coal had been left in the coal-bin and the landlord wanted another five dollars for it. That was a lot of money.

Sam argued back and forth, but the landlord won. So, for fifty dollars, in cash, we were ready to move into our new "mansion."

Even with all the extra space, their wasn't enough room for me in any of the bedrooms, so I slept on a wicker sofa in the ante-room, below the main staircase. I didn't mind, because it was fairly large, and like having my own private bedroom.

Directly across the street from our new house, was Fox's Woods, but we kids called it "Foxey's Woods." We never met "Old man Foxey," but we were afraid of him just the same, because we often "trespassed" on his property. It was a great playground for us. The land that bordered Churchview Avenue was level and grassy, for a few feet, then came a fairly steep slope, and, after that, was the glorious woods where we kids could go and have our adventures.

It was a fairly small woodland, but just the right size for pre-teen kids to play in. We never, or seldom, entered the woods directly from Churchview,

we were too afraid of the mythical "Foxey."

There was an entrance on Wildwood Street, which was the eastern border of our "playground." The western border was Sankey Avenue. If you hiked straight through the woods, you would reach Saint Wedelin's Catholic Church, School and Cemetery on Custer Avenue. There was a main path through the woods, starting on Wildwood Street, that the Catholic kids used to get to school. It was the entrance we other kids would use to get into the woods to play.

At the top of Sankey Avenue, even on a higher hill, stood a Catholic Convent, The Sisters of Something-or-other, I don't remember their name. Behind their property was the beginnings of "The Woods." The caretaker at the Nunnery was Mr. McGibben. He had a young son and a red headed daughter, Pearl's age, named Helen, who grew into a ravishing beauty.

Going east on Churchview, from the convent, toward our new house, was another big church. I think it was Presbyterian. Across the street from it was Cunningham's Candy Store where you could get a big, twelve ounce bottle of Pepsi Cola for only a nickel, and where the locals voted on election day.

A few houses down was the house where my future best friend, Ray Harmoning, would soon live. He and I never went to the same school, because this part of Churchview Avenue was in Carrick, and I lived in Brentwood.

Continuing east, at a curve in the road, Waidler Street began. If you stood in the middle of Churchview Avenue, at that juncture, you would be in three towns at the same time: to the west was Carrick, to the east was Baldwin Township, and the southern side of Churchview was the Borough of Brentwood, where we lived.

At that intersection, on the Carrick side, lived a Syrian family named Joseph. They had a dirty little daughter, called Lulu, who grew into a beauty. Their son's name was Joseph Joseph, but they called him Joe-Boy. There seemed to be so many people existing in that "falling apart," shanty of a building. They were boisterous, fought a lot, but were always cheerful, spouting Syrian at each other, and laughing. Their house was noisy and chaotic, but filled with love.

Where Baldwin began stood Foxey's house, a duplex. Prayer meetings were held there once a week, and soon Mama would begin attending. We kids thought they were "Holy Rollers," because when we spied on them, they were always on their knees, swaying. Mama assured us that they were not Holy Rollers, that they were merely praying. She enjoyed going there because it was "just across the street," and she could get out and socialize one evening a week.

To the left of us was the Obringer family, who were Irish Catholic, and probably everything you'd expect an Irish Catholic family to be. He drank a little, played cards a little, and fought a little. She stayed home taking care of the kids. They ate no meat on Fridays, and attended mass at St. Wedelin's, every Sunday.

Pearl had an instant friend with their daughter, Lois, who was Pearl's age. She was a chubby, jovial sort, with freckles, and a boyish bob hair style. I used to tease her by singing, "Obringer back, Obringer back, oh bring 'er back my Bonnie to me, to me." Somehow, she never saw the humor in it. She was a very serious Catholic girl, always studying her lessons, because if she didn't, the Nuns, who taught in the school, would whack her across the knuckles with a ruler. They were very strict disciplinarians, those Nuns.

The Obringers had a crippled son, Bob. He had a terrible limp, and when he walked, his arms flailed all over the place. How he managed to stand at all, let alone walk, was a miracle. He was one of the most cheerful people you'd ever want to meet. Nothing ever got him down. I don't think he realized just how crippled he was. He played ball, went on hikes with us guys, and, really, did everything all the other fellows did, except maybe, he did them a little slower and with greater animation.

Their son, Jack, was a year or two younger than I, while Bob was a year or two older. Jack was a quiet kid, and I don't remember him too well, probably because he was too young to play with the bigger kids.

Our neighbors, on the right, were the Viemans. Mrs. Vieman was a cultured American lady, with no accent. Her house was the most beautiful I had seen, to date. When she hung her curtains, she actually measured each fold, so that they hung perfectly. Perfection, it seems, was her mien. Nothing was ever out of place.

Earl was her son, who was probably Ed's age. We didn't see him too often, but occasionally, we would talk over the back yard hedges. He entertained me one day, by eating an apple and blowing out smoke, as if he got the smoke from the apple. After being amazed, he showed me how he did it. He took a deep drag of a cigarette, that he had been hiding, then a bite of the apple, then he would blow out the smoke.

The Bowdens lived about five or six houses down, from there. Mrs. Bowden, I thought, was beautiful. She was probably in her early thirties, who had coal black hair, pulled back tightly into a chignon, and wore bright red lipstick. The red and black, with her white, white skin, made quite a contrast. And to me, she was the most beautiful woman I had ever seen. She had three children, and was American born, with *no* accent.

I used to say a terrible thing to Mama: "Why aren't you young and pretty like Mrs. Bowden? And, when are you going to get rid of your accent, and speak good English?"

How cruel that was, and how hurt Mama must have been.

Joe Bowden was the oldest child, who had sugar diabetes. He was Pearl's age, and had to give himself an insulin shot every day. As a result, he was super serious, and aware of everything he ate, keeping track of each bite that entered his mouth. We never saw too much of him, because he stayed indoors and studied. He did have a paper route, however.

When I was ten or eleven, he took me along on his route, to teach it to me, so that I could do it when he went away on a vacation. I accompanied him for several weeks, and at the end of each day, he would take out a coin purse, and pay me a penny. When he went on vacation, I took over the route, and was paid three pennies a day. Paper delivery, I decided, was not for me, although I did try selling *Liberty Magazine*, at one time.

Miriam Bowden, like her mother was pretty, but not too friendly. She was two years younger than I, and for all practical purposes, she and I should have paired up. We never did. Although, she did "save my life," once. Like her brother, she too was so serious, and studious.

Charlotte Bowden was the polar opposite of her siblings. She was funny, outgoing, and knew how to enjoy herself. She was Sue's age, and the two of them became fast friends, keeping that friendship going for many years. You couldn't help but like "Charley." She had a little lisp, which was quite becoming. Though I teased her mercilessly, she was always a good sport, and kept her sense of humor.

Mrs. Bowden took an interest in her kids, and encouraged them to do practical things, as well as fun things. Each summer, Miriam and Charlotte would buy lemons and sugar, out of their allowance, and set up a lemonade stand in front of their house. They did quite well, and built up a following of passersby, walking home from work. I tried to give them a little competition, one year, but was not very successful. The "customers" seemed to prefer buying from two "perfect" little girls, rather than from a little boy, with a dirty face and hands.

Each summer, Mrs. Bowden would get most of the kids in the neighborhood to "put on a show" on her back yard porch. She would hang a curtain between the two porch posts, then open it when each kid performed his act.

I remember teaching Suzie a poem to recite, when she was about five: "I'm a little Dutch girl, I'm no so very fat. Come around the corner and I'll give you some of that." She was supposed to make a fist, and shake it threateningly at the audience when she said, "I'll give you some of that."

She froze, and couldn't do it, then she began to cry. She was so cute that the audience loved her, anyway. Little did I realize that that poem is from an old burlesque skit, where the "talking lady" does a "grind" and a "bump" when she says, "I'll give you some of *that!*" That was the end of Sue's Show Biz career!

Further on down Churchview Avenue, there was another small candy store, called Willet's. Across the alley, from Willet's, stood the Steinbecker's property, which stretched from that alley, all the way down to Willet Road, and down to Brevard Avenue, a whole city block. That property was, at one time, part of a large farm, that had been sub-divided. The Steinbeckers were poor paper hangers, with a bunch of dirty kids, who lived in the big, rundown house that remained on the property. I guess they weren't too poor, if they owned a whole city block! They sure as heck did look, and act poor, though. Perhaps, they only rented.

Where the Steinbeckers property ended, and across Willet Road, on Churchview, was Feld's Ice Cream Parlor, where Pearl broke her arm. Willet Road was the boundary line of Baldwin Township. Next door to Feld's was a very handy butcher shop, where Mama would do her last minute shopping for meat.

Once, she sent me there, with ten cents, to get a dime's worth of steak for Sam's dinner. After the butcher cut and weighed it, he told me it would cost eleven cents. I panicked, having only a dime. That sent him into a rage.

"How the hell do you expect me to cut exactly ten cents worth of steak?" he screamed.

All I knew was that, I only had a dime to pay for the meat, and couldn't go home without it. He shoved his knife toward me and ranted.

"Here, you cut it, see if you can cut exactly ten cents worth, you stupid kid!"

I declined. Still furious, he wrapped the meat and shoved it at me saying, "Here, take your Goddamned ten cent steak! And don't come back here, ever again!"

One day, Mama forced me to return, this time for cold cuts. I was scared to death to re-encounter that butcher. After entering the shop, my heart was beating fast. Trying to disguise myself, by changing the way I walked and stood, I lowered my eyes, and asked for my five cents worth of spiced ham.

He couldn't have been nicer. But, what if he sliced too much? I only had a nickel! There was no need to fret. He handed me the spiced ham, I handed him the nickel, he smiled nicely, and thanked me. My fears were over.

Beyond the butcher shop, Churchview Avenue continued to run on for miles, through the Baldwin Township farmlands and countryside. After I got my first bicycle, that stretch of road became my favorite riding route.

Usually, I'd ride alone, but sometimes I would ride with one of the neighborhood kids. We'd steal those beautiful, luscious Concord grapes and gorge ourselves on them. We never brought any home because Mama would be furious if she knew we were stealing. It was always an adventure riding on that old, country road, exploring the various farms, and eating their produce.

"Joe," Jogeese, was still courting Martha when we moved to Churchview. Sue and I always looked forward to his visits because he brought

37

us, each, a big, nickel candy bar. He was crazy about Suzie, but only tolerated me. I tried so hard to please and amuse him, but I *was* probably a little too hyperactive for him.

He tried to be nice to me, but it was Sue he really made the fuss over by picking her up and kissing her, and bouncing her on his knee, while pretty much ignoring me. That didn't bother me, so long as he brought me my big candy bar.

One week, he came to visit and only brought Sue a candy bar. I asked him where mine was, and he snapped, grabbed me, threw me over his knee, and began paddling the Hell out of me. What had I done?

"You brat. You terrible brat! I'll teach you to talk to me, and your mother, the way you do. She works and slaves for you, and you treat her like an old work-horse. Who the Hell do you think you are?"

He ranted on, and on, while beating me. Mama wasn't even in the room, how could I have been "talking back" to her? She came into the room and joined in on the chiding, urging him on, agreeing with him that I was such a bad boy.

All I ever wanted to do was be nice to everybody, to amuse and entertain people. They thought I was being "smart Alecky." I cried, then sulked into the corner to get away. Then, quietly, I stole away to the top of the staircase.

After my departure, Joe continued playing with Sue, flattering Mama, and flirting with Martha, as though nothing had happened. From the top of the stairs, I spied on them, listening to everything they said. When the conversation got too soft, I leaned further over the banister to hear better. I leaned too far, and over the railing I went, "flying," again.

It was a short flight, landing on the floor behind my "bed." An old gas jet, about two inched high, jutted out of the floor, and gouged me in the back of the head. Blood poured out profusely. Joe would have to stop griping and get me to a doctor.

They took me to Dr. Uptagraff's office, at the bottom of Sankey Avenue, near Brownsville Road. Fortunately, he was still in his office, and he sewed me up. After that night, Joe Jogeese was avoided by me. The only thing I missed about the relationship, anyway, was the candy bar.

Martha and Joe got married and moved into a nice apartment on Brownsville Road, just above the hill from where Marie and Art Tombs had their house. It seems that Martha and Marie would forever be entwined in each others lives. They were still in business together, and had a love/hate relationship, all their lives.

In September of 1938, I began third grade at Elroy Elementary School. Pearl started the fifth. We continued there for the next four years. It was located on Elroy Avenue and Bellecrest Street, about a half a mile from where we lived. It was a long, pleasant walk, except in the winter when ice and snow were on the ground.

At first Pearl and I would walk to school together, then she met Frances

Ferri, who would become her life-long friend. Frances lived right around the corner, near the top of Waidler Avenue. How convenient! After they started walking to school, together, I saw no reason why I couldn't continue walking with them.

They did everything they could to prevent me from accompanying them. I was not easily discouraged. After much bickering, we decided that I would walk ten or fifteen feet behind them. That way they could have their privacy.

The only teacher I really remember was Miss Sefton. She was my third grade home-room teacher. Besides her being so kind, what I remember most about her was that, each day, she read to us from the L. Frank Baum "Oz" books. We were all enraptured with the tales, and looked forward to each day's installment. This was before the 1939 motion picture of "The Wizard of Oz" was released.

I do remember some of my classmates. Several of them lived right on Elroy or Bellecrest. There was a real beauty called Marcella Daelhausen; a snooty little girl named Nancy Tear; and a cute, vivacious Betty Ann Griffin. I saw them all fairly recently, at our fiftieth fifth High School Reunion, of the class of 1948.

Also, from the third grade, I remember Joan Carnahan, Ken Eskey, Sheila Forrester, Jim Harrold, Lindy Becker, Ray Dunsey, Lois Marsh, Mary Ann Carpellucci, Ron Clark, Dick Amerhein, Norma Hedrick, Joan Dunbar, Loretta Siefort, Jean Bishop, Norma Yeager. and my very first girlfriend, Barbara Hiller.

One day, Barbara and I started sending "love notes," back and forth, to each other, during one of our classes. Her note simply said, "I love you." And I responded with, "I love you, too." Or, was it the other way around. Did I start the "romance?" This "love affair" went on for months, perhaps even the entire year.

I told sister Pearl about my infatuation with Barbara Hiller, and pointed her out.

"What do you see in her," Pearl asked. "She's not very pretty. You can do better than that."

This shocked the heck out of me, I thought she was beautiful. I decided to "end it all," the next day, by writing her a note that said, "I hate you."

Without missing a beat, she responded exactly the same way: "I hate you, too." So ended my first love affair.

At our fifty fifth high school reunion, we reminisced about our torrid romance. Jokingly, she said that she was "available," and that we could start over, again. She still looked pretty good.

There was this delightful, happy-go-lucky boy in our third grade class, named Louis Consilla. He had coal black, strait hair that fell in his eyes, wore short, short pants, was always so disheveled, but had the greatest smile.

One day, the teacher had him at the blackboard,

harassing him into giving an answer to something he obviously didn't know. Poor Louie got so scared and bewildered at the teacher, that he peed his pants.

A week later Louie was gone from Elroy, never to return. I felt so sorry for him, and missed him after he went. He and Jim Harrold were the only two boys, in our class, who were smaller than I. Jim and I remained the shortest up through the eleventh grade, then I got taller.

Years later, when I was living in Hollywood, California, I met Louie, again. It must have been 1958 or 59, at about 2:30 in the morning. I had been out drinking, "hitting the joints," and now I was hungry. I stopped at an outdoor coffee shop, on Vine Street, for a cheeseburger and a cup of coffee.

I looked up, and sitting directly across from me was this cheerful looking fellow, with straight, black hair, smiling at me. He stared at and me, and I stared at him. Could it be? I asked, "Louie?" He asked, "Bill?" Then I inquired further, "Louis Consilla?" He queried, "Bill Bordy?" We had actually recognized each other, after all that time. This was not the sloppy, little beleaguered kid I knew in third grade. He was still short, but very suave in appearance, and quite good looking.

What had happened to him after he left Elroy? He told me that his family moved to Hollywood, and that he had played a little Indian boy in the motion picture, "The Last of the Mohicans" (or was it "Drums Along the Mohawk?")

Wow, was I impressed. I had come to Hollywood to "break into pictures," too. We gave each other our phone numbers, and promised to get together. We never did. I really liked Louie, and still wonder whatever happened to him.

Martha and Joe could no longer afford their apartment on Brownsville Road, (or was it because she was pregnant with Marilyn?). Supposedly, to "help out," they left there, and moved into the front bedroom of our Churchview Avenue house.

Now, that miserable brother-in-law would be under foot, all the time. Actually, the move worked out pretty well, because Joe was on the road a lot.

Because Martha was pregnant, it was better that she was home, with Mama, in case of an emergency. She was good company for Mama, and we kids all enjoyed her being around, too. She was much friendlier than Marie.

Martha and Joe enjoyed a cocktail, now and again. Mama was a teetotaler, and didn't allow alcohol in the house. One hot summer evening, Martha offered to make Mama a "lemonade," which she spiked with gin. Mama drank it, and I never saw her so relaxed and jovial.

What a lovely, friendly evening that night had become. The following evening, Mama asked Martha for another one of her special lemonades. She had really enjoyed it. Maybe if Mama had had a drink, once in a while, she would have lived longer than her fifty-three years.

The Jogeeses only lived with us for the duration of Martha's pregnancy. After the baby was born, they moved into a new apartment, at the bottom of some hill in Brentwood. Marilyn was born on May 9th, 1940, and I became a proud uncle at the age of nine and a half.

Each year, on May 1st, Elroy had a big Mayday Celebration. The pretty young girls looked forward to Mayday, with hopes of becoming Queen of the May, or as they called it, May Queen.

To be eligible, you had to have perfect teeth. Miss Stilley, the dental hygienist, who cleaned and examined the teeth of every student, once a year, was the one to decide who was eligible.

Sister Pearl had a big gap between her two front teeth, but somehow or other, she won the title that summer of 1940.

Mama made her a "gown," that she hated. It was made out of taffeta, with a huge hem. Mama didn't want to waste the material. Pearl was not very happy.

On Sunday mornings, Art Tombs began bringing his son, Bobby, to our house, so he could go to church with Pearl, Suzie and me. Bobby was a nice quiet kid, who lived with his grandmother, way out in Baldwin Township.

Marie wasn't going to get bogged down with the raising of a kid, not yet anyways. Bobby sure as heck looked like a Bordy, and fit right, in age wise, between Sue and me.

Bobby, along with all the Bordys, looked forward to Mama's Sunday feast. Like me, he loved the red Jello dessert, with cake and ice cream. These happy days only lasted a year or so. Marie divorced Art, I know not why.

Pearl and I had never seen our new niece, so one Sunday, after church, we made the trek to Martha and Joe's new apartment, to see her.

41

It was way out Brownsville Road, and down at the bottom of, yet, another hill. We knocked and knocked, but no answer. They had to be home, maybe we weren't knocking loud enough. Bang, bang!

Martha, angrily, came to the door, in her blue silk kimono, and let us in. Was she still in bed sleeping? She told us to wait, then returned to her bedroom. How long did we wait? It seemed like an hour. What was she doing in that bedroom? Did she go back to sleep?

Finally, she brought out our new niece. What a disappointment! She was all pink and ugly, with only a few wisps of blonde hair. On top of her head was, what appeared to be, a huge red lump.

What the heck, she was our first niece, and we were still happy to spend some time with her, even though she didn't smile very much. She was not a happy baby.

Marilyn was born with that "strawberry" on her head; that's what they called it. It was a small, strawberry-sized aneurysm. To reduce its size, she was given radiation treatments. It seemed to recede, but she would always have a tender spot on the top of her head.

All went well until she was in her mid thirties. While taking a shower, she fell and hit her head. The aneurysm burst, and she died. What a sad end, to a very sad girl, with a very sad life.

As a kid, **my ears protruded**. After "Dumbo," the Walt Disney Movie was released, in 1941, some of the mean kids started calling me by that name.

"Dumbo" was the story of a baby elephant, with giant ears, who was shunned, and humiliated, by the other elephants. Thus, I was called Dumbo, by a cruel few. My ears weren't really big, they just stuck out.

On the walk home from school, I often encountered a nasty hooligan, called Roy Potts. I didn't know his name at the time, nor did he go to my school. He would sit on his front porch, on Pyramid Avenue, waiting for me to pass by, in order to could call me Dumbo. I would ignore him, and keep on walking, but his insults followed me.

One day, in the middle of winter, with much snow and ice on the ground, I was, once again, accosted by Potts. This time, he actually got off his porch and stood directly in front of me, on my left foot, screaming in my face.

I still don't know why he hated me so much, but he did. When he was done lashing out, he pushed me to the snowy ground, while still standing on my foot. He stormed off, leaving me in the snow with, what I thought was, a broken foot.

Not being able to get up, I remained on the ground for a good ten to fifteen minutes. Then miracle of miracles, Miriam Bowden ventured by. I told her what had happened, and that I couldn't walk. Not to worry, she would get help.

Sure enough, she and her brother, Joe, returned, pulling his little red delivery wagon. I got into it, and somehow, they managed to pull me, and that wagon, up Pyramid Avenue, then up that very steep Waidler Avenue, to Churchview Avenue, and then finally to the Bordy house.

Poor Mama was panic stricken. Somehow, she got me to St. Joseph's hospital, in South Side, which was quite a distance from home. Why she took me there, and how we got there, I can't recollect. Had we actually taken a taxi? Possibly.

I do remember being placed on a gurney, in some kind of a waiting room, without Mama. There was a guy, in his twenties, sprawled out on the gurney next to me, singing "Blues in the Night." He kept repeating the phrase, "….from Memphis to Saint Joe, wherever the trade winds blow…." What an appropriate song to sing in Saint "Joe's" Hospital.

It seemed like I was there for hours, waiting for the doctor to put a cast on my foot. It wasn't broken, but it had been cracked in three places. A cast was needed, which the doctor proceeded to apply.

Until that time, I had never owned a pair of long pants. All the boys wore "knickers." American knickers, not to be confused with English knickers, which are women's panties, were trousers that all American boys wore, in those days. They had elastic bottoms, and came to just below the knees, so they could hold up your stockings. To put the cast on, the doctor had to slit the elastic on the left pant leg, in order to apply the plaster of Paris.

The cast covered most of my foot, except for the toes. It went up my leg to the knee. Neither my shoe, nor my stocking, could be utilized, so I had to leave the hospital, with my toes exposed to the elements.

It was a cold day and my toes were freezing while we waited for the bus to take us home. Afraid to put my weight on the new cast, I hopped all the way to the bus stop, with Mama's help. After the bus arrived, I hopped up the stairs, and we were on our way home.

The bus-stop, on Churchview, was not near our house, but Mama sweet talked the driver into stopping in front of it. I hopped down the steps, then slid and fell on the icy ground. The bus sped off and, believe it or not, Mama reached down, and picked me up in her arms, carrying me up the five snow covered steps, up the fifteen foot walkway to the three steps of the porch, then up those steps, and into the house. How could she do it? She had super strength, when she needed it.

On our next visit to the doctor's, he added a metal brace, that ran down the two sides of the cast, and joined together under the foot. There was rubber on the bottom of the brace, which allowed me to walk on it. Now, I wouldn't have to hop around, anymore.

Papa had returned from California, and reopened his shoe repair shop, in Homestead. For a while, he was living in its back room. On week-ends, he was allowed to come home for his Saturday night bath ritual, in which he scrubbed himself raw, with a brush, and left a big, black ring around the tub.

On Sunday mornings, he would get dressed-up in a suit and tie to go to "Jew Town," to see his friend and leather supplier, Mr. Ferber. I never understood how they could conduct business, buying and selling leather, on a Sunday. Yes, "Jew Town" was "open for business." It absolutely amazed me, the first time I accompanied him there. Gee, you could buy *anything* on a Sunday, just like Saturdays in downtown Pittsburgh.

Mama asked Papa to make me some kind of a shoe that would fit over my toes and the lower part of the cast. He took a large leather sole, sewed soft leather to it, and added shoe strings. It fit, quite well, over my toes and lower foot. Now, I could walk on my new brace, and go to school. And, I finally got my first pair of long pants. No more knickers for me!

On Christmas Eve of 1941, Doctor Emmett Duane Carmalt came a-wooing Marie at our house on Churchview Avenue. This was the first time any of the family had ever seen him. He was very serious, and perhaps a little intimidated by the big Bordy family that Marie had sprung on him.

He was rather diminutive and soft spoken, exhibiting a large, black moustache. To me he looked like a cross between Hitler and Charlie Chaplin. Everyone was impressed that he was a Doctor, someone who immediately deserved respect. Mama was enthralled.

Even though this was Christmas Eve, he barely spoke. Marie made up for it, though, by doting over him, and nuzzling up to him. Her trap was set!

The good doctor brought with him, the largest red, Christmas stocking, ever seen. It was jammed solid with beautiful, meticulously wrapped gifts. After we kids opened all of our presents, it was time for Marie to start unwrapping everything in her stocking.

Many of the "gifts" were toys, or gag items. Aha, the doctor had a sense of humor! Suzie and I were ecstatic because Marie gave the gag gifts, and toys, to us. The glamorous and elegant stuff, she kept for herself.

Then, finally, the *coup de grace*: in the toe of the stocking was the final gift. It was an elegant, twenty-four jeweled, Elgin wrist watch. Very impressive, and expensive!

Of course, Marie blubbered all over her new beau. She was ready to reel him in, and she did. Soon they were married, and moved to Charles Street, in Knoxville, where she, immediately, began renovations on his impressive old house.

Philco Radio Corporation transferred Joe to Atlanta, Georgia, for about a year. That's where Marilyn got the Southern nick-name of "Mame." At last, she was growing into a cute little girl.

Martha seemed to have really enjoyed her time there, because when she returned to "The North," all of a sudden, she became Scarlett O'Hara. All the southern belle mannerisms, and ways of innocent flir-tation, had become hers.

When she returned to Pittsburgh, they moved in with us, again, on Churchview, until Joe got his next transfer.

It was so much fun going out with my Southern Belle sister. I remember a bus trip we took, together, to downtown Pittsburgh. Instead of her accent going away, it got thicker. And, the thicker it got, the more demure she became, and the more she fluttered her eye lashes.

She asked the bus driver if his bus went past Kaufmann's Department Store; she knew darn well that it did. After saying, yes, he asked her what part of the south she was from.

"Wha, dear me, Ah'm not from the south, Ah'm from right he-ah in Pittsburgh," she responded. "What accent? Wha, yes, I did live in Atlanta for a little while, but Ah'm sure Ah don't have any accent." Flutter, flutter!

It was good having Martha home, she was always so much fun. Even Mamie was developing a friendly personality, with a touch of Georgia about her, too. They didn't stay too long. Philco would, again, transfer them, this time to Philadelphia.

Ruth had been working at Isaly's, in South Side, not the best neigh-borhood to work in, but she enjoyed it there. The guys were a little rougher than in Carrick, but that never bothered her. Blackie could always take care of herself.

One day, during the war, she met a fly-boy named Delwyn "Dale" Peterson. He was home on leave, was lonesome, asked Ruth to marry him, and she accepted. She was only seventeen or eighteen at the time. They were no sooner married than he had to return to his base. Ruth was doing her part for the war effort, and got an allotment check, as well. That would help Mama.

RAY HARMONING

My new buddy, Ray Harmoning, moved to Churchview Avenue, about six houses away from Cunningham's Grocery Store. At that time, he was twelve or thirteen, with two older brothers, Earl and Howard. Howard became brother Ed's best friend, and Ray, mine.

Their father was a very gaunt and emaciated coal miner who came home covered in coal dust every evening. Their mother was the fattest woman I had ever seen, up to that time. She could barely walk, and spent her life sitting at the kitchen table, preparing food, holding court, and conducting family business.

When she had to go to the bathroom, Ray would to help her down the stairs to the basement toilet. He'd wait for her, while she urinated or defecated. Her arms were so fat and short. that he'd have to wipe her. It didn't bother him at all.

He'd go to the store for her and, conveniently, forget to give her the change. When he needed money, he thought nothing of taking it from her purse, that way he always had enough money for his soda pop and candy.

Mrs. Harmoning was like no one I had ever met. She was loud, course, and flatulent. Whenever Ray asked her what they were having for dinner, her standard response was, "Fried farts and pickled ass holes!" I still gasp thinking of that reply.

Mama felt sorry for her and conned her into accompanying her to a weekly prayer meeting held at Foxey's apartment. After one trip, Mrs. Harmoning begged off, citing her difficulty with mobility. She wasn't, really, what one would call religious. Why the Hell should she have to hang out with those damn Holy Rollers?

Ray had his own room up in the attic, where he kept his stash of dirty pictures and Jo-Jo Books, under his bed. Jo-Jos were little books of famous cartoon characters doing all kinds of sexually graphic things. Where he got this stuff, no one knows, but all the gang was always anxious to see anything new.

He was very good at making model airplanes, and taught me how to make them out of balsa wood and paper. It was very difficult to meticulously cut out all those parts with an x-acto knife. Once they were cut out, the fun began by putting it all together with airplane glue, and painting the fuselage with banana oil. We would get very woozy from the fumes, and were probably "high," without knowing it. The smell of airplane glue and banana oil really was a "turn-on" for us.

The completion of my first model airplane couldn't have come at a more opportune time. Corporal Delwyn Petersen, Ruth's new husband, was coming home on leave. Being a flyer in the U.S. Army Air Corps, I was sure he'd be excited to see my first model airplane. He ignored it, and me, completely, as though neither existed. I didn't like Delwyn Petersen very much, and apparently Ruth didn't either. They divorced shortly after, and we never saw him again.

Ray and I stayed friends for many years. When we got older, we would play hooky from high school and go downtown to Jaffe's Casino. "Jaffey's" was not a gambling casino; it was an old fashioned burlesque house. We loved it there. They had the proverbial four shows a day, with all the old time comedy acts, and of course, the strippers!

By going as often as we did, we got to know who all the comics and all the permanent chorus girls were. Some of them weren't very attractive, but they sure tried hard. After all, they were in "Show Business!" They actually had a pretty good choreographer who created some very interesting routines, so even the lousy dancers excelled, with her choreography.

Each week, there was a star stripper. Some were fantastic, some not so hot. What really got Ray mad was when they tried to pass off one of the regular chorus girls as the star.

Many of the old Burlesque Stars did play Jaffe's, but at that stage of our lives, we didn't know one from the other. If they looked good in their photos, we went to see them. As the years passed, we got to know them all.

I especially remember one of the comics. He was Billy "cheese n' crackers" Hogan. He played often at Jaffe's, was extremely hilarious, and would say some of the most outrageous things, that could really shock the uninitiated. His remarks sounded "dirty," but weren't, really. It was very clever how he stayed just within an inch of the law.

Yes, I loved the comics. Ray, on the other hand, physically matured earlier than I, and his purposes were purely prurient. His main desire was to watch the girls "take 'em off." Soon he "graduated."

As we reached our late teens, occasionally, on Saturday mornings, I would accompany Ray to downtown Pittsburgh, then walk across the Allegheny River to, what was called, The North Side. There, he could visit one of the many whorehouses, and get a girl for two dollars.

He liked to get there early, because the girls were fresh as a daisy, and horny, after a good night's rest. I'd wait for him, outside, until he came out, always with a big smile on his face. One time, I did go in to "window shop," but I wasn't about to pay two dollars for some old bag of twenty. Two bucks was a hell of a lot of money!

Papa pulled up stakes and moved to California for his health, again. He had developed a terrible cough that he blamed on the dirty air from the steel mills' emissions, and the leather dust he inhaled when he ground the soles of the shoes that he repaired. Once more, he asked Mama to go with him and, again, Mama refused.

This time he set up shop on Figueroa Street in downtown Los Angeles. Papa was never out of business long.

His new shop was about twenty-five miles from the mineral baths in Lake Elsinore. He loved the sun and the mud! On weekends, he would go there and stay at the Lake Elsinore Hotel.

Years later, I would live in that very same hotel, for a short time. During the 1967/68 school term, I taught Arts and Crafts at the Lakeside Lodge, a reform school for "the worst boys in the state of California." The State of California said that, not I. Most were very smart, just a little too hyper, or too imaginative. I got along well with the boys; it was the management that needed disciplining. That teaching sojourn only lasted two semesters.

Sue was finishing up her second year, and I was finishing up my sixth year, at Elroy Elementary School. Our lease on Churchview Avenue ran out, so it was time for our family to move, again. What a perfect time! In September, I would be a freshman at Brentwood High School. Pearl, by this time, had already gone there for two years.

CARRICK AVENUE

THE SUMMER OF DIRTY OLD MEN

CHAPTER THREE

It was the summer of 1942, and the Second World War was on. The house on Carrick Avenue was as close to a mansion as any of us had ever seen. It was built of yellow bricks, and was located half way up a very steep yard. This yard was even steeper, and higher, and wider, than Maytide Street. There were ten or fifteen steps going up to the massive front porch. The yard was beautifully manicured with rose bushes and lush green foliage. It was located directly across the street from an empty lot, where the Carrick Grade School had once stood. The "basement" had been filled in, and the irregular terrain became the neighborhood playground.

The inside of the house was laid out similarly to the Churchview Avenue house, only larger and grander. The ante room was one and a half times the size as the one on Churchview. There was not only a "grand" staircase in the front of the house, but there was a servants' staircase, as well.

The rent was a little more than we had expected to pay, but we were only going to stay there until we could find another house and move back to Brentwood. Pearl and I had already enrolled in Brentwood High School, with the hopes that we would find a new place to live before the end of the summer. Of course, we did not tell the landlords that.

The house was perfect, except for two things: The landlords! They were two ancient brothers who lived there with us. They inhabited a room on the second floor, and did their cooking and bathing in the cellar. The house reeked of a foul odor that came from their kitchen. We never did find out what they cooked there that gave off such a vile emission.

They did keep the outside of the building gloriously beautiful, though. At least it smelled fine. It took them the entire week to mow and prune the yard. On Monday morning, one of them would start pushing the lawn mower at the top of the yard, while the other pruned the plant life. By Friday, they finished their chores, then on Saturday and Sunday, they would listen to the ball games. This was their only other interest, beside their house and yard, except maybe Mama.

They were baseball fanatics. I never really cared for baseball, but one Saturday, they insisted I listen to the game with them, in their room. Mama would not let me get out of it. It must have been the longest baseball game in history.

They kept saying, "The balloon's gonna go up, now!" I assumed that meant that the game would soon end. It didn't. "Ah, the balloon's gonna go up any minute, now!" It didn't.

There must have been twelve innings in that darn game. Finally, it did come to an end. I was exhausted. They invited me to have dinner with them.

No way! That was one of the longest, and most boring, afternoon I ever spent in my life.

There was one other bad habit the old geezers had: They loved buxom Mama, and chased her all over the house. Certainly, she was flattered, and in her own inimitable way, encouraged them. If they caught her, surely they wouldn't have known what to do with her.

They had a cat that they called Pussy. Being a cat, she was always missing from the yard, cattin' around somewhere. When they missed her, they would call out, "Pussy, Pussy, Pussy, where are you? Get home, right now, you dumb cat."

They both had much excess skin under their necks, so naturally, I would imitate them by pulling down the flesh under my chin and call out, as well, "Pussy, Pussy, Pussy. Come on home you dumb cat."

Mama was afraid they would catch me imitating them, but they never did.

Before Marie married Emmett, she had his house completely remodeled. It, too, was a grand old, three story house, located on Charles Street, in a nice, suburban town, called Knoxville, about five miles south of Carrick Avenue. The doctor had office hours in the house, and saw patients every evening, after he got home from the Shadyside Hospital. He had been doing this for years. Marie would have preferred otherwise, but it was the one compromise she would have to make for this prestigious union.

There was a large ante room as you entered the Charles Street house; this was utilized as the waiting room for the patients. Two enormous, sliding doors separated the waiting room from the rest of the house. Down a short hallway, Emmett had his examination room. There were no nurses, no receptionists, no accountants. He did it all by himself.

The patients let themselves in and waited for the doctor to finish with the previous patient. Then, the doctor himself would usher the old patient out and the new one into the examination room. No appointments necessary. The whole procedure ran pretty much like your local, friendly barber shop. And, it was all in cash, too. No such thing as credit cards.

The top floor of the Charles Street house had been used, at one time, as a mini hospital/laboratory, for Emmett's patients, who needed "special" care. With Marie's arrival, there were to be no more, in-house, "guests."

She turned the space into a secretarial office, where she did mimeographing for many of her old clients who still needed her services. She seldom did the work, herself. Ruth was, usually, drafted to do it, for her. Mama always volunteered her children to work, especially for Marie.

On the corner of Carrick Avenue and Brownsville Road, stood a hamburger joint called "Villella's, were Ruth went to work for Mr. Villella and his daughter, Eva. She and Ruth became very good friends and "Pop" Villella treated her like another daughter. Eva lived in a duplex, behind the café, with her Irish husband Bill Flynn, and their two small daughters, Barbara and Patty.

50

It was nice having Ruthie working so near. Villella's was a great place for older kids to hang out, have a hamburger, dance, and play the pinball machines. I was a little too young to patronize the place in the evening, but Ruth allowed me to visit there in the afternoons.

She made me my very first hamburger. 'Til that time, I had only eaten hot dogs. Villella's didn't have hot dogs, so I had to settle for a hamburger. How could anyone eat that awful red stuff? First, Ruth took a round ball of ground meat and threw it on the hot grill.

The meat sizzled while she smashed it flat with the spatula. Sizzle, sizzle. Then she turned the patty over, squishing it, again. She threw the hamburger bun on the grill, covering it with a lid. Sizzle, sizzle. It started smelling pretty good. Then a little salt and pepper. Did I want ketchup or mustard? No, nothing, just the meat, and bun, and some sweet relish. It wasn't bad. It didn't take long to develop a taste for hamburgers, and replace the relish with dill pickles and fried onions.

 **Ruth tells the story about that summer of '42,** when Ed was still in his teens, and hadn't, yet, joined the Army.

It was pouring down rain when a customer came into Villella's to tell her that her brother, and his buddy Howard Harmoning, were literally, fallen down drunk on Brownsville Road, in front of the cemetery. Ruth got two male customers to go with her to where the two boys were sprawled out.

They were moaning in the gutter. Ed told me that he had shit his pants and was vomiting all over the place. It seems that he, and Howard, had met some guy in front of Vitale's drug store who had a bottle of booze. The three of them had a grand old time swigging the contents of the bottle. Neither Ed nor Howard had drunk much liquor, so they really got smashed.

It began to rain and was time to amble back to Carrick Avenue, before the deluge. The quarter mile walk proved to be more difficult than imagined, and they collapsed at the cemetery. How *apropos!*

Ruth found "the boys," and managed to get them back to the Carrick Avenue house, up the long flight of stairs to the porch, where they passed out. At least they were out of the rain. Ruth would come back, later, to tend to them.

After work, she wakened the boys and snuck them into the cellar were she hosed them off. They took off their clothes and swaddled themselves in some old rags. Ruth snuck them up the back staircase to the attic, then put them to bed. There, they, immediately passed out, again.

How they managed to get past Mama's room, and the old geezers' room, without rousing them, we'll never know. "Blackie" had come to the rescue of "Dutch," one more time. When the guys awoke in the morning, naked in Ed's bed, they could not figure out what had happened. And why were they naked?

That summer, Pearl had gotten herself a job at Isaly's on Brownsville Road, two doors down from the bowling alley where Ed used to shine shoes. Pearl just turned fourteen, but was very tall for her age. She was assigned a double shift on Saturdays and Sundays, and was given the key to open the place in the morning, and close it at night. How the manager got away with this, no one knows. The important thing was that he could have his weekends off. Poor Pearl was all alone slicing meat, selling dairy products, making sodas and sundaes, and then cleaning up at the end of her shift.

One Sunday afternoon, the boss stopped by to check on her. Pearl loved to read, and had been reading the Sunday Newspaper in the back room, which he soon discovered. Rather than say anything to Pearl, he ripped up the entire paper and threw it in the trash.

Later, when she discovered this, she furiously telephoned him and *ordered* him to "return immediately!" When he got there, she ranted and raved at him, threw the key in his face, and told him to keep his lousy job. Then, she stormed out of the store, never to return, not even for her pay. Her summer sojourn with Klondikes, buttermilk, and chipped chopped ham, had ended.

It was a pleasant, lazy summer that year. Beside playing in the empty lot, that once housed my grade school, what I remember most was sitting on the swing of our front porch and singing at the top of my lungs, in my high, soprano voice. Secretly, I was hoping that someone would "discover" me. I remember singing "Johnny Doughboy Found a Rose in Ireland," "Chickita, Markita, Lolita, Papita, Rosita, Juanita Lopez," and, of course, "Somewhere Over the Rainbow."

After joining the Cub Scouts, they asked me to sing at one of the meetings. I chose the very macho military song, "Over the Sea, Let's go Men." How ridiculous it must have seemed with this tiny, effete little guy, "leading his men to war," in this high pitched, soprano voice. No one laughed, but I was not asked to sing, again.

Other than the dirty old men chasing Mama, not much else happened that summer. September came around and it was time to enroll in Brentwood High School. How were we going to do that when we were living in Carrick? We deluded them into thinking that we were still living on Churchview Avenue.

When school reopened, Pearl and I began the long trek from Carrick Avenue to Brentwood High School, dropping off Suzie, at Elroy grade school. It was a long distance, but we did walk it. After turning left on Brownsville Road, we walked past the Birmingham Cemetery, past Sankey Avenue and the Melrose Theater, past the Lutheran Church, to Bellecrest Street (where Elroy School was located), then up and down many small hills, passing many homes. After that long trek, we would arrive at Brentwood High School, my future alma mater. Fortunately, by the time winter came, we found a new house and moved closer.

Sam would joined the Marine Corps on September 11th. He went to

boot camp at Parris Island, South Carolina. Later, he served on an aircraft carrier where he was an aide to Admiral Montgomery. Of course, he got all the razzing about being a "sea going bell-hop," to which the correct response was: "The only belle I ever hopped was your mother, and she was a bum lay!"

He did see plenty of action, though, and lost the hearing in his right ear because of a near-by explosion aboard his ship.

Ed hadn't joined the Army, yet, but he "signed up" in December, and was inducted on January 20, 1943. He went for his basic training at Ft. Meade, Maryland. Later he was stationed at Fort Bragg, where he became a "tank destroyer." He was sent to Guam, in the South Pacific, and then to the islands of Pelau. He hated it there! He hated the "Gooks," he hated the climate, he hated everything, but he did survive. They both survived.

With the war on, Mama could no longer be a German. She had to become a good American, so she started her studies, passed her exams, and became a proud American citizen, with two boys fighting for *her* country.

BREVARD AVENUE

THE TEEN AGE YEARS

CHAPTER FOUR

Marie came to the rescue, again. In October of 1943, she got the down payment from her new husband, Dr. Carmalt; and, Susan Elischer Bordy became the proud owner, almost, of 2946 Brevard Avenue, in Brentwood. It was just behind the Steinberger's property, near where we lived on Churchview Avenue. Sam and Ed's allotment checks from the government, would be enough to pay the monthly mortgage.

This house was not nearly so grand as our two previous houses, but it was comfy and cozy. It was located on a jog in the road, so two sides of our house faced Brevard Avenue. There was a small front porch with a glider, a nice size, slanted side yard, and a steep, triangular shaped back yard, where Mama could plant her "Victory Garden." During the war, everyone was encouraged to grow their own produce. Mama always planted tomato plants, green peppers, radishes, carrots and corn. In our back yard there was a large elderberry bush and a lilac bush, so we had fruit, vegetables and flowers. The entire side of the house was covered with ivy, (not shown in the above photo because it was taken thirty years later).

Coming in the front door was a small ante room. To the left was a narrow staircase to the second floor. Straight ahead was a small kitchen, then the sun porch. To the right of the foyer was the living room, with dark, Royal blue carpets, which would accommodate the elegant furniture that Marie bought when she was married to Art Tombs. This room would soon become "untouchable" to any of the family. It was to be used, strictly, for company.

Through the double arch of the living room was a good sized dining room, just perfect for our family dinners. Then, there was a swinging door into the other end of the sun porch. The sun porch became the "family room." It had a studio couch, a small table and chairs for meals, and a radio. Television sets weren't being made, yet. From the table, you could see the unpaved part of Brevard Avenue, running to Willet Road.

From the back windows of the sun porch, you could see our back yard and the pathway that ran almost a mile, through some farmland, all the way to the back of Brentwood Park, where we would go swimming in the summer. Up a steep hill from the park stood the rear of Brentwood High School.

The third side of the sun porch had no windows, but it did have a large closet that ran the entire length of that wall.

Below the sun porch, in the cellar, was a "finished off" room with wooden floors and a door to the side yard. It was furnished with odds and ends, and it became my *pied a terre*. We stored our huge McCausland player piano there, that we kids would pretend to play for hours on end. I wanted to take piano lessons, but was refused because Martha's lessons, on the violin, were a waste of time, as will as Pearl's, with the piano.

"Ve don't have no money to vaste on no more lessons," Mama told me.

For hours on end, I would pretend to play, "Miss Annabel Lee," "Big Tin Pan Parade," "The Unknown Soldier's Grave," "Just Let a Smile be Your Umbrella on a Rainy, Rainy day," and many other player-rolls, that we had collected.

My favorite piece of furniture was stored in the basement room, as well. It was a huge arm chair that had two lions' heads at the ends of each arm. By sitting in it, your fingers would find themselves in the mouths of the lions. The back of the chair could be tilted back to several positions, as well as all the way down, which would make into a kind of cot, for napping. When I was fourteen, I did sleep on it one night, when I ran away from home.

This room became Mama's ironing room, and my private playpen. The two of us spent many hours together there, she ironing, and I doing my art work, or hand crafts, or making model airplanes.

Next to this room was the regular cement cellar that held Mama's washing machine and wash tubs. At the base of the cellar steps was another complete bathroom. How great to have two bathrooms in the house!

Above the kitchen, on the second floor, was a small bedroom that Ed slept in until he went into the Army. Then, I got it for a short while.

Next, to that room, was a larger bedroom for Pearl, Ruth and Suzie, and whoever else came home to stay, or visit. From this bedroom, there was a doorway out to the roof of the sun porch, which was great during the summer for sun bathing.

Next to the girls' room was Mama's bedroom, then the bathroom, which was located over the small, front porch. The house was small and compact, but somehow, large enough for all of us: those who moved in initially, and those who "came and went," over the years.

There were a couple of boys, on Brevard, that I hadn't met, yet. Two doors down lived Johnny Soukup, a big, husky blond kid. Up Brevard Avenue, another buddy lived. His name was Bill Ackerman. Next to him lived a younger kid, a "baseball-nut," called Frankie Frisch. Baseball was all he ever thought about and talked about. He wore a baseball hat, a Pirates' jersey, and carried his ball and mitt with him, wherever he would go. After all, he did have an uncle who was the manager of the Pittsburgh Pirates baseball team.

We didn't play baseball, but we did play softball in the front of our house. There wasn't much traffic, so it was an ideal place for us to play. One day, Bill hit a home run, breaking a neighbor's stained glass window. We all ran, except for Bill, he owned up to the dreadful deed and paid for the repair.

Johnny Soukup and I, soon, became fast friends. He looked years older than me, but was actually a little younger. Along with the old gang from Churchview Avenue, we ventured to explore Hesse's Woods, which was really a small forest, several miles down Sankey Avenue. It was a glorious place, a veritable jungle, compared to Foxey's Woods.

It had a much bigger creek, monkey vines for swinging out over the dale, many big trees for climbing, and a waterfall! It wasn't really much of a waterfall, but its water did fall off a steep cliff, about thirty feet high, straight down. Above the falls, "the gang" would usually pitch camp and look for Indian arrowheads. There were quite a few to be found around there.

In one section of the thicket, there was an abandoned coalmine which had a tram car in its passageway. We would take turns pushing each other deep into the mine. Water seeped from its crevices and the cave's floor was often flooded. As a result, we didn't play there too often.

One day, we found some old dynamite sticks, way down in the excavation, and tried to explode them. We'd throw them as far as we could and run like Hell. They never exploded. No one knew why.

There was a steep slag dump outside the mine entrance. That became more fun than trying to explode dynamite. We climbed up, and slid down, that sooty heap. What did it matter? We had our own private waterfall to shower in.

On one of our camping trips, we found a huge dead tree on the ground that had been struck by lightning. By the time we discovered it, the leaves had all dried up, and the whole tree was ready to be kindling. What a great find! We pitched our camp there and started a fire, nearby. Believe it or not, we began to bake an apple pie in front of it. I had learned how to do it at the Boy Scouts, and was anxious to see if it worked. While the pie was "baking," we played in the dead tree.

Shortly, Johnny yelled, "Look out! The whole damn camp's on fire!"

Sure enough, the fire had spread along the ground and was quickly coming toward the tree. We no sooner got out of it than it ignited into a huge fire ball, shooting skyward, blocking out the sun. Surely, it was going to envelop us.

We were scared shitless, grabbed our "stuff," and ran like hell to get out of there. Was the whole woods going to catch fire? We were sure it would.

After reaching the road, we looked back to see if the fire was going to catch up with us. Somehow, it didn't.

Several weeks later, Johnny and I hiked back to the woods, and were astonished to find that it was still standing, still verdant. We sheepishly ventured back to our burnt out campground, giving a sigh of relief to find that the fire didn't spread any further, and that it had burned itself out.

On my thirteenth birthday, I was given permission to go to work at the bowling alley. Ed's shoeshine stand was still there. I didn't shine shoes, but I did go to work as a pin setter. This bowling alley used what were called duckpins. They were much smaller than the regular tenpins, but much easier for boys, with small hands, to set up, when they were knocked down.

There was another Bill working there, so the boss, remembering my brother Dutch, decided to call me Dutch, too. That suited me. What bliss! I had a nickname, a job where I earned money, and I could stay out until eleven o'clock at night.

Fifty years to the day, I walked down that same flight of stairs of the bowling alley, during a visit to Pittsburgh. How eerie that was: my thirteen year old spirit descended those steps with my sixty-three year old self. The facility looked the same, except that, now, the alleys are automated, and they use tenpins, rather than duckpins.

I had my own bedroom, but not for long. Papa was found (or he found us, I'm not sure), and moved in. As the story goes, Papa had returned from California, again, and set up shop, again, in Homestead. Somehow, he found out that we were living on Brevard Avenue and asked to move in.

Mama, it seemed, had no alternative than to invite him to stay. She could always use the extra money. But, she was not going to get pregnant, again, so he was assigned my bedroom, and I had to move in with Mama. My new bunk was a spring and mattress, on the floor, next to Mama's bed. Oh, woe!

Marie and Dr. Emmett Carmalt were living on Charles Street with their new baby. Martha, Joe and Mamie, were living in Philadelphia. Ruth was working in Isaly's dairy store in the South Side. Pearl went to work as a part time sales girl at the new Murphy's five and ten cent store that had just opened on Brownsville Road. And, of course, Sam and Ed were away at war.

Kay was now a Captain in the Salvation Army, and would soon return to Pittsburgh to work in downtown Pittsburgh, at the Salvation Army Headquarters. This was a wonderful facility. It not only had its executive offices there, it had an extensive meeting hall for Sunday services, a large gymnasium, tennis courts, a swimming pool, and a "canteen," where Servicemen could spend their free time writing letters, conversing with cute, young things, and getting something to eat.

Above all these facilities, there were seven or eight floors of living quarters for women, where Kay moved, when she was transferred back to Pittsburgh. Later, she moved in with us on Brevard, because she would be doing a lot of traveling for the Girl Guards, The Salvation Army equivalent of the Girl Scouts. It was great having her home, again, because she always entertained us kids, by playing games with us.

Papa was determined that one of his sons would learn the shoe repair business. I was the only one left. Ed gave it a try several years earlier, but he ruined a shoe by stitching right through it, while trying to attach a new sole. His repairing days were over, so he went to the bowling alley to shine shoes, instead. At least, he learned how to do that in Papa's shop.

As the last son, I was amenable to "learning the business," by accompanying him, many Saturdays, to his new shop at 603 Amity Street, just around the corner from where we used to live on Seventh Avenue, in Homestead. Papa worked long hours. His business card stated that he was open, Monday through Saturday, from 8 a.m. to 7:30 p.m. Unbelievable!

Learning the trade was easy for me. Within weeks, I could do any of the procedures, but he only let me repair heels. He had learned his lesson with Ed, and wouldn't let me replace any soles. Leather was too expensive, and he didn't want any more costly mistakes. Nevertheless, I finished his repairs by grinding smooth the edges of the soles and heels, stitching together any rips or tears, and buffing the shoes to a bright shine, becoming quite proficient in all aspects of the job.

The favorite part of my Saturday's with Papa was lunchtime. I would eat my two delicious hot dogs, and drink a bottle of pop, at the Blue Goose Café, which was located at the corner of Amity and Seventh. This was a café that actually sold beer and wine, so I felt quite grown up to be eating in such an "adult" place. Gus, the owner, was a jovial, kindly Greek fellow, who always had a pleasant word for me, and who made me feel, very much, at home, there.

After lunch, I would have to walk past the poultry store. This store had live chickens that they slew, right there, in the front window. There were five or six inverted funnels with bloody buckets beneath them. After a customer chose his chicken, the butcher would shove its head down, through the funnel opening, and slit its throat. The bird would scream, and jump, and flutter its wings, while the blood ran from its body. After a while, it would stop jumping, and stop bleeding. Then, it was ready for the plucking. That was another bloody task that was done "while you wait." It took me many years before I could eat chicken.

There was a back room, in Papa's shop, with a loft above it. On Saturday nights, I would sleep over with him, so we could go to see his leather supplier, Mr. Ferber, in the morning.

Papa had a ritual he performed each night and each morning. He read the Tarot cards, which made me think he really was a gypsy. After reading the cards, at night, he knelt down by the bed, to pray. He wasn't taking any chances.

There was a sign on the door of the back room. It was made it with wrapping paper and black shoe polish, which read, "Kip Auth." It was there for such a long time that I didn't pay any attention to it. I thought it was something in Hungarian.

One day, I got curious, and asked Papa what the sign said. He became exasperated with me. "Vat's the matter mit you. Don't you understand Anglish? It says, 'kip auth, keep out!'" Ooooh.

When Papa got tired of teaching me, or had no work for me, he'd send me to one of the local movie theaters. I always enjoyed going there, but preferred my own movie house, the Melrose Theater. I missed my Saturday morning serials of Flash Gordon, and Jungle Jim, and the rest.

Once Duane Emmett Carmalt was born (or is it Emmett Duane?), on May 11, 1943, Mama volunteered me, to baby sit my new nephew. On Saturday nights, when "Doc" and Marie went out for a nice dinner, I'd sit. Actually, I loved doing it, it made me feel so grown up, but not grown up enough to call Dr. Carmalt by his first name. Suzie and I called him Doc.

Usually Duane would be fast asleep before they'd leave, Emmett must have given him a little sedative, because he never woke up. I was given instructions on what to say, to various patients, if they called. If there was an emergency, I would have the number where the good doctor could be reached.

When the phone rang, I answered, "Doctor Carmalt's office." My voice hadn't changed, yet, so most people thought I was the doctor's nurse. After trying so often to explain that I was a boy, I just gave up, and admitted to being, "the nurse." What respect I had. People talked to me like I was an adult. So, I became an "adult."

Usually, I would sleep over on those Saturday nights, in Emmett's bed. He loved it when I stayed over, because that gave him the opportunity to, actually, sleep with Marie, in the same bed. How often he would try to get "close" to her, but was always rebuffed, supposedly because I was in the next room.

After joining the Cub Scouts, I needed a physical examination to attend their summer camp. Wasn't it nice that we had a doctor in the family? And, it wouldn't cost Mama anything. Doctor Carmalt took me back into that dank, dark examination room, and was very professional and efficient.

He did notice, however, that my testicles had not yet descended. Was this the reason I was so tiny, and had such a high voice? He would start testosterone therapy on me, which consisted of two injections a week. I had no idea what that meant, at the time. All I knew was that it was a pain in the butt, literally, to go there.

These shots were very expensive, so I had to do extra work for the Carmalts, to pay for the them. My new job, each week, was to play gardener and cut their grass, with a hand lawn mower, no less. Power driven mowers were not, yet, invented, or too expensive, I don't know which. This puny, little kid had to push, and pull, that enormous contraption, and sweat his punctured *tush* off.

I hated doing anything so manual, but the therapy did work. Soon my voice descended, as well as my testicles. I developed a beautiful, deep bass voice in a few years, and was complimented on it, so often, and told that I should "get into" radio, which would become my intention.

I'm deeply grateful to Doctor Carmalt. Had he not caught my "ailment" in time, I don't know what I would have become. Perhaps, I would have beaten Wayne Newton to the draw and had a recording career, singing *"Danke schoen."*

SCOUT CAMPING

Soon, after my physical examination, I did go to Cub Scout camp for a week. It was my first time away from home, and I really enjoyed it. After we arrived, we were each given a long, colorful cloth, about twelve inches wide, and four feet long. The councilor called them "breechcloths." We were instructed to put all of our clothes away, including what we were wearing, and to keep only our belts and breechcloths. We were going to dress like real Indians, by draping the cloths over our belts, in the front and in the back. Then, we were each given a headband, with a feather, to complete our costume. That's what we wore all week. What freedom!

How easy it was to get dressed each morning. Actually, we didn't have to get dressed, we already were. Luckily, it didn't rain, or get cold that week. The only annoying part, of the week, was when I had to go to the camp doctor, for my shots.

A year later, when I became a Boy Scout, our troop went on a weekend hike and camping trip. I had flat feet and never enjoyed the hikes, but I did like the camping, and living outdoors in the great fresh air. We had many activities, but the one I enjoyed most was when I got to "fly!" Yes, I was going to "fly," again.

One afternoon, we were to have a broad-jump tournament to see who could jump the farthest. I was still quite small and didn't even think to enter the contest. There were too many bigger boys who were much more athletic than I. Still, in high school, Coach Crevar always called on me, in gym class, to demonstrate any tumbling or acrobatic feat that he would dream up. I could, usually, do all of them. I was quite agile, and acrobatics came easily to me.

After watching all the clods trying to jump, I thought to myself, I can do better than them. And I did. I got in line behind the guys, and started jumping. Each time I "flew" further, and further. I was flying, again, higher and higher, and farther and farther. As I remember it, I jumped over twenty-five feet. I don't remember how far, exactly, but I was told that it was further than most of the top broad-jumpers, of that time, could do. I *adored* the attention and adulation. Of course!

Martha, Joe and Marilyn had returned from Philadelphia, In the spring of 1944, for a visit with Marie. Duane was a not quite a year old, and another baby was "on its way." On the Saturday that they visited, I was there, as usual, to baby sit, so the adults could go out to dinner.

During the afternoon, Duane and Marilyn were sent upstairs to take their naps. Marilyn went to sleep in Emmett's bed and Duane in his own. When Emmett came home from the hospital, he was tired and decided that, before dinner, he would go upstairs to rest a few minutes. Off he went, while Martha, Marie, Joe and I remained downstairs, visiting.

Shortly, there was a blood curdling scream. It was Marilyn. It sounded as if someone was trying to murder her. Joe and Martha ran up the stairs. Marilyn was hysterical. Soon Joe was berating Emmett, calling him a sex pervert who was trying to molest his daughter. Marilyn continued screeching, Martha joined in. You could tell that she was beating on him, calling him a dirty, disgusting sex maniac who molests children. Duane, frightened and shaking uncontrollably, ran downstairs to me, while the berating upstairs continued.

I had never seen Emmett angry, nor had I ever seen him shout, but not this time. He came storming down the stairs, protesting his innocence, with Martha and Joe in pursuit. What the hell was Marilyn doing in his bed, anyway? He was only trying to take a nap.

Marie joined in the fracas, accusing him, also, of being a molester. Marilyn continued howling, while Joe tried to placate her. Emmett could take it no longer. Still protesting his innocence, he took a big swing and smashed a table lamp that went flying across the room: "I am *not* a goddamned pervert!"

A bright light flashed as the lamp splattered against the wall. Duane became hysterical at the flash of light, and jumped into my arms. I hugged him, and took him into another room to get him away from all the crazies.

Soon, all was quiet. After a few drinks, they made up. They *did* go out to dinner that night, leaving Marilyn and Duane with me. Neither slept well. I don't thing that either of them ever, completely, recovered from that experience.

Mama was diagnosed with cancer of the rectum. She wasn't too worried because, after all, she had a very distinguished son-in-law to take care of her. And, he did. Emmett took care of everything, since he was one of the top surgeons at Shadyside Hospital. A colleague of his did the colostomy surgery.

It was a terrible thing for Mama to go through. She was fitted with a colostomy bag, which would fill up at the most inconvenient times. Poor Mama, she'd rush to the bathroom to clean out the bag, immediately. Nowadays, this operation, I understand, can be reversed, but not then.

For the next year, Mama dealt with her illness as best she could. Her one joy was visiting with her little grand-son, Duane. One day, that summer before the war ended, she was proudly strolling with him in Murphy's Five and Ten when she slipped on the newly mopped floor, and fell. This fall must have triggered a new outburst in her cancer.

It was sad to see this once big, bosomed woman, shrivel to a hundred and twenty pounds. Her new figure pleased her. Ruth gave her one of her best Sunday suits, which fit Mama like a glove. She had never been so svelte. Her new found glamour didn't last long.

In May of 1945, Sue became May Queen at Elroy School, just like Pearl, several years before. Mama didn't make her gown, it was store bought. That made Sue very happy. Charlotte Bowden and Duane attended the ceremonies with her. She looked quite pretty.

DAVIS DRUG STORE

Emmett did most of his business at Davis Drugs Store. It was located three or four long blocks away from his house. In the summer of 1945, Old Man Davis needed a kid to work, so I was volunteered. As well as being a baby sitter, "nurse," and gardener, I became a "soda jerk." My calling, at last! Being a soda jerk/clerk was like being in show business. It meant being "on stage" all the time, "performing" for all the customers. The only problem was the pay.

Old man Davis was a cheap son-of-a-bitch. The going rate for kids working was twenty five cents an hour. I assumed that that's what I would be paid. I worked my tail off that first week. There was a lady there, who taught me how to clean all the equipment, each morning, with Bon Ami cleanser (it didn't scratch), how to fill up the syrups and sundae toppings, how to do all of *her* duties. Little did she realize, that after several weeks, she would no longer be needed, and was let go.

It's embarrassing to tell you how much I was paid, but I will: a dollar a day! Apparently, when Mr. Davis was a boy, that was good pay. I was too shocked to decline the offer, not wanting to embarrass the good doctor, so I stayed and worked for that dollar a day.

Once he fired the lady who trained me, certainly he would pay me what was coming to me. He didn't. So, I did the only thing I thought right. I stole the rest. How did I manage to do that? Well, I'll tell you.

There were three cash registers in the drug store. The main register was in front of the pharmacy. It had different keys to punch for drugs, toiletries, newspapers, magazines, etc. The two registers, on either side of the soda fountain, were supposed to be: one for the fountain items, and the other for tobacco items. The tobacco case was next to the fountain. I, like a good employee, would ring up everything in its proper register, which was very difficult to do. All this was done in the head, there were no adding machine capabilities, on any of these registers.

By mid-afternoon, each day, the newspapers were delivered. Mobs of people would come in to buy them. Arnie "Long-crazy-Italian-name-that-no-one-could-pronounce," the other pharmacist, would come to the fountain to help me when the mobs descended. We would take their money for the papers and place the coins on the back counter, to ring up at the main register, later.

Sometimes, he would forget to ring it up, so I would do it, and help myself to a share of the pot. I hated being a thief, and hated Mr. Davis for making me one. Hell, it cost me half of my dollar for streetcar fare and lunch; I was owed that money!

What really irritated me was that my classmate from school, Dick Greene, worked from seven in the evening until closing time at eleven, for the same pay that I got. Of course, the soda fountain was busier, and made more money in the evening, but that was all Dick did, he made sundaes and sodas. Half the time, he left the dirty glassware in the sink for me to take care of in the morning. I would have to clean up the mess from the night before.

Mr. Davis was an old codger of sixty-something. He was very small, but perky and jaunty, with nice features When he was young, he must have been handsome. He had a large wife, who adored him. Several of her front teeth were missing, but where a top one was missing a bottom one filled in.

She brought him his lunch each day, and was quite pleasant to me. Occasionally, she would sit in one of the booths, act like a customer, and order an ice cream soda. I loved it when she did that because she always left me a ten cent tip.

Old man Davis had a filthy habit. He chewed tobacco! Ugh! Not only did he chew constantly, but when he needed to spit, he came to the soda fountain and spit down the chute where we threw old straws, and trash, from the fountain. This chute was next to the receptacle that held the ice cream scoops, and next to the water where we washed the glassware.

His aim was terrible. Half the time, he would miss the chute opening and the spittle would land beside the ice cream scoops, then run into the dish water. Nonchalantly, he'd pick up the wipe-cloth, wipe up the spittle, wring it out into the water, and walk back to his drug compound. Sometimes, I would have to change that water five or six times a day.

PHILADELPHIA

Martha had invited me to come to Philadelphia for a visit, in late summer of 1945. It would be my first train trip. I didn't have any problem leaving Davis Drug store behind, for two weeks.

The train traveled around the Horseshoe Bend, up into the Allegheny Mountains. It actually made a U-turn, where you could see its other side, as it went around the curve. That was a little frightening because, below, there was a deep chasm where the train could have plummeted at any minute. I held my breath.

My seat was shared with a nice looking older woman, probably around thirty. She wore a pastel yellow, two-piece suit, with a little pink hat and veil, looking like she just came from church, on Easter Sunday. She was very friendly, perhaps a little too friendly. The only thing that was distracting about her was that she had a slight, brownish moustache on her upper lip. It certainly distracted from her appearance. That was all I could see when I looked at her. Disgusting!

During the trip, I roamed all over the train, checking out everything, including the Dining Car, which I couldn't afford. It didn't matter, Mama had packed me a nice lunch of ham salad sandwiches, made from her own special recipe.

When she baked a ham, nothing went to waste! She cut every iota of remaining flesh from the bone, and ground it by hand, adding relish, onions, celery, mayonnaise, and whatever. The conglomeration actually tasted pretty good.

There was also a Club Car where the adults drank and played cards. I didn't drink, but they did allow me to play cards with them, for a short while, until they started playing for money. I felt so grown up!

Upon returning to my seat, the "pastel lady" was curled up on her side of the seat, seemingly trying to nap. When I sat down, she immediately started nuzzling up
to me. Certainly, it was accidental, she was only trying to sleep. She kept on nudging me, and snuggled further. I edged away from her, she continued her pursuit. Soon, her face was close to mine as she begged, "Kiss me."

What was this old bag trying to do to me? I got up and left, spending the rest of the trip in the Club Car. Had she not had that moustache, I probably would have stayed.

Martha, Joe and Mame picked me up, and drove me back to their apartment in Upper Darby.

"This is the very exclusive area of Philadelphia," Martha related to me.

After we got there, it didn't look very "exclusive" to me. There are movies of where she was living, and it looked more like "welfare housing," than an upscale living facility. It was, however, quite comfortable, but teeming with pregnant women and young couples with their children and pets.

Martha was always a good hostess, and treated me royally. She cooked all my favorite foods, and made Joe take me all over Philadelphia to show me the sights: the Liberty Bell, Independence Hall, etc. It was a good history lesson for me, but I knew how bored Joe was doing it. Hah, hah!

We drove to Beach Haven, New Jersey, for a few days. They loved the ocean, especially Marilyn. This would be my first time. I didn't like the salty water or all the sticky sand. Give me a pool any day.

I had to get my movie "fix," so I was allowed to go the local cinema. "The Picture of Dorian Gray" was playing. I sat through it twice, and was absolutely fascinated by the evil character of Dorian, who never aged.

That would become one of my goals. Like Dorian, after I became an adult, I didn't age at all, for twenty years. Unlike Dorian, I didn't have my portrait in the attic.

For the trip back, Martha had packed two sandwiches made with thick slabs of roast beef and loaded with butter, on soft, white bread. I was accustomed only to Mama's ham salad, baloney, or spiced ham cold cuts for my sandwiches, and couldn't imagine eating cold roast beef. I hid the sandwiches under the seat, figuring I'd leave them when I left the train.

During the trip back, I became famished, and soon reached under the seat for the sandwiches. Never before had I ever tasted anything so delicious! Cold roast beef, loaded with butter, became one of my favorite sandwich. Not very Kosher, I'm afraid.

SHIRLEY JORDAN

During the early fall of 1945, after school had resumed, my buddy, Bill Ackerman, and I went to a Saturday Matinee at the Melrose Theater. On this particular Saturday afternoon, we entered and walked down the right hand aisle, to sit behind what, at first glance, looked like a couple of young, good looking girls, around our age.

Immediately, we started flirting. Actually, only one of them was our age. That was Shirley Jordan, who was quite a stunning and mature looking fourteen-year-old. She was "baby sitting" her chubby younger sister, Beady (Beatrice), her cute little sister, Donna, and her pint-sized cousin, Marsha.

"Dick Tracy Verses Cueball" (or some other Dick Tracy movie) was playing there, that day. Throughout the first showing, Bill and I were typical boys, acting like jerks, flirting and joking with the cute blonde. Under it all, I could see that Shirley really like me. I invited her to come back and sit with Bill and me, to get away from "her children." Instead, she invited me to come down to sit with her. I was nervous, and yet exhilarated, with the anticipation of that which might come. And, there was no sign of a moustache, either. What Heaven!

When the first picture ended, Bill and I went up to the lobby, hitting each other on the back, and laughing. After getting our candy "fix," we nervously paced the lobby, almost afraid to return to our seats. Stupid me, I asked him for his permission to sit with the cute girl. He was just as eager as I was and, of course, gave me his permission.

On the way back down the aisle, I decided to sit next to her. Immediately, I put my arm around her and rested my hand on her shoulder. If I didn't do it then, I'd never have done it. She was quite receptive. So receptive that, during the screening of "Dick Tracy," the first time something "exciting" happened, she screamed and grabbed my hand, which accidentally (on purpose), gently brushed against her breast. Wow! My first feel! We even kissed, not once but many times.

This went on throughout the rest of the movie, as well as the rest of the afternoon: cuddling, caressing and kissing. By the time the movie was over, we had become pretty "close," and made arrangements to meet the following Saturday.

66

Walking up the aisle, I was so weak in the knees, and exhausted, that I lost my equilibrium. I kept falling, forward. Luckily, Bill grabbed hold of me before I could fall. Nothing like that had ever happened to me, and boy, did I like it.

We met the following Saturday, and the following Saturday, and the following Saturday, and "went together" for three years, while we were both "growing up."

Often, we would get together, and go for walks. Usually we met at Bard's Dairy, across the street from the Melrose Theater. Hand in hand, we would walk up Brownsville road to Brentwood Park, then back to the Melrose, and then on to her house, behind St. Wedelin's Church.

To get to her house from the Melrose was quite a walk. By the time we got to her neighborhood, it was usually getting dark. After passing St. Wedelin's Church, and going down the deserted back road to her house, we would stop and "neck." When a car came by, we'd stop, and walk a few more feet, until the car was out of sight. Then we'd go at it again. That was our big date, when we were young.

When we got older, we went to Sully's Swingland, on Saturday nights. There, we kids could dance to all the latest records, played by the host, "Sully," Jack Sullivan, in his beautiful, dimly lit ballroom.

"Sully's" was a great, inexpensive place for us kids to go. It was located on the second floor, over the dressing rooms, in Brentwood Park, directly overlooking its shimmering swimming pool.

We didn't have an ocean to gaze at, but we did have a romantic view, from the second story porch, of the sparkling pool, below. And, when "Goodnight Sweetheart" played, we knew it was the last dance of the evening. Huggy, huggy, kissy, kissy.

In June of 1948, she and I went to the prom together. Then in September of '48, I left her behind when I moved to Florida.

THE SECOND WORLD WAR

Sam was the first to go to war. He enlisted in the United States Marine Corps on September 11, 1942. After going through Boot Camp at Parris Island, South Carolina, he was sent to "Sea School" in Portsmouth, Virginia. While there, the *USS Essex* aircraft carrier was being built at nearby Norfolk Navy Yard.

On December 23, 1942, his Marine Attachment was assigned to the *Essex*. They were called "light aerial aircraft crewmen" and were each assigned a position at the anti-aircraft guns. To test the ship, its first cruise was taken around the Caribbean Sea. This was called the "Shakedown Cruise."

After the Shakedown Cruise, and before the ship went through the Panama Canal, the crew was given Liberty. Sam had "duty," and had to stay aboard the ship.

When his buddies came back, they told him what the Panamanians called aircraft carriers. They referred to them as "Floating Coffins," and, just recently, three carriers had been sunk. What terrible news to hear just when you're about to be shipped out to the War Zone.

Sam, and five other Marines, were assigned to Admiral Montgomery, as his personal orderlies. Even with this exalted position, Sam and his fellow orderlies still had to man the anti-aircraft guns whenever the ship was attacked, which was quite often, from November 1943 through February 1944.

Apparently, the Admiral liked Sam so much, that when he got transferred to the *USS Bunker Hill,* on March 4, 1944, he took Sam with him. He hadn't done Sam any favors, because, almost immediately, the action began, which included strikes against Palau, Tinian, Guam, Rota, Bonin, Truk, and the Caroline Islands.

He participated in the capture and occupation of Wakde and Hollandia, in New Guinea, as well as Saipan, Guam, and the Marianas Islands. His anti-aircraft crew, also, repelled many attacks through August 11, 1944.

He received eight bronze stars, each representing a major battle in which he was involved. Then, Sam was transferred back to Camp Le Jeune, North Carolina, where he stayed until his discharge on September 11, 1945.

Ed was the next to go to war. Shortly after his nineteenth birthday, he "signed up" to go into the United States Army, and was "inducted" January 20, 1943. On January 27, he arrived at Fort Meade, Maryland for his basic training. From there, he went to Fort Hood and Fort Bragg, Texas, for the rest of his training.

When he went into the service, he was listed as an electrician's helper. Soon, he was to become an automotive mechanic, an "Auto Mech 014."

He was a member of Company C, 819th Tank Destroyer Battalion, and stationed in the Asian Pacific from March 1944 through November 1945.

At first, he was stationed in Hawaii for eight months, where he was assigned to Island Security, doing patrol work. After that, he was stationed,

predominately, on the Islands of Pelau, and then Guam, before being shipped home.

For six months, he was stationed on the Island of Anguar, fifteen miles from Pelau. He was part of the invasion, and retaking, of the Island of Pelalu, another one of the Pelau islands.

Ed's LSTs landed, and he and his fellow solders, dressed in full battle gear, were let loose to recapture the island from the Japanese Imperial Marines.

After the retaking of the island, he was kept on for another six months to cleanup the remaining Japs, who were still hiding out in the caves.

On November 27, 1945, he boarded a ship to be sent home. He arrived in the good old U.S.A. on December 12th, and was discharged on December 20th.

Sam and Ed both received the same decorations: the American Theater Ribbon; the Asiatic-Pacific Theater Ribbon (Sam's with two bronze stars); the good conduct medal; and the World War II Victory Medal. Luckily, neither was wounded.

During the war, Ruth worked as a welder at Dravo Shipbuilders, on Neville Island, just outside of Pittsburgh.

She was small, agile, and not afraid of anything. While building the LSTs at Dravo, she volunteered to climb to the highest positions on the ship, in order to do the intricate welding. Most of the men were afraid to go there, but not our Ruthie. She was unflappable.

Perhaps, she even worked on the very ship that Ed was on, during the invasion of Pelalu. "Rosie the Riveter" may have gotten all the glory, but "Ruthie the Welder" was the top dog in our family.

Writing letters to the Bordy servicemen became my chore. Mama couldn't write English, so I had to write for her. It was a long drawn out affair to get them to make any sense. All the letters started out the same: "Dear Son. Vee are fine, how are you? I haven't written in such a long time because dat bad boy Beely von't sit down and write for me. He knows I can't write Anglish."

Half the time, I composed the whole letter, myself. Then, I would read what I had written back to Mama, and she'd say, yes, that was exactly what she wanted to say. That Hungarian-Gypsy mind-reading, we possessed, sure came in handy.

Pearl claims that writing letters was her job, too. I'm sure she did write once in a while, but I don't remember it that way. To me, I was always the "chosen one."

Not only did I write to Sam and Ed, but, occasionally, to Katy, as well, because she did a lot of traveling for the Salvation Army. I came across a letter that was written to her while she was stationed at Camp Cornplanter, in Kane, Pennsylvania. It was dictated by Mama, written by me, and mailed to Katy, with two three cent stamps attached. It reads:

August 18, 1944

Dear Kate,

I got your card. We are all well and hope you are the same. I starting to miss you. It is starting to get cold in Pittsburgh. How is the weather at Cornplanter? I was away 3 days at a church convention. I'm glad I'm home again. I got a letter from Sam. He isn't coming home yet. I don't know when he is coming home. Marie's baby is getting bigger, sweeter, and fatter. He crawls around on the chairs and he wears me out. Take good care of yourself.

Love,
Mom

In our front window, Mama had a service flag with two blue stars. That meant that this household had two sons in the Service. If a silver star was placed over a blue star, it meant that a son had been wounded in the war; if it was a gold star, then that son had been killed. It was always so sad seeing a gold star in someone's window. We were lucky; both of Mama's sons survived.

And, like everyone else, we gladly endured the shortages of sugar, meat, gasoline, and all the rest. We were helping to "bring our boys home!" Life went on.

V.J. DAY, SEPTEMBER 2, 1945

First came D-Day on June 6, 1945. It was imminent that soon the war would be over. Then came V.E. (Victory in Europe) Day, shortly after, and then came V.J. Day (Victory in Japan Day) on September 2, 1945. The war was officially over.

The radio reported on all the celebrations in Times Square, and all across the country. I wanted to celebrate, too, so off to our "Times Square," I went. The square in front of the Melrose Theater had amassed a huge, happy crowd.

At home, I had a carved cocoanut with a grotesque face on it, that we called Tojo. Tojo was the general in charge of the

Japanese Army. With this "head," and my Boy Scout uniform, I created an effigy of the Jap leader, which I hung from a long clothes prop. Like I was carrying the American flag, I brought "Tojo" to "Melrose Square" for all to ridicule.

What a great time we had with Tojo swaying in the breeze every time he was belted by the happy throng.

Soon, my brothers would be home from the war. Sam was discharged on September 11, 1945, and Ed was discharged, from Camp Atterbury, Indiana, on December 20, 1945. Mama was going to have a happy Christmas, even though she had become very ill.

THE BOYS COME HOME

After the war, both Sam and Ed returned to Brevard Avenue. For the time being, both of them enjoyed being in the "52/20 Club," where each service man was given Twenty Dollars a week for a fifty-two week period.

At first, Sam tried working as a private detective for Nick Carter (Capone) Detective Agency. That didn't last long, but soon, he would find his calling.

He got a job at the Bel Air Cleaners, at 2910 West Liberty Avenue, in Dormont. There, he learned to be a spotter. A spotter, "spots" stains in the clothing, and removes them.

His boss was so impressed with him, that he sent him to the National Institute of Cleaners and Dyers in Silver Spring, Maryland, for his training. He stayed with Bel Air Cleaners until he moved to Florida, in 1947.

Ed went back to work as an Electrician's Helper, at Mine Safety. That's where he met the mother of his children, Helen Smith. After nine months, he was laid off, and went to work as a Mechanic's Helper, for Hertz-Rent-a-Car. Shortly, after Easter of 1947, Ed took off for California, to pursue his career as an auto mechanic.

Mama had a great Christmas. Her entire family was there. Besides Mama and Papa, Sam, Ed, Ruth, Pearl, Sue and I were all living there. Kay was living at the Salvation Army, downtown. How did so many family members manage to live there in that tiny house? No one remembers exactly who slept where. Somehow, we managed.

Pearl told me that she and Ruth slept on cots in the dining room. On Brevard Avenue, it seemed that we were always playing "musical beds." Over the years, one family member would come, and another would go. It's impossible to figure who was living "at home," at any one time. But, on this Christmas,

almost all the single members of the family were living there.

Marie, Emmett, Duane, and the new baby, Cordell Ley, were there for Christmas celebration, as well as Martha, Joe and Marilyn. Sam saw what a tough little kid Cordell Ley was, and immediately started calling him "Butch." The name stuck, and since that day, he has remained Butch.

Even though this was Mama's last Christmas, none of the remaining members of the Bordy Clan can remember any of the particulars of that day. How strange! Could it possibly be that all of us were on our best behavior and nobody fought? Mama really had quite a family. Thankfully, she enjoyed that day to the fullest.

After having two children in her thirties, and carrying around such a big bosom while trying to stand erect, Marie had developed lower back problems. It was decided that she would need an operation on her two lower vertebrae. After the operation, Mama offered up Ruthie to stay with Marie while she recuperated. After all, Mama had volunteered Ruthie, many times before, to do Marie's stenographic work in the Charles Street house. So, Ruth moved in.

When Marie became mobile, she decided that she needed a vacation. The weather was starting to get cold in Pittsburgh, so she, Duane, Butch, and Ruth took off for warmer climate in St. Petersburg, Florida, leaving Emmett behind.

Marie loved the sultry climate — and the sultry men. She recuperated quickly, and was soon socializing and flirting with all the attractive guys. She met a New York jeweler named Tom Marino, who, immediately, fell in love with her. He was rich, but not really Marie's type. She liked tall, sophisticated, good looking men. Tom was none of these. He was bald, short, had an Italian accent, and definitely was *not* sophisticated, but he loved her, all his life.

While Marie "socialized," Ruth tended to the boys. During the day they played around the pool, and before she knew it, she was surrounded by all the other kids staying in the complex. She seemed to have inherited the job as the hotel baby sitter. What was she doing there with all those kids? She was disappointed, too, that no one ever asked her out. She was sure everyone thought that she was the mother of the two children. How could they? She was only twenty.

When they returned to Charles Street, Marie told Emmett to "settle up" with Ruth, for her work in Florida.

"You mean I've got to pay her, too? I've already paid for her trip, and everything else, while you were in Florida. What am I, made of money?"

It was always difficult for Emmett to open his wallet.

"Just pay her. She worked very hard for me."

He took out his wallet and gave Ruth a twenty dollar bill. Ruth got so furious that she threw the twenty in his face.

"Keep your goddamn money, you cheap son-of-a-bitch!"

Sweet, lovely Ruth could cuss like a sailor. On second thought, she reached over and took the money back, vowing to never work for them, again. She never did.

I won a free trip to Niagara Falls on August 9, 1946. *The Pittsburgh Sun Telegraph* held a contest for teen-agers to sell subscriptions. About a hundred kids won the trip, and we all met at the train station for an overnight trip to Niagara. There were no bunks for us, so we had to sleep, as best we could, on the seats. It didn't matter, no one slept, anyway. Everyone had a jolly old time.

In the morning, we, and our chaperones, were met by a bus, and given the tour of The Falls. It was quite breathtaking, and the thrill of a lifetime. By late afternoon, we were taken on a side trip to Fort Ticonderoga.

Then, we returned to the train, and rode all night, back to Pittsburgh. This time we slept. Wow, my second train trip in a year! How *The Sun Telly* got away with that "cheapo" trip, amazes me. That could never happen today.

Mama's cancer had reemerged in her lungs. After I returned from Niagara Falls, she got even sicker and was hospitalized. She was placed in an oxygen tent, then deteriorated fast. Emmett's associates did all they could do to save her.

Suzie and I initially were not permitted to visit her. But, she kept asking for her Suzie, and her Billy. She wanted to know if we were getting off to school alright, and if we were eating okay. When we were finally allowed to visit her, I was aghast at the sight of her. In that oxygen tent, her tiny skeletal body lay gasping for air that she could not get into her lungs. It was a horrible sight for Suzie and me to see. She died the next day. But, at least, Mama got to see her two "babies," one more time.

Mama was laid out in Slater's funeral home, on Brownsville Road, in Whitehall, a mile beyond Brentwood High School. The funeral home was a large mansion, and was quite lovely. The Slater family lived upstairs and the downstairs was the Mortuary. As of 2010, they are still in business, with my high school classmate, Fred Slater, now in charge.

I can still see Mama, laid out in her coffin. The first thing you noticed was the overwhelming aroma of all the flowers. There were many, all displayed around the coffin. She was dressed in an ugly pink, ruffled, "funeral" dress, that showed absolutely no signs of a bosom. Where did it go?

Kay, Ruth, and Martha fussed over Mama, adjusting her, and trying to make her look more natural. One of them noticed that Mama's chest "crunched." Apparently, she had been stuffed with newspapers, to give her shape, because of the cavity in her chest, left by the operation. No wonder she had no bosom. Also, she was wearing lipstick and rouge. We had never seen her in any kind of makeup, other than a little face powder.

The body was on display for several days. It was a long ordeal, spending those days there, talking to the guests who had come to pay their last respects. They were all so worried about what would happen to Suzie and me, now that Mama was gone. Martha wanted to take Suzie to live with her, but Suzie adamantly refused.

"I ain't goin' to be no baby sitter for her brat!"

Of course, she was referring to Marilyn.

I was the odd-ball. Nobody knew what to do with me. I was fifteen and a half, and felt I could take care of myself. Why couldn't I stay on at Brevard Avenue, and continue going to Brentwood High? Even though I had an adult brain, I still looked like a child, and was often treated as such.

It was decided that Suzie and I would move in with Katy. She had been working as the Western Pennsylvania "Commander" of the Girl Guards, the Salvation Army's equivalent of the Girl Scouts. She traveled all over the state tending to its business. In order for Sue and me to live with her, she had to leave the Girl Guards, and get a transfer to her own facility.

As soon as the transfer could be arranged, the Salvation Army gave Captain Bordy her own tabernacle to run, in Tarentum, some twenty miles west of Pittsburgh. There would be plenty of room for both Suzie and me, and we would each have our own private bedroom. That would be nice.

Jefferson Memorial Park was the burial site for Mama. The actual funeral would be the hardest ordeal. Mama's coffin was sitting on straps, over the deep hole in the ground, that would soon receive it. Would I be able to control myself, or would I break down during the lowering? I needn't have worried. When the services were over, the coffin was left there, to be lowered later.

After the funeral, there was a get-together, for all the family and friends, who had attended. Pearl went directly upstairs to her room, where she slept the rest of the afternoon. She had been working for Bell Telephone, as well as attending the visitations, and was exhausted. Suzie and I sat on the staircase, observing all.

Papa was completely ignored by everyone. He didn't cry, but he was visibly shaken. After all, he and Mama had been married for thirty four years. He sat quietly in a chair, observing.

The wake soon turned into a wild, drunken brawl, or so it seemed to me, at the time. Booze was a plenty. Sam's first girlfriend, Annie, was feeling lovey-dovey, and had Sam pinned against the wall, ravaging him. He didn't fight too hard.

She could never resist him.

Kate and Ruth were stuck in the kitchen feeding everyone, while the rest were drinking, and partying, and kissing, and carrying on.

Marie had her hands full. She was sitting on the sofa with nine month old Butch, and with three year old Duane, who was tugging on her, while she calmly sipped her drink, Emmett close beside her. *Noblesse oblige!* Her best friend Ethel Sloan, with her husband, Buzz Brady, were on hand giving her moral support. There were quite a few other people there, coming and going, who I cannot remember specifically, but the house was crowded, and the liquor was flowing.

Joe was the worst drunk. He stayed in the kitchen downing shots, because he didn't like the taste of whiskey, just the effect. He always had a yen for Katy, she did have big boobs. So, after a few shots, watching her preparing and serving food, he could resist no longer. He felt free enough to grab a quick feel of her boob. Katy hauled off and slugged him across the kisser, and screamed at him to never touch her, again. I think she even swore at him. Wow, our Salvation Army Lassie could really "let go," if need be. He giggled, and continued trying to snatch at her. She slugged him, again, and pushed him away.

Martha, who by this time was pretty drunk herself, joined in the fight, taking Joe's side, berating Katy, and doing her best to pound on her back. Marilyn, near hysteria, pulled at Martha, and begged her to stop. To Joe it was a big joke, he just kept laughing, enjoying the "cat fight."

Suzie and I were on our perch in the stairway, observing all, and wondering about the sanity of our family. After all, Mama's funeral had just ended. What was wrong with these people?

LIFE GOES ON

Until Katy's transfer came through, Suzie and I returned, temporarily, to school, in Brentwood. Pearl left Bell Telephone and went to work for a Jewish Deli in East Liberty in the accounting department, she did like working with money. Ruth got her the job there.

She had been working in East Liberty, as a short order cook, in an Italian restaurant called The Circle Bar and Grill. She told me that the owners, there, were a little "shady," whatever that means. Pop Villella, had gotten her that job, even though she still worked for him on Saturday nights, at his hamburger joint.

Ed was still working at Mine Safety Tool and Die Corporation as an electrician's helper, where he started dating his co-worker, Helen Smith.

Sam continued "spotting" at the Bel Air Cleaners, in Dormont. Papa returned to repairing shoes at his shop on Amity Street, in Homestead.

Martha and Joe moved back to Pittsburgh, and would soon go into business for themselves with a Lewis-Sheppard franchise, selling battery operated "trucks."

The Carmalts continued on, as before, living on Charles Street, for a short while, anyways. Soon, Marie would return to Florida, to build the Carmo Apartments with her new found "friend," and business partner, Tom Marino.

TARENTUM

"THE SALVATION ARMY HAS
THE RIGHT TO BEAT THE DRUM"

CHAPTER FIVE

Mama died on August 26, 1946, and by the end of October, Suzie and I moved in with Captain Katherine Bordy, in our new "home."

The Salvation Army was a two story building on the Main Street, in Tarentum, at the bottom of a steep hill. There was a wonderful bakery next door, that would, soon, give us all their leftover bake goods, every Saturday.

Halfway up the hill was the Movie Theater, which became my new refuge, and at the top of the hill was this white, brick high school, that looked like a castle.

Walking through the main entrance of the Salvation Army building was an ante room, with a long staircase leading to the second floor. To the left of the ante room was the Tabernacle, where Sunday services were held. To the immediate right was Captain Bordy's office. Behind the office was an auditorium, that was used for Sunday School, and non-religious gatherings. Behind the auditorium were various other rooms, used for classes, or other small meetings.

The first room at the top of the stairs, to the left, was my room, with an entrance both into the hall and into the living room. Next to me was the bedroom of Lt. Marion Smith, a small chubby redhead, who was to be Kay's assistant. Then came Suzie's room. To the rear of the staircase was a huge living room, that ran the length of the front of the building, except for Kay's bedroom, at the far end.

I plastered my stark white walls with a montage of movie star photos, and a montage of sports banners, not that I was into sports, but somehow, I had acquired them somewhere, and they were colorful. It was quite wonderful to have a room to myself, and be able to decorate it, any way I wanted.

Suzie fit in right away, but it took me a while to adjust. I was still small, and looked years younger. They had a terrific acrobatic program at the school, and I thought I'd fit right in. I could not get on any of the teams, because all the spots had been taken, I was too late. That's too bad, because that is one sport in which I excelled.

Word got around that I was "with" the

Salvation Army, which seemed to make people treat me differently. It actually embarrassed me, for people to know that I was living at the Army, and tried keeping it a secret for as long as I could. Therefore, because I didn't get too involved in the High School activities, I got more and more involved in the activities at the Army.

It was enjoyable sitting in the front office, taking care of the transients, when Kay had places to go. In the previous regime, the officer in charge let some of the bums stay over night in the building. Kay would not permit that. Instead, we would give them a food chit to eat at a café, and a chit to stay in a local hotel for the evening. Kay did not want any strangers sleeping under her roof.

She conscientiously did her work for the Army, but any time she could get away, we would get in the station-wagon, and go on a little trip, somewhere. That Gypsy blood, again! Shortly after we got settled, Kay informed us that we were going to go apple picking at the Salvation Army Summer Camp, in West View.

When I was five or six, I learned to swim there. Someone tied a rope around my waist, holding it while I splashed through the water. The system worked. Soon, I was swimming like the proverbial fish. "Look, Ma. No rope!"

On this day, Kay seemed in a particularly good mood. How could she be so happy about going apple picking? She wore a white angora sweater, which overly exaggerated the size of her bosom. Why was she wearing a dressy white sweater to climb trees? As it turned out, she didn't climb any trees at all, Suzie and I did. She took off with the blondish caretaker, who was going to "show her around."

After a while, Suzie and I got bored picking apples, and returned to the main house, to see if we could find Kay. She wasn't there, but shortly, she came strolling back, hand in hand, with the young, good looking German stud, named Clarence. Ah ha! Katy had found a boyfriend!

Clarence Schotter, and his brother Richard, lived in the camp with Richard's wife, Ruth, and their two sons, Richard, Jr. and Carl. They acted as the caretakers, and did handy work around the camp. They were painters by trade, and soon, Kay had an idea. She decided that the Salvation Army interior, in Tarentum, was in dire need of a paint job (it wasn't, really), so she hired them. And boy, did their romance bloom!

Soon, the brothers were underfoot, painting the entire interior of the two story Army building. It was going to take months to complete the job. because Kay insisted that they use paint brushes, rather that rollers. Paint brushes were more "professional." That suited her, the longer, the better. Katy's sights were set.

Every Saturday night Kay, Marion, Sue, and I would get into the Army's old broken down station wagon, to hit the bars, in order to sell *The War Cry,* the Salvation Army weekly newspaper. Marion and Kay would go into the bars, vending their papers, while Sue and I sat out in the car, keeping the engine going, by pulling on the choke. If the engine stopped, we would have been "up the creek." Somehow, we always kept it running.

The bar patrons enjoyed these two shapely babes, shaking their tambourines, and selling them *War Crys*. The girls usually did quite well, and the customers always looked forward to the two Salvation Army Sallies, visiting each week. They enjoyed it, too, especially our plucky little red-head Marion. She was a natural flirt.

Kay had great posture, but was always a little self-conscious of her protruding chest. Whenever she had to walk across a stage, she would always "fix" her hair, with her down-stage hand, so that her arm would "mask" her bosom. It was so subtle, that no one ever noticed. How clever she was!

During the Sunday services, she would accompany herself on the guitar, while she, and the congregation, sang, "It is summertime in my heart, it is summertime in my heart . . ." Some of the girls would shake their tambourines, Katy might even play her cornet, and I would beat the drum. " . . . since Jesus saved me, new life he gave me, when it's wintertime it's summer in my heart."

These prayer meetings were exhilarating and, often, fun. The Salvation Army certainly believes in making "a joyful noise unto the Lord."

After Sunday Services, Sue and I would pass out the cakes and "goodies," that the bakery gave us. We always had a good crowd. Did the people came to hear Kay's sermon, to enjoy the music, or just to get their free sugar fix?

At Christmas time, I was assigned the task of ringing the Salvation Army bell, and collecting money. This did not please me. The guy who was supposed to do it didn't show up, so I was conscripted. My "uniform" was a navy blue coat, and a cap, that had "The Salvation Army" written on it.

It was a busy Saturday afternoon, and I was assigned to ring the bell in front of the local five and ten. It was so embarrassing, that every time someone from school came by, I would turn my back to them, hoping they wouldn't recognize me. It was a long, boring, tedious job standing there, for a four hour shift, ding-a-linging. I only did it once, and refused to do it, again, even though a percentage of the money was paid to me. That was nice.

Of course, my favorite place to visit was the Movie Theater. One Saturday afternoon, "Madonna of the Seven Moons," an English film with Phyllis Calvert and Stewart Granger, was playing. It was about a very religious lady, with a dual personality. Every so often, her lascivious side would erupt, and she'd return to her lover at The Seven Moons Café, in Italy. It was "based on" a true story, and, absolutely, captivated me. Naturally, I sat through it twice.

Kay loved the movies, too, but didn't think it was right for any of her congregation to see her attending the cinema, in Tarentum. Whenever we went into Pittsburgh, usually on the way back, we would stop to see a film.

During our sojourn in Tarentum, Katy had to go to an Army Conference, in Atlantic City, for a few days. While she was gone, she had

Ruthie come to stay with Suzie and me. The day after Ruth got there, we got a call from the Tarentum Fire Department. It seems that Siegfried's Furniture Store had caught fire. How soon could we, The Salvation Army, get to the scene of the fire, to take care of the fatigued fire fighters?

Ruth tried to explain that Captain Bordy was out of town, and that she didn't know what to do. Not to worry, I could handle the whole thing, including showing her where the big coffee urn was located, and instructing her on how to make the coffee.

I went next store to the bakery, and begged them for goodies, to feed the fire department. They were, as always, quite generous. Neither Ruth nor I drove, so we had to get someone to drive the station wagon for us. I called Howard, a guy who was crazy about Katy. He obliged, anything for Captain Bordy!

We loaded up the station wagon, and drove to the fire. Howard dropped us off, and would return later. Immediately, we set up shop. Ruth was wearing shorts and a "busty" blouse. The firemen seemed to enjoy the coffee and cake, and kept returning for refills. They sure loved our coffee, or was it Ruthie?

During all this activity, the press happened to come by, and snapped her picture, while she was pouring coffee. We didn't notice, we were too busy doing "the Lord's work!"

The next day, in the local Tarentum newspaper, there was a picture of glamorous Ruth, serving a fireman a cup of coffee, with a cigarette dangling from her mouth. How shocking! The headline read, "Salvation Army Lassie Comes to Aid of Firemen." The story praised us for doing such a good job. We all got a big laugh out of it, including Kay, when she returned.

Clarence and Richard came to paint the Army interior on the week-ends, because they still had duties at Camp West View. The two of them, often, bickered with each other, neither thought the other was doing his share of the work. Kay did not always act as peace maker, and usually took Clarence's side. Of course, she was enamored with him, and had an ulterior motive. Richard was a rather burly man, who really *didn't* "pull his own weight."

As time went along, Kay and her future husband, got friendlier, and friendlier. Clarence would stay late on Saturdays, "courting" her in the living room. I'd hear them outside my door, whispering "sweet nothings" to each other, for hours on end. Why didn't he go home, so I could get some sleep? Katy had to get up and preach in the morning, which she always managed to do.

At the end of January, Kay and Clarence decided to spend some quality time together, by going on a drive across Pennsylvania, to New York City, and then back. Sue and I were to go along on this adventure. Clarence had a

pretty good running car, so we left the old station wagon behind, piled into his car, and off we Hunkies went on our little trek.

The first night, we drove all night, with Suzie and I in the back seat, and Kay and Clarence in the front. Whenever Clarence got "tired," he'd pull off to the side of the road to "rest." Oh, is that what they call it?

On the morning of February 1, 1947, we drove through Harrisburg, Pennsylvania, then into New York City. It was the first time Suzie and I had ever been to Times Square. What a thrill it was. The theater facades were impressive. There was a huge colored mural, covering the side of a building, of Maureen O'Hara, in her low-cut dress, with Douglas Fairbanks, Jr., at her side. The marquee displayed the name of the film, "Sinbad the Sailor."

After driving around Times Square, we turned around, and went back to Tarentum. When you're in love, even a silly trip like the one we just took, is exciting, I guess. It was for Sue and me, too, even though we didn't get much sleep.

The rest of the winter was filled with our usual routines: selling the *War Cry*, holding services, feeding our congregants, taking care of the bums, holding our arts and crafts classes, and then, preparing for our special Easter services. Naturally, I decorated the church for the occasion.

The choir was to sing some special numbers for the service, so I made little song booklets, with large crosses, painted in florescent paint, on the covers. At the end of the singing, the lights were turned out for the "spectacular" effect of the crosses glowing in the dark. It didn't work well, at all, too much daylight.

When spring arrived, the Schotter boys were transferred from the West View Camp to Camp Allegheny, in Ellwood City, near New Castle. Coincidentally, for the two previous summers, Kay had worked there teaching "woods lore," leading her Girl Guards on hikes through the countryside. This summer, she would not be teaching there, because of her duties in Tarentum.

The boys were to build an outdoor tabernacle, and renovate the camp by doing carpentry work, and generally getting the place into shape. Another brainstorm! Why couldn't I work there during the summer, too. I was very proficient with the handicraft classes, that I taught, in Tarentum, and they could use an assistant handicraft instructor, so I was hired.

Papa came to call on us. He brought with him a nice looking Italian woman, that he had been dating. She looked and talked like a more Americanized version of Mama, and was quite nice. In his own way, Papa wanted to provide a home for Suzie and me by

81

marrying again. A little companionship for him would be nice, too.

We spent a pleasant afternoon together, walking around Tarentum Park, but I don't think this woman was ready to take care of an "old" man, and his two teen-age kids.

Papa did marry, again, but not to this woman. Soon, he would meet a nice, sheltered Hungarian/American woman, in her forties, who had never been married, named Margit. Suzie, Kay and I would attend the ceremony.

Before starting my stint at Camp Allegheny, I was allowed to spend a few days with the family, on Brevard Avenue. It was nice to get away from the Army for a few days. Papa, Sam, Ed, Ruth, and Pearl were all living there. The family members came and went, but always seemed to return to Brevard, myself included.

It was April of 1947, and Ruth was preparing herself for a move to Atlantic City, where she would work the summer season, as a waitress. She had heard that good money could be made there. Pop Villella and I drove her to the train station, in downtown Pittsburgh, to see her off.

Years later, she told me how her heart was breaking, at how sad and forlorn, she thought I had looked, when she left. She felt that *she* should have, some how, some way, taken care of Suzie and me, instead of going off to New Jersey. Hell, she wasn't yet twenty-one herself, how could she have taken care of us? Ruth was always such a big mother-type, taking care of everyone.

When she arrived in Atlantic City, she got a job right away at Betty's Restaurant, on Virginia Avenue, quite close to the Boardwalk, and across from the Virginia Bar and Hotel. Around the corner, on the Boardwalk, was a game called Fascination. All of these places would soon become very important in her life.

The Virginia Bar was owned by jovial Paul Swetkoff, and friendly John Heaton. It was a fun place where Ruth, and her girlfriend Virginia, could go to relax after work. They seldom paid for a drink, both were quite attractive and popular.

Fascination was a mechanical Bingo game, that was run by a dark, brooding gambler, named Solomon Mintz. The girls would often go there for a little divertissement. Sol was charming, handsome, and loved by all. Ruth fell victim to his charm, and when the summer season ended, the two of them got married on November 3, 1947.

Ed decided to move to California. Several days after Easter, of 1947, he left for Los Angeles. Ed already had a job lined up, and a place to stay, when he reached L.A. He moved in with Ann and Paul Nowicki, a nice, friendly couple with many kids. Their two families stayed life-long friends, celebrating Christmas and

Thanksgiving, together, for over thirty years.

He got on-the-job training at Fox Automotive, in Huntington Park, where he, finally, became a full fledged mechanic. Once he got settled, he sent for his girlfriend, Helen Smith, and married her.

With his partner, Mickey Cannata, he would go into the automobile repair business. It was in a town called Norwalk, where they managed to establish Liberty Motors.

After returning to Tarentum, Kay decided to take one last trip to visit Ma Hayman in Rye Beach, New Jersey. We would be able to stop over in Atlantic City to see Ruth, as well. When she was at her Conference in Atlantic City, earlier that year, the Major, there, invited her to come for a visit, and "bring the kids," so we obliged.

We left Tarentum early on a June morning of 1947. Katy got behind the wheel of that old, beat-up station wagon, and in no time at all, we were on our way to "romantic, enchantic Atlantic City."

We made pretty good time, Clarence wasn't around to distract her. When Kay got behind that wheel, she could, and did, drive like a maniac. "The Lord will protect us," she always said. And he always did.

We arrived in Atlantic City, later that day, and went directly to The Salvation Army, on New York Avenue. They gave me a cot to sleep on, in the Major's office. On the wall was a picture of Christ, with his eyes closed. What a spooky picture it was. Even though his eyes were closed, they seemed to open, and follow you all over the room. I didn't sleep well that night, because The Lord spooked me.

The next morning, we were all up, bright and early, ready to explore the Boardwalk. We strolled from New York Avenue. down five or six blocks, to Virginia Avenue, so we could see Ruth, at Betty's Restaurant. After a quick visit, we returned to the Boardwalk, where some kind of a parade was about to take place. We didn't know what the occasion was, but it must have had something to do with a rodeo, or a horse show.

In the parade, we saw Dale Evans, the Queen of the Cowboys, as well as several equine "stars:" Thunderhead, Smoky, and Flicka.

After the parade, I did what I always do. I got off by myself, and went to the movies. "Duel in the Sun" was playing, and it was the sexiest movie I had ever seen. That was, also, the day I discovered Dmitri Tiomkin, the composer. What a magnificent score!

Jennifer Jones wasn't bad, either. By the time the movie was shown in Pennsylvania, some of the more provocative scenes had been cut. Luckily,

I had seen the original, and bragged to my buddies about those extracted "hot scenes."

We stopped by to see Ruth, one last time, before returning to the Army for the night. She was sorry she couldn't spend more time with us, but when you're "working the season in Atlantic City," time is limited, and your work comes first.

The next morning, we drove to Rye Beach, where we spent a few nice, pleasant days with "Ma" Hayman. She really was a kind lady, and everyone loved her.

Kay had told me about when she first graduated from college, and was stationed with Mrs. Hayman. Often, they would have nothing to eat, which kind of frightened young Lt. Bordy. Ma never worried, she would tell Katy to go ahead and set the table for dinner.

"What are we going to eat?" Katy would ask.

"Don't worry. The Lord will provide."

Apparently, he always did, and Kay never doubted her faith, again.

Sue, Kay, I and Mrs. Hayman had a grand old time going to the beach.

She introduced Suzie and me to ice cream cones with "jimmy" on top. Jimmies turned out being very tiny bits of chocolate, covered with a multi-colored sugar coating. The cones were dipped into that mixture. How delicious!

After our few days in the sun, it was back to Tarentum for us Bordys.

CAMP ALLEGHENY

Camp Allegheny was going to be quite an adventure. This was to be my first "adult" job. Upon arriving, Clarence and Richard had just about finished building the tabernacle, and had begun renovating the porches, of each of the cabins.

Both sides of the porches were being enclosed, in

84

order to have private quarters built for the councilors.

It took most of the summer to complete this task. Therefore, all of the male councilors were assigned to stay together, in one of the cabins. I was consigned to stay with them, even though I was a "teacher." How devastating!

Miss Betty Herbertson was hired as the handicraft instructor, and I was to assist her. She didn't look like the typical Salvation Army Lassie; they didn't wear dark red lipstick, and have bleached, blonde hair. She smoked cigarettes, too! Good heavens!

Our first several days were spent cleaning up the Craft Shop. It was quite huge, and fairly well equipped with various tools and equipment. On our first meeting, Miss Herbertson eyed me rather skeptically, and wondered why the Hell had she been given an assistant. After seeing me work, cleaning up the shop and putting everything in order, I became her best friend, and confidante.

When our first class arrived, I gave a "tour" of the shop, explaining what each piece of equipment was, and what its usage was, while walking around with a yard stick gently striking my leg, as I talked. It sent quite a message to the students: that they had better behave. I didn't even realize what I was doing, the yardstick just happened to be in my hand, when the first class commenced. I saw how effective it was, so continued carrying it with me, at all times.

After my indoctrination speech, "Miss Betty," as she would have the children call her, gave a nicer, more pleasant welcome. Then the class would begin. Naturally, all most of them wanted to do was make lanyards. There were many other things lined up for the kids to do, but most insisted on making lanyards.

A lanyard is a kind of sliding necklace, with a clip on the end for holding keys, or a whistle, or whatever. They were made with four strands of "gimp," long narrow strands of shiny, imitation leather. I taught the kids how to "bondoggle," which is a four strand braid. Everyone loved making these useless adornments. On my lanyard, I had a small pair of scissors attached, in order to easily snip the gimp.

Another popular item for the boys was banging those big, tin can lids, that we got from the kitchen, into ash trays, with a mallet, and a wooden mold. Miss Betty was not pleased with this "craft," but it did help so many of the boys, and a few of the girls, to get rid of some of their aggressions.

Often, Miss Betty and I would work late, preparing for the next day's classes. "What was that 'floozy' doing with that young, innocent boy so late at night?" Naturally, rumors began to fly. Really, we were quite innocent, just conscientious.

Each evening, the entire camp came together around a campfire for evening services, and then, usually, some kind of entertainment. Often, the powers that be would seek me out to participate in these programs. My natural flair for theatrics had been discovered. One of the more spectacular events that I staged included an Indian torch fight.

The banks of the waterway were made of red clay. A group of us boys smeared the clay all over our bodies, to make us look like Indians. We wore only breechcloths, to cover our privates, and a feather in each head band. Before the program started, we had one of the guys hide in a nearby tree. Two "torches" were hidden in a small campfire. Next to that, we constructed a huge pile of wood, which would soon become our bonfire.

After everyone was seated, and the campfire program began, one "Indian" came into the campground, beating his tom-tom. Four other Indians followed him, and danced around the little fire, to the sound of the drum. Soon, the Indian who was hidden in the tree. gave out a blood curdling scream, and swung down to the dancers, grabbing a "torch" out of the fire. All ran off except me.

I grabbed my "torch," and the two of us began fighting. My enemy fell to the ground, throwing his torch into the prepared bonfire, which had been secreted with gun powder and kerosene. Immediately, it blew up and lighted the sky.

Across the lake, our "Indian Chief," in full war bonnet regalia, was rowed across the river by his "tribesmen," while the drums continued beating, and the Indians chanted. It looked like that painting of Washington crossing the Delaware. The whole thing was quite dramatic and exciting, until the "Chief," the camp commander, opened him mouth and gave a boring sermon; that no one had control over. All in all, a good time was had by all.

Not all of our campfire meetings were quite so spectacular. Often they were little more than telling ghost stories, or having sing-a-longs, or amateurs performing songs, or doing "acts." Occasionally, I was conscripted into singing, "Mammy," a la Al Jolson. The imitation was terrible, but the squares loved it.

Toward the end of the summer, Miss Betty had a terrible experience. While in the ladies room having a cigarette, and using the facilities, a couple of boys, who were in the men's room next door, decided to climb up the wall, and peek over the top. Miss Betty was changing a sanitary napkin, and saw the boys.

She screamed, and became hysterical. The trauma must have really gotten to her, because the next day, she left the camp, for good. That meant that I would be "in charge," for the rest of the summer. Though I still looked like a kid, adult responsibilities were always mine.

Kay and Clarence got married on July 25, 1947, at Clarence's parents home, in West View.

The house was on top of a bluff, covered with beautiful, lush foliage. I managed to get the time off from the camp, so that I could attend the wedding (or was the summer session already over?).

While there, I decorated the yard, the food tables, and the interior of the house, using many of the decorative "tricks" with crepe paper, that I had learned by observing the window trimmer at Davis Drug Store, when I worked there.

The rear window overlooked the luxuriant back yard, where the wedding was to take place. That's where I would observe the wedding, while playing the ceremonial music. Everything fell into place. The wedding was really beautiful, and went off splendidly, with Major Tripp performing the ceremony.

Many Salvation Army friends attended, along with Clarence's father and mother, Majors Alfred and Lina Schotter. They sponsored the wedding, and prepared a delicious array of food for the festivities. Clarence's sister Louise, brother Richard, and cousin Gunter attended, too. Pearl was Kay's maid of honor. Also, in attendance, were Kay's girlfriend Mildred, with her husband Don Peterson, Sam, Suzie and me.

In the back yard of Major Schotter's house stood a tiny cottage. It had been built as the servants' quarters for the main house.

It was quaint and picturesque, enveloped by many trees and bushes. It was perhaps a little too small, and too cozy, to be used by a "honeymooning" couple, with a twelve year old girl.

Sue slept on the couch in the narrow living room, while Kay and Clarence occupied the adjacent bedroom. There was no door between the rooms, only a drape. How awkward! This is where the three of them would live for the next three or four years, until they were able to buy their first house. It, at one time, was an old rustic log cabin, way out of town, on Old Perry Highway, in a place called Wexford.

BACK TO BRENTWOOD

The Senior Year

Chapter Six

After proving myself at Camp Allegheny, that summer of 1947, it was agreed that I was "adult" enough to move back to Brevard Avenue, and return to Brentwood High School for my senior year.

Papa was still living there, as well as Sam, and Pearl. Ruth had gone to Atlantic City, and would marry Sol Mintz. Ed had gone to Los Angeles, followed by his soon to be wife, Helen. Suzie was living with Kay and Clarence, in West View, Martha and Joe were living in an apartment, a quarter mile past Brentwood High, and Marie and Emmett were still living on Charles St. in Knoxville, but not for long.

Even though Kay just got married, there was a standing invitation for me to visit on Sundays for dinner. Suzie and I always had a good time horsing around together. Often, the clan would go swimming and picnicking at North Park, or just hang around the new, "honeymoon" cottage. Clarence had a ready made family, and *no* privacy.

Papa still went to work, each day, on Amity Street, in Homestead. I, no longer, went with him, being too busy, having the time of my life, growing up.

Sam continued working at Bel-Air Cleaners, in Dormont. He was seldom home. At twenty-six, he was really sowing his wild rice; for awhile, he dated a Chinese girl. His buddy, Jack Smith, and he were running around, most evenings, "entertaining" all kinds of women.

During my stay in Tarentum, the only thing I remember about school was March 4, 1947. I played a cowboy in a school show, with a huge monologue about Pecos Bill. There's not too much else to remember, except that I wasn't too happy there. All that changed, after returning to Brentwood High School.

It was great to be back. I hadn't realized how many friends I had made in Brentwood. About half of my class mates were my same class mates in the third grade, when we all went to Elroy Elementary. The other half had gone to Moore Elementary School, on the other side of Brentwood High. A few

had been transferred there from Mount Oliver.

One of the first things we Seniors had to do was have our photos taken for the year-book. Why so early? As it turned out, my photo looked nothing like me when I graduated. Starting out the year as a scrawny, little kid with long legs, by graduation, I finally matured into a five foot, ten and a half inch, one hundred and forty five pound man, still a little scrawny, but not for long.

Almost right away, I rejoined the Chess Club, the Theatrical Make-up Club, and the Stage Crew, and auditioned for the Choral Group. At the audition, Mr. Munn, the music teacher, accompanied each person up and down the scales, to find out his range. When it was my turn, we started around middle C, and went up, and up. He seemed to be impressed. "Now, let's try your lower register."

"Not yet," I begged him, "I can sing a lot higher than that."

We started up the scale, again, gliding right into my soprano voice, to high C.

"Okay, now let's try the lower notes," I instructed.

Down we went, way down into the *basso* range. So, what was I? A bass or a soprano? Mr. Munn had a dilemma, where should he place me in the choir? He didn't have any strong sopranos, so he put me in the midst of a bunch of giggling girls, because my voice could help carry them. That didn't last long; after performing in the Christmas Cantata, on December 11th and 12th, 1947, I quit.

Soon, they would be auditioning for "The Hasty Heart." The setting of the play was in a military hospital, and there were plenty of men's parts. Certainly, I would get one. I didn't. I still looked like a child, and there was a huge selection of other guys, who looked and acted older, so they got the parts. Maybe the next play?

One of the transferees, from Mount Oliver, was Shirley Weinhaus. We met in our P.O.D. (Problems of Democracy) class and became fast friends, not romantically, I was still going with Shirley Jordan, from Baldwin.

We sat in the last two desks, of the first two rows. Our teacher, Mr. Moore, was a shy, good looking, but rather awkward man, who droned on and on about "Democracy." Shirley and I entertained each other, "reacting" to Mr. Moore, and writing each other notes. This went on for the entire year.

Marie decided to return to St. Petersburg, to go into business with Tom Marino. They were to build a new apartment building. This time, she took Pearl with her. Unlike Ruth, Pearl had a good time in St. Pete. Marie had rented a house, and hired a maid to take care of Duane and Butch, so Pearl only had to baby-sit, evenings, when Marie went out.

Being an attractive nineteen year old, she

was having the time of her life. One afternoon, at one of Marie's social functions, Pearl met Tyrone Power. She was not impressed. No one ever impressed Pearl; she treated all celebrities just like they were real people.

Tyrone and she got along well and spent a pleasant afternoon together. Years later, when Pearl worked for me, at my newspaper, in Hollywood, she met many celebrities, who loved to sit and chat with her: Susan Strasberg in particular, as well as Nina Foch, Guy Stockwell, and many other, lesser known "stars."

After staying in Florida a few months, she came back to Brentwood, and went to work as a hostess/cashier in the Pittsburgher Hotel restaurant. Across the street from the hotel was Kaufmann's Department Store, where she also worked, Mondays and Saturdays, in the accounting department. Pearl still loved "handling" money. Later, she worked at Child's Restaurant. That girl sure did move around, a lot.

"UNCONQUERED"

On October 3, 1947, Cecil B. DeMille came to town for the world premier of his latest epic film, "Unconquered," starring Gary Cooper and Paulette Goddard. It was an historic film about the settlers, and the Indians, of Pittsburgh, in the 1700's. The film premiered at one of Pittsburgh's grandest movie palaces, the Loews-Penn Theater, now called Heinz Hall.

A huge platform, about six feet off the ground, had been built in front of the theater for the pre-premier ceremonies. After a big, two hour parade, that afternoon, the festivities would begin there. During the parade, I stationed myself in front of that stage, directly under the microphone, so I wouldn't miss a thing. It's a good thing I did, because mobs of people showed up. Many movie celebrities were to be there; unfortunately, the two stars did not attend.

One by one the "guest stars" were introduced by Hedda Hopper. She was a well know Hollywood Gossip Columnist, who was known for wearing unusual hats, that was her trademark. Right before she started to introduce Cecil B. DeMille, I called up to her, "Hey, Hedda. How about giving us your hat?" She was quite amused and even wrote about the incident in her column, after returning to Hollywood.

"C.B." talked about "his greatest picture, yet," Then, Hedda continued introducing the guest-stars, who were "so happy to come to Pittsburgh for this very special occasion."

There was funny Billy De Wolfe, surly Howard da Silva, pleasant Macdonald Carey, pert Olga San Juan, pretty Virginia Welles and then, finally my favorite, sexy

90

Lizabeth Scott. I stood directly under her, in front of that stage, looking up into her nostrils; such beautiful nostrils I had never seen. I gasped for breath, she was absolutely stunning! Pitter pat, pitter pat!

Naturally, I couldn't afford to attend the premier, later that evening, but I could hang around their hotel, and try to meet some of the stars, afterwards. The word was that they were all staying at the William Penn Hotel, and would leave later that evening, to return to Hollywood.

That gave me time to go home, put on my baggy, chocolate brown suit, and get my autograph book. Later that evening, I stationed myself in the lobby of the hotel, "acting" as if I belonged there, and just waited for the celebrities to come by.

Macdonald Carey was sitting in the lobby reading a magazine. All the other stars were in their rooms, waiting to make their "entrances." He was very friendly to all who talked to him. I asked him for his autograph, and he obliged.

Howard da Silva came roaming through the lobby. He was the only actor there who was actually in the movie. He seemed just as threatening in person as he was in his movies, *but* he did give me his autograph.

Then Billy de Wolfe came into the lobby to visit with the fans. He was quite funny, and everyone laughed at his carrying on. Getting an autograph from him was easy; he obliged us all. Then, all the stars were instructed to go back to their rooms, leaving the fans to await the next "activity."

Soon, the first "star," Virginia Welles, made her entrance from the elevator, with two chaperones on either side of her. They walked her briskly through the lobby, trying to wave off the kids asking for autographs.

"Miss Welles has a train to catch, please let her through."

The escorts rushed her out the Penn Avenue entrance, down the stairs and into a waiting limousine. Then, off they drove, but not before I got her autograph..

Ah ha! My brain started working, overtime. Why don't I become one of the chaperones? So, I did. The next star getting out of the elevator was Hedda, with only one chaperone. Seeing my opening, I walked directly up to her, put my arm around her, and rushed her to her waiting limousine, pushing the fans aside.

"Please, let Miss Hopper through. She has a train to catch," I dared to say as I pushed the fans away. Right before she drove off, I asked for her autograph.

The women all carried bouquets of roses, and wore sleek, silky mink coats. How soft and luxurious they felt, when I put my arm around both Hedda Hopper and Olga San Juan, while escorting them to their limos.

C. B. de Mille didn't bother with escorts. He just roamed through the lobby by himself, stopping and visiting with whomever wanted to talk to him. When he was ready, I walked beside him to the limo, and had no trouble acquiring his autograph.

Howard da Silva and Billy De Wolfe both needed escorting, so I obliged them. So far, I had "escorted" all the stars, and was successful in getting their autographs. There was only one that I really wanted, so I waited and waited.

When the elevator door finally opened, revealing Lizabeth Scott, I grabbed her, and, perhaps, held her a little closer than the other women. She was charming and friendly to all, but adamantly, she was not signing anyone's book.

"Let Miss Scott through, she has a train to catch. No autographs, please."

Once she was seated in her limo, I was sure that I would be able to get her to sign my book. I was wrong. The limo driver was impatient, and started to drive away, even before I could get completely out of the car.

How disappointing! But, at least, I had held that ravishing woman in my left arm, sniffing her lightly scented hair, while stroking that luscious fur with my right hand. I did manage to get one souvenir, though, a petal from her bouquet of roses. It is pasted in my autograph book, in lieu of her signature.

Christmas time in Pittsburgh was always delightful. Usually, the weather would turn chilly and snowy, by then. The downtown streets were always strewn with multi-colored lights, and laurel decorations. All the department stores tried to outdo each other, with their window decorations and gimmicks.

Going from Kaufmann's, to Gimbel's, to Boggs and Buhl's, to Horne's, and all the rest, to see their displays, was the highlight of the Christmas Season.

My favorite display was at Kaufmann's. All their windows were nicely decorated, but the *coup de grace* was, that one of their windows was turned into a theatrical stage, where they presented its annual marionette show. The audiences gathered outside, around the window, to watch the continuous performances. Each year's show got better than the year before.

Maybe, after I got out of high school, I could get myself a job decorating windows at Kaufmann's, and work with the marionette show. After all, I had learned to decorate windows at Davis Drug Store with crepe paper, and had already made my first marionette. Why *couldn't* I work there? How naïve! As a matter of fact, several years later, I did have an interview for a job in Kaufmann's decorating department, but nothing ever came of it. I really wasn't qualified.

The marionette show did inspire me to finish my puppet, that was begun in my "craft room" when I was thirteen. It was an ugly, skinny man, almost two feet tall, that needed operating controls, and strings. The head was solid clay, covered with *papier-mache*. It had two sunken eye sockets, into which I put two pearls, giving it the appearance of a zombie. The boots were made of clay, too, attached to two dowel rods, and covered with *papier-mache*, also. The hair was made from shreds of an old "rat" Mama used to wear in her hair, during the war. The entire monstrosity, including the clothes, was made by me. Now, it was time to finish it.

With the aid of my shop teacher, Mr. Kuhn, the controls were fashioned out of pine wood. Afterward, I got some strong shoe thread from Papa's shop, for stringing. Now, "the zombie" would be ready for me to entertain "the troops," when I returned to Camp Allegheny.

My dreams of Show Business did not abate. My theatrical itch had to be scratch somehow, some way. While riding on the buses and streetcars, I had noticed an advertisement for the Vera Liebau Dance Studio. They taught all types of dancing. Being flush with the money earned at Camp Allegheny, what better way to spend it but on dance lessons. I could envision myself as another Gene Kelly, not Fred Astaire. Dancing was always something I wanted to do, and now, I was going to do it before it was too late. Scratch, scratch.

After signing up for my lessons, they asked what style of dancing I wanted to study. I didn't know one from the other, so "acrobatic dance" sounded like it would be the one for me. Pauline Wray became my teacher. With muscles bulging everywhere, she looked like a weight lifter, and scared the hell out of me.

The first thing she did was sit me on a mat, got behind me, bended me over as far as I could go, and started to stretch my body into the strangest contortions. That must be how she got all of those muscles. Boy, was she strong. This was our routine at the beginning of each lesson.

Soon, she had me doing hand springs, cartwheels, back bends, head and hand stands, the "spider," and my strong suit, "butterflies." Butterflies are similar to cartwheels without any hands. We worked on doing the split, but my legs never quite allowed my crotch to hit the floor, no matter how hard Pauline shoved me down. I had to contend myself with faking a split, by putting my hand on the floor to mask the space in front of my crotch, and "acting" as though I could, actually, do it.

So, when was I going to actually dance? In June, the studio was to present it's annual dance recital at the Nixon Theatre. Wow, the Nixon Theatre was *the* legitimate theatre in Pittsburgh. How prestigious! Finally, I was going to dance, and at the Nixon, no less. Pauline began to choreograph a dance for me to "Fun and Fancy Free." Up on my toes, arms extended, head up, turn, turn. Boy, did I fly, or flit, or whatever! Man, was I terrible.

As the winter got colder, more and more people were catching the flu. Papa was no exception. He usually didn't give in to any illness, no one in our family did. Whenever he got a cold, his usual remedy was to work up a sweat, by getting a bottle of whiskey, and swigging on it all night. This usually worked, even though he would get quite drunk, and start moaning about imagined, or real slights. His favorite "victim" was usually Mr. Ferber, his leather supplier. Papa would hurl such awful insults at him, and call him such terrible names. How could he? Mr. Ferber was such a nice man.

In this particular winter of 1948, Papa did not recover quickly He stayed home from work, which he never did, and was bed ridden. I waited on him, bringing his meals and drinks, and a bucket of water when he needed to defecate. Yeah, he wouldn't walk down the hall to the bathroom, he was too ill, and too weak. I didn't mind bringing him a bottle to urinate in, but the bucket, that was too much. But, I did it. He begged me to call Dr. Pfaff, the Hungarian doctor from Homestead, to come and make him well. I think Pfaff was married to the midwife, who birthed most of us.

"How do you spell that, Papa?" I asked.

"Pfaff, Pfaff, puh, fuh, faff. How do I know? You're the smart one. Call Dr. Pfaff," he screamed. "What are you trying to do, kill me? *Call Dr. Pfaff!*"

I looked in the phone book for Dr. Faff, Dr. Pufaf, every imaginable spelling I could conceive of, but no luck. Then I remembered Dr. Uptagraph, the doctor who had sewed up the back of my head, and had set Pearl's broken arm. The best part was, his office was nearby. I called him, and he came immediately. How fortunate. That would never happen today. The best part, it only cost two dollars.

He gave Papa some syrup, and told him to stay in bed, drink plenty of liquids, and get lots of rest, everything we had already been doing. Soon, Papa was well enough to go back to work, and everything went back to normal, whatever that was.

While Marie was away in Florida, building her new Carmo Apartment complex, Emmett was left alone in Pittsburgh. Surely he missed her, and needed some kind of companionship, so he started seeing other women.

He had just bought one of those snazzy, new Studebaker automobiles, that looked the same in the back as in the front; you couldn't tell what direction it was going. One evening, after finishing his duties at the Shadyside Hospital, he went out to have dinner and drinks with a young woman.

It had been snowing, and the streets were slippery. They probably had a little too much to drink, because he lost control of his Studebaker, and smashed into the rear end of a streetcar, while it was turning a bend. They were killed instantly, and he was decapitated.

Marie was informed, and came home to take care of the identification and burial. There was no funeral. Apparently, his body was in pretty bad shape, so she had him buried immediately. I don't know where. I don't even think she had a memorial service for him, being anxious to get back to Florida.

She stayed around only as long as it took to dispose of their belongings, and put the Charles Street house on the market. Emmett had bought a new light, blue gabardine suit, some shirts, and underwear, that were delivered after he died. Marie offered the new clothes to me, along with all his other attire. He was a little shorter than I, and not really wanting to wear a dead man's garments, I declined saying that the clothing wouldn't fit me. The new suit, however, would be perfect, once I had cuffs put on it. It was a summer suit, so it was left it in the box until then.

Before returning to Saint Petersburg, there was a newspaper article in the *Pittsburgh Press*, with the headline saying, something to the effect that: "Well known doctor leaves $85,000 estate to wife." Wow! That was a hell of a lot of money!

When the Carmo Apartments were completed, she would have enough money to buy another apartment complex. So, she bought Bexley Hall, and two empty lots on Hendricks Island, in Fort Lauderdale. After completing their work on the Carmo Apartments, she and Tom Marino moved to Bexley Hall, on "The Island."

The Jogeeses were fully ensconced in their new Lewis-Sheppard office, across the street from Brentwood High School. Joe couldn't afford a staff, so Martha went to work as his private secretary, once or twice a week. They shared an office with Flo Menges, Martha's best friend from high school. Her sister Betty was in my class at Brentwood, although I never really got to know her well. I did like Flo, she was not only pretty, but sweet as could be.

For years, Joe had worked as a salesman for Philco, and was an expert with industrial batteries. They kept transferring him to other cities, so he and Martha thought it was time to branch out on their own, and go into business for themselves.

The Lewis-Sheppard Company sold "trucks," that was the broad term for fork lifts, and other battery operated machinery. The big profits came from selling, and servicing, their batteries. Clark Trucks had been in business for many years, and was their major competitor. Lewis-Sheppard had the edge, though, because most of the Clark trucks were run on gasoline, not batteries.

Usually on Fridays, Martha and Joe would work late, so they'd have me take Marilyn home, after school. We'd leisurely stroll to their apartment, about a quarter mile away. At first, Marilyn resented her uncle chaperoning her, but, soon, started to enjoy it.

She forgot that I was her uncle, and started treating me as if I were her beau, by sashaying and fluttering her eyes at me. And, she was only eight years old. Oh my, a blonde, miniature Martha!

Television had been invented, but wasn't, yet, quite on the market. But, it would be, soon. We had to amuse ourselves, as best we could, she by reading, and I by listening to Joe's classical music collection, sometimes getting up and trying to be Gene Kelly.

"Oh, Uncle William," she would deride, "You look so foolish." It didn't bother me at all, I had to keep in shape for my dance recital. Ha, ha!

When Martha got home, she started dinner right away. She and Marie turned out to be pretty good cooks. They learned, initially, from cook books, then followed the Hunky way of cooking by just "throwing whatever was available together and experimenting. I cook the same way.

She had just bought a pressure cooker, and loved it. Most of her meals were prepared with it in mere minutes. One of my favorite dinners, that she would make anytime I wanted, was her special chili con carne.

She fried up her ground chuck (never hamburger), with onions and other ingredients, poured off the excess fat, then added a can of Campbell's tomato soup, and a can of kidney beans. When it was finished, she would place a huge pile of mashed potatoes on a plate, with a big glob of butter on top. Then, she would surround the potatoes with the chili. It sounds terrible, but it was delicious. Even after living in California, and eating real Mexican Chili, I still prefer Martha's.

It took several years for their franchise to really start paying off. When it did, they moved their office, a few miles away, to the more business oriented, Wilkinsburg, and rented a home in nearby Edgewood. That was their first house.

In the spring, the students at Brentwood High went on strike, only Heaven knows why. They had gone on strike two times before, so this year was no exception. The organizers came around to each class room, dragging us out, and dictating to us that we were on strike. We didn't care why, it was spring, a nice day, and we were just glad to get out of class, and go outside into the nice, fresh air.

Most of the throng "protested" from the south end of the campus, to across Brownsville Road, to in front of Joe's business. The exuberance of the crowd reminded me of the crowd that had celebrated the end of the war, in front of the Melrose Theater.

Backing up, I bumped into a fellow classmate, who would become my best friend. His name was Bill Weinhaus, and the brother of my P.O.D. class cohort, Shirley Weinhaus.

Bill played the clarinet in the school band, and was teaching himself how to play the piano. He said the magic word, piano. My love affair with the piano was ongoing, and even though I never learned how to play, it was still enjoyable to listen and sing to. I dragged him across the street, into the school auditorium, and sat him down at the piano.

He really wasn't very good, because he was still learning, by teaching himself. That was okay, because he learned to "fake it." He could read music, because he played the clarinet. So with his right hand, he played the melody, then with the back of his left hand, he would clomp the lower keys, up then down. It actually didn't sound bad. He called it Scheibel-style, named after Gracie Scheibel, the eight year old neighborhood kid, who taught herself to play that way.

Lunch hour at school was always the same: eat lunch, then watch the girls dance, at the far end of the cafeteria. Of course, we boys were allowed to dance, too, but most of us were too shy to ask any of the girls. A group of us would watch Margie Snyder and Elsie Dornberg dance, day after day, and vowed that, today would be the day that one of us would cut in, and actually dance with one of them. We never did.

After the strike, and after lunch, one day, I got Bill to come into the auditorium, again, to try his luck on the piano. He didn't have to be coaxed too hard, to sit down, and start playing. Soon, there was a crowd around him, singing along. He had been practicing, and was getting better. He loved the attention, and soon was playing the piano, like the professional that he would become.

We started spending much time together, he was very funny, and we just "hit it off." My lurid Saturdays, with Ray Harmoning, were soon replaced with my wholesome Saturdays, with Bill Weinhaus. Ray and I would continue to play hooky from school to go to Jaffe's Casino, during the week, but he would have to go the North Side cathouses on his own.

Bill Weinhaus and I met downtown for our weekly gad-a-bout. He was anxious to introduce me to Tillie Fichter, the lady who demonstrated sheet music on an old upright piano, in Volkwein's Music Store. She was quite nice to him, answering a multitude of questions, showing, and demonstrating everything in the store. That music store was his Saturday haven.

After leaving Tillie's, we would go to Woolworth's, to hear Marie Moss play all the new sheet music that had just arrived. He was friendly with her, too. We'd both laugh to ourselves when we saw her left hand banging up and down on the lower register. She had "Scheibel-style" down to a science, although, she actually played the correct chords. It was her technique that had inspired Bill to persevere.

Afterwards, sometimes we'd go to a movie, especially if Bette Davis was playing. Usually, we just spent the time roaming around downtown, soaking up that special Pittsburgh aura (or was it its dirt) that we both loved? Saturday days, I spent with Bill, and Saturday nights, I spent with Shirley Jordan at Sully's Swingland.

"Ten Little Indians," by Agatha Christie, was going to be the second semester play at Brentwood High. There had to be a part in it for me. There was. I was cast as the middle aged, Cockney butler, Rogers. I still looked a little young for the part, but Mr. Murphy, the director, figured we could get a skull cap to make me look bald, then age me with makeup.

One Saturday morning, we met in a theatrical makeup shop to get the wig. It didn't work well, at all. Being in the makeup club since the tenth grade, I was fairly proficient at applying it, so I decided to do my own make-up, and just "act" older.

We performed the play on April 15th and 16th. What a ball, chewing the scenery with my fake British accent: "There's plenny a beer in the 'ouse."

At last, I was in Show Business! And, soon, I would be making my dancing debut in the Nixon Theatre.

KENNYWOOD

Pittsburgh is blessed with one of the best amusement parks in America, perhaps even the world. Kennywood Park was entertaining kids decades before the advent of Disneyland. From the third grade on, every summer, Brentwood High and Elroy Elementary held their annual picnic at Kennywood.

It had, and still has, three of the most exciting and dangerous roller coasters in the world: The Jack Rabbit, The Pippin, and The Racer. There are some new steel coasters there, now, but nothing like the old rickety, wooden classics. It has/had all the standard rides, as well as two of the spookiest fun houses: The Old Mill and Noah's Ark.

Buying ride tickets, in advance, cost a lot less than at the park. Students got a tremendous discount. For years, a dollar or two dollars worth of tickets would, usually, last the entire day.

It was a long streetcar ride, over an hour, to get to the park. Once there, the first thing you saw was the "biggest swimming pool in the world." It had a huge island in the middle, that held a grand, flowing waterfall, that was beautifully lit up at night.

At one end of the pool was the high-dive, with two regular diving boards

on either side. On the far side of the pool was a crag, that you could climb up on, right out of the pool. It was covered with rocks and vegetation, and was the most popular diving spot there. As a little kid, I spent hours climbing that rock, imitating the good divers. Soon, I could do the swan dive, the jack knife, the flip, and all the rest. It's sad that diving has been banned at most pools; it was so much fun.

There was no admission into the park, it was free. To enter, you had a long trail to walk, through an underground tunnel, that went under the railway tracks, and into the park. Upon exiting the tunnel, the first thing you saw was the penny arcade, and the dance pavilion.

The first ride was The Old Mill, where small boats would take lovers, or kids, through the mill, past "horrifying" sights. The Jack Rabbit was next. It was probably the creakiest and scariest roller coaster in the park. There was always a long line of expectant daredevils, waiting to ride, and be scared to death.

To the right of The Jack Rabbit was the picnic area, with hundreds of picnic tables. That's where the parents would stake out a table, and set it up for lunch. Mama always brought a huge basket of food, stayed at the table visiting with the other ladies, and feeding any of us, whenever we got hungry.

In the center of the park was a large, man-made lake, where you could rent, and row, a boat, with your sweetie. In the center was an island, where twice a day, circus acts performed. Beyond the lake was Kiddee Land, with rides for the youngest kids.

Near the swimming pool was Noah's Ark. It was a boat that rocked back and forth, on an imitation sea. Old man Noah fishes from one of the windows, while various animals poke out their heads. The inside had all the typical fright gags, but keeping your balance in the dark, while the boat rocked, was difficult and fun.

Then there was the loop-de-loop, the caterpillar, the skooter bumper cars, the Ferris wheel, one of the prettiest merry-go-rounds in America, and all the other great, standard rides to entertain you.

For my senior year picnic, I splurged; I bought five dollars worth of tickets. Baldwin High and Brentwood High were to have their picnics on the same day, so I brought my girlfriend, Shirley Jordan. Her sisters Beadie and

Donna, and cousin Marsha, tagged along.

We ditched them by taking a canoe ride. Rowing a boat was more difficult than I had imagined. The three girls managed to entertain themselves for the rest of the day, so Shirley and I did have a fun filled day together.

In 1998, during my fiftieth high school reunion, I took a final trip to my favorite place in the world. It was miraculously the same, but different. The swimming pool and the pond were no longer there, they had been replaced with new attractions. Most of the old rides were there, but many new, spectacular, exciting, breath-taking ones had been added. They were nice, but I still liked the old ones best.

After the picnic at Kennywood, Shirley and I went to the prom. Like all good graduating seniors, I bought Shirley a rose corsage (couldn't afford an orchid).

Sam gave me five dollars to spend on prom night, and believe it or not, we came back from the prom with the five dollars still in my pocket. What a cheap son-of-a gun I was, still am.

There's not much to remember about the prom except that we did have a good time. Neither of us drank booze, that's probably how we came back with so much money. The only thing I remember about the prom was that it was held at the South Hills Country Club, and we did have a nice, lovey-dovey time.

On June 2nd, I graduated high school. It's all a blur, but it must have happened, because I still have my diploma and the gold tassel from my cap.

THE NIXON THEATRE

The Nixon Theatre was a grand old, lushly gilded, legitimate theatre, with plush red seats, carpeting and walls. It was built circa 1910, across from where Mellon Square Park is today.

In the early twenties, it was the Pittsburgh location of George White's "Scandals." In 1931, Oscar Hammerstein had his world premier of "East

Wind" there, not that anyone remembers it. Now, on June 8, 1948, Vera Liebau was to present her "Dance Tempo Revue."

After many attempts, my dancing instructor, Pauline Wray, got tired of trying to get me up on my toes to "Fun and Fancy Free." She very cleverly came upon the idea of teaming me up with a young acrobatic dancer, named Dauphin Bohn. That way, each of us would get twice the lessons for the same money. That sounded good to me. Dauphin and I got along well, and soon, I would be picking her up, while she contorted into all kinds of artistic positions. Thank God, she was tiny. Pauline began choreographing a kind of adagio dance, for the two of us.

We were to be part of a large production number, "In a Persian Market." I was the Master of the Slaves, and Dauphin was one of my slave girls. It was quite a spectacular number, with all the girls dancing around the Sheik, and then me. In the middle of this display, it was just Dauphin and me.

Her parents were filming our dance routine for posterity. At last, I was going to be in the movies, again. I picked her up, high in the air, and threw her all over the place. First, up on my shoulders, then down on the ground, getting into all kinds of exotic, acrobatics positions, while I, in my bare feet and bare chest, sneered at her. She did some impressive stunts, and I did a series of six spectacular butterflies. Then, the performance was over.

Within a three week period, I had acted in a play, picnicked at Kennywood Park, gone to the prom, graduated high school, and made my dancing debut in The Nixon Theatre. Hollywood, here I come! I never did get to see the film.

Mae West, once again played the Nixon, just two years later in 1950. She had staged a touring revival of her favorite play, "Diamond Lil." Her second motion picture, "She Done Him Wrong" was based on the play. This revival was to be her swan song in the legit theatre. It was also to be the swan song of the Nixon Theatre.

Papa told me that he had attended her final performance on June 29th. After the curtain came down, scavengers immediately started ripping the place apart, gathering up souvenirs. It was a mad house. Papa didn't want any souvenirs, he just wanted to see Mae, again.

He worked his way backstage; the place was in chaos. Mae escaped, before the throng could get to her. It must have been a harrowing experience for her, but Papa was satisfied. He saw his Mae one last time. The theatre was halfway demolished that night, and completely demolished within the week.

101

RETURN TO CAMP ALLEGHENY

It was great to be back at Camp Allegheny. From the year before, I had finally grown to my full five foot, ten and a half inch height.

The year before, I was the second to the smallest guy on the ball team; this year I would prove to be the second from the tallest.

Our hardball team consisted of Gene Wilson, Ralph Stephenson, Walter Fahey, David Riley, Cliff Hall, Wayne Pierce, myself, Louie Conte, and Vern Clete. Naturally, they put me in right field, because I was such a lousy player. But, I was a terrific hitter, and had a high R.B.I. stat. That meant that I could knock the home runs in.

I was a terrible fielder, who could barely catch a fly-ball. My "peg" was worse; the ball seldom found its target. However, the last game of the summer, after making so many errors, my past record was rectified. After catching the final fly ball, of the final game, we won, and I became the team's hero.

The Schotter boys had finished adding the private rooms to the front of each cabin. This year, I wouldn't have to share a cabin with ten other guys. They gave me my own private room. It didn't do much good, though. When I overslept, and missed going to breakfast, the guys would break into my room, pick me up, and throw me into the creek. Why they didn't do it before breakfast, I'll never know.

Mrs. Grace Lodge was the new craft teacher, that summer of 1948. When we first met, she eyed me warily. Had she heard all those nasty rumors about Betty Herbertson and me? I'm sure she had. She was about thirty, but seemed older, and was probably a widow, I'm not sure. She brought with her the most adorable little blonde girl, of about eight, named Mary. What a delightful, cheerful child she was, nothing like her sad mother.

Before they arrived, I had already scoured the craft shop clean, and put everything in order for the upcoming classes. After giving Mrs. Lodge the grand tour of the shop, and grounds, she seemed to relax a bit. Certainly, she must have been impressed.

That summer was like the one before, with all the campers wanting to bondoggle a lanyard, weave baskets, or bang out ash trays. Once the classes got underway, Grace relaxed when she realized that no attempted seductions were going to take place. She relied more and more on me. As always, I just dove in and "did my job." After all, I was the one with experience, there.

The Campfire programmer needed some new entertainment, so I got involved, again. This year they were going to get something special: an acrobatic exhibition with Mary Lodge and myself. Almost immediately, we started working together doing a truncated version of the routine Dauphin Bohn and I did at the Nixon Theatre. She caught on beautifully. So, at one of the campfire programs, we performed. Her mother was captivated.

I had brought my zombie puppet with me, but hadn't, as yet, figured out what to do with it. Mrs. Lodge had a solution. Mary had a collection of store bought marionettes at home, in New York. She would send for them and, perhaps, we could put on a puppet show. How nice to see her warming up.

When the marionettes arrived, we began rehearsals. With my huge zombie puppet, and Mary's small puppets, what better show to put on than "Jack and the Beanstalk." My zombie would be the perfect "giant."

From there on, the zombie was officially named "The Giant." I still have him stashed away in my storage bin, in need of restringing.

A new refrigerator had been delivered to the kitchen, which had been packed in a large, wooden crate. Aha! What a stage that box would make! I lugged it back to the front yard of the craft shop. It had a big porch, extending the length of the building, with a six foot wide staircase leading up to it. What a great place to mount our stage. The crate fit perfectly between the two center porch posts.

With the opening facing the yard, I removed the top side and nailed it to the two front posts, to hide the actors. It worked perfectly, too. Miracle of miracles, Mrs. Lodge wrote the script, and would play the part of the

103

mother in "Jack and the Beanstalk." Mary played Jack, and I was the big, bad giant.

In front of the shop, there was a large yard, with plenty of room, for all the kids to sit and enjoy the show. So, instead of being at our usual campfire sight, that one night in July, we performed "Jack and the Beanstalk," instead.

When the summer session ended, I think Grace was genuinely sorry to leave. She had enjoyed the summer, despite herself.

FLORIDA

LIFE IS A CIRCUS

CHAPTER SEVEN

All the older brothers and sisters had gotten together and decided that if, and whenever, the house on Brevard Avenue was sold, the money gained from the sale would go to Suzie and me. I didn't get the logic, but that is what was decided. Apparently, that was one of Mama's last wishes. It went a little to Suzie's head, she was looking forward to receiving her "inheritance."

Family members were still living there, so there was no need to be concerned about "the inheritance," yet. The mortgage was only forty-two dollars a month, so Papa, Sam and Pearl didn't have too difficult a time paying it. I hadn't officially moved back in, so wasn't asked to pay any rent, yet.

Ruth and Sol were living in a tiny walk-up apartment, on Congress Avenue, in Atlantic City, just a block or two from the Atlantic Ocean. On August 8th, Ruth gave birth to her first son, Bruce Alan Mintz, who they called Cookie.

In California, Helen and Ed Bordy had bought their first house, with a G.I. loan, in a town called Compton. On June 17, 1948, Helen gave birth to a little girl they called Jayne.

WHITHER BOUND?

Now that I had graduated High School, where to from there? Deep down, I wanted to go off to Hollywood to become a movie star, but wasn't quite brave enough to go way out there, yet. I was too old to play kid parts, and not mature enough to play leading men. Maybe in a few years . . .

Marie came up with the solution. She came across the Ringling School of Art in Sarasota, Florida. The price was right, and it was fairly close to her. She would advance me the tuition until the house was sold. It all sounded pretty good to me, so off I went to see Marie, in Ft. Lauderdale, in late August of 1948. It was my first airplane ride.

Stepping out of the plane was like hitting a wall of broiling, clammy air, I could hardly breath. Is this what it was going to be like to live Florida? Marie and her "partner," Tom Marino, met me at the Miami Airport. Then, back to Ft. Lauderdale we drove, twenty-five miles north. Tom did not seem too happy to have had this chore imposed upon him, but he did anything Marie required.

When we arrived at Bexley Hall, it was beginning to get dark. Bexley Hall was the eight unit apartment building Marie had bought, on Hendricks Island. She had the lower left apartment, and Marino had the upper left. Across the street, Marie's new house was being built on one of the two lots she had purchased.

Marino went directly to his apartment, leaving Marie with me for only a minute or two, before she followed him. She did not show me where I was to sleep, she did not offer me anything to eat or drink, she did not even turn on any lights. Without a word, she left me there, alone, with my bag, in the middle of the living room.

Neither Duane nor Butch was there, they were with some baby sitter, somewhere, so I was all alone. Soon, it became night. I sat there in the living room, in the dark, waiting, waiting, waiting for over two hours. Nothing.

It was exciting coming to Florida, and I wanted to visit with my big sister, and find out all about the art school I would be attending in a few days. And, I was hungry. How rude! Where the Hell was she? Did she forget I was there? There was nothing left to do but go upstairs and inquire. When I got to Marino's apartment, it was dark and there were no lights on. Did they go out for the evening, and forget about me? I tapped on the door. Nothing. I rapped again, harder. No answer. One last time, I really banged.

Marino came to the door, shirtless, in a panic, and buttoning up his shorts. He was a very emotional man. I could hear Marie storm into the bathroom, slamming the door behind her.

"What's the matter? What's wrong?" he gasped.

Uh, oh. What did I interrupt? Marie came out of the bathroom, disheveled.

"How rude of you, William Bordy! How dare you come banging on Tom's door like that? Where did you learn your manners?"

Manners? Me? Marie always did tend to overreact when she was caught with her hand in the proverbial "cookie jar." She ordered me back down the stairs. Then, another half hour or so later, she finally deigned to come home. By that time, I lost my appetite and just wanted to sleep, which I did. I was seething.

Early the next morning, Butch and Duane awakened me, and were quite excited to see me, again. Yes, the two boys had miraculously reappeared.

Marie fed us a great, big breakfast of French toast and bacon, the boys' favorite dish. She was cheerful and did not mention the night before. After breakfast, there were chores to do. All the apartments had to be cleaned, scrubbed, and readied for the winter tourist season, This, I could do. This was something I was born to do, clean up other people's messes.

Marie drove me to the train station for my trip to Sarasota. The train

106

did not go directly there. In the middle of nowhere, I was let off the train, and had to wait for a bus. Then, after the bus trip, I had to take another train, to get to Sarasota. What a bother!

The train station was right in the middle of the town. After checking my bags in a locker, and walking the half block to Main Street, I proceeded to walk up and down, getting the lay of the land. It was mid-afternoon when I arrived, and I had no idea of what to do next. So, I did what I usually do, I went to a movie.

It was a nice little town with three movie theaters, and plenty of shops. I'll worry about getting to Ringling tomorrow, today I wanted to see a movie. "The Luck of the Irish," with Tyrone Power and Ann Baxter, was playing, so I went.

It was nighttime when I exited the theater. Now, no more procrastinating, It was really the time to figure out what to do next. Walking around some of the side streets, I noticed several homes that rented out rooms. In a nice little house, I managed to rent a room for the night, for one dollar. The husband and wife were an agreeable, old couple, and were really looking for a steady roomer, but they did put me up for the night.

Over breakfast, the following morning, I informed them of my intentions to register, the following day, at the Ringling Art School. Could they tell me how to get there. They were most informative, and gave me directions, assuring me that finding a room would not be a problem. Many room listing would be posted on the bulletin board, in the lobby of the school. The time had come for my new adventure.

RINGLING SCHOOL OF ART

LIFE MAGAZINE PHOTO

Ringling School of Art was located just off the Tamiami Trail, Rte. 41, on 27th Street in North Sarasota. It was nothing more than an old hotel made into a school.

The various store fronts, of the hotel, were utilized as the classrooms. The upstairs rooms were the girls' dormitory, although several of the male teachers lived there, too.

At first, I was a little disappointed. Is that all there was? Upon further inspection, I found that off the main lobby, of the ex-hotel, many of the "shops" were used for "rest and relaxation." There was a music room, a reading room, card and game rooms, always a place to be entertained, or to read. or rest, when classes ended for the day.

There was a bulletin board, right outside of the enrollment office, that had listings of room rentals. Private rooms were fairly expensive, but if two people shared a room, it was a lot cheaper. Searching the board with me was an ex G.I. When we discovered that neither of us had a roommate, we decided to search together. We found a place, immediately, several blocks away, on Central Avenue, three doors down from 27th.

A pleasant, old couple, probably in their seventies, had a home there, and rented out a large room to Joe and me. Their smaller room had already been taken by another ex-G.I. The two ex-service men soon would become good drinking buddies.

The following day, we walked down 27th Street to the school, for enrollment. What an odd assortment of people there were, waiting in line. There were many "Bohemian" types; that was the vogue then, being a Bohemian. Beatniks and Hippies came much later.

There were several enrollees in their forties, most were in their teens and early twenties, as well as a few veterans, like Joe. Also, there were many torridly demure Southern Belles; why did they all look so ripe? What a plethora to choose from, although most seemed a little too worldly, for me.

Where were the uncomplicated girls, who were more my style and age? Before leaving Pittsburgh, Shirley and I had a mutual understanding. Knowing how anxious she was to get married, and not wanting to hold her back, and figuring that I might never come back to Pittsburgh, we decided to end our relationship. After so many years with the same girl, it was time to sow a little wild rice, or oats, myself.

Standing at the head of the line was this "kewpie doll," with beautiful, lush red, bow lips, and long, curly blonde hair, trickling over her shoulders. Her green-blue eyes had that wide-open, surprised look, and she had the stance of a chorus girl.

The incongruous part was that, she was standing with a matronly woman, and that she was wearing a girl's gym suit, that masked her voluptuous curves. Wow! What a hot number! None of the other girls looked quite like this.

Naturally, I made it a point to meet her. Her name was Sue Gressing, a

Hunky girl from Cleveland. The "chaperone" was her mother, a pleasant American born woman, whose husband was from Hungary. "Zsuzsi" was nothing like what she appeared to be. I thought that she might be a little "loose," she wasn't. The exciting part was, she was a Hunky, just like me!

We immediately bonded, becoming close friends, not lovers. She was always on the "look-out" for someone who would be just right for me, and I for her. Because of her demeanor, she attracted too many of the wrong kind of guys, so I became her guardian,

Included in our tuition was both breakfast and dinner. The dining room was in a separate building, attached by a canopy. At dinner, that first evening, was a good time to get acquainted with many of the other students. Everyone, of course, was on his best behavior. I thought I fit right in. Ha!

In the morning, they served grits for breakfast. I thought it was farina, the same stuff that Mama made her "gum boats" out of, for her gum boat soup. Why did everyone put butter, and salt, and pepper, on their Cream of Wheat? After trying it, I loved it, morphing into a Southern "cracker." It was later, I found out what I was really eating, grits!

Everyone sat in the same seats, as the night before. That way, we could become better acquainted. They all seemed so self-confident, especially those Southern girls, and I felt so grown up being with them. That didn't last long. I was not nearly so sophisticated, or rude, as they. None of them was destined to become my friend.

Soon, I had my own coterie of chums, who were naïve, and less experienced, like myself. Sexy Sue was one of them, along with Beverly Bradley, a sweet local gal from Bradenton, Ken Trimble, a short, hirsute "sunflower" from Kansas, who would become her boyfriend, and Mary Alice Bunch, from Mobile, Alabama.

She looked exactly like a seventeen year old Bette Davis, but much sweeter. Her girlfriend was named Mary Alice, too. They both pronounced their two first names as if they were one. Instead of Mary Alice, the name became "Mayralice." We Yankees thought it was cute as could be, so we called them both "May Ralice," as well.

Before starting our classes, we had to purchase all of our art supplies, which were sold from a shop, just off the lobby. It was run by an effete wanna-be ballet dancer, named Pappy. He lived upstairs with the commercial art instructor, Mr. Blake, who was actually much older than he.

Pappy was a rather obnoxious, surly sort, who didn't give us much choice when we ordered our art supplies. He asked each new student what classes he was taking, then quickly, he ran around picking out the needed supplies, and shoved them at each new pupil. He proved to be right, almost all of the time. Nobody knew the business like he.

Once classes got underway, and after a few drinks in his room with Mr. Blake, Pappy, oftentimes, would come down to the lobby and dance "Swan Lake." He was actually pretty good, considering he was handicapped with a club foot. That never seemed to bother him, though, and when he danced, he seemed genuinely happy.

Classes were small, so having them in the storefronts was quite adequate for most classes, such as Still Life, Portraiture, and Advertising Layout. For the Life classes, there was a larger room where the nude models would pose.

The guys were anxious to get to their first Life Class to watch the female model disrobe. Our first nude model was named Peggy. She lived upstairs, in the girls dormitory, and ate her meals with us.

For that first Life Class, we all waited patiently, and with bated breath, for Peggy to disrobe. She climbed up on a small platform, sat down on a stool, and dropped her robe to the floor. That's all there was to it, nothing prurient at all. No gasps, no clapping!

Peggy was very shy and demure, never looking any of the men directly in the eye. She was a marvelous model, beautifully proportioned, and could sit perfectly still for thirty minutes at a time Occasionally, she would come down to dinner, wearing a tight, T-shirt or sweater, and all the guys would gawk, some would whistle, like they'd never seen her before. Of course, she would blush.

As much as we loved Peggy, we wondered when we would get some new blood. We did get some new models, occasionally, but not often. The women models seldom, completely, disrobed. The male models were a strange assortment, some muscular, but most old and flabby. They didn't actually pose nude, either. Like Charlton Heston, when he modeled, they wore "jock-straps."

Mr. Blake, having worked in advertising during the Art Nouveau period, taught Advertising Layout and Design. He was a bald, little old man, who wore a miniscule white moustache under his nose, and was just plain cute, a perfect example of Mr. Milquetoast.

Sue Gressing flirted with him outrageously, by fluttering those big baby-blues, and purring in his face. He would always blush, and smile happily. Even though Sue was an innocent lamb, she certainly knew how to turn men on. Needless to say, she got straight "A's" in his class.

The Still Life Class was where we learned to paint with oils. First, we had to draw in charcoal any of the many busts, statuettes, and curios, that were strewn around the class room. There were a couple of dozen small, wooden alcoves, that were built on tables, in the middle of the room. Those mini-cubicles were where we could set up our still life displays, that we intended to draw, or paint.

I painted two oils that year: one was of an Egyptian bust, that, at one time, had been part of a Circus wagon, with a piece of driftwood, and two kinds of draped material; the other was of a wine bottle, a small bowl, and two different kinds of draping. They still hang in my living room.

110

Some of our best classes were held away from the school. The Ringling Museum of Art was very nearby, and we had free access to it at all times. It is laid out like an Italian Renaissance Villa, with a huge garden in the center. At the far end is a bronze casting of Michael Angelo's David. In the beautifully manicured courtyard, there are many reproductions of classic statues, and several Roman fountains. There, we would take our sketch pads to draw the statues, or paint the scenery.

The surrounding interior rooms have the largest Rubens collection in the United States, as well as many other notable paintings. Inside, we could try our hand at sketching or painting the "masters."

Also, located on this large estate, is a grand old mansion called the *Ca d' Zan*, Italian slang for "House of John." John Ringling built this manor as a winter home for his wife Mable, in the late '20s. It was used as Ann Bancroft's dilapidated house in the 1998 American version of "Great Expectations." Unlike what you see in the movie, it is not rundown.

It has been renovated, and is decorated with many works of art, from around the world, sort of a miniature Hearst's Castle. We art students had free reign of this rambling home, too. There were no guards, as there are today.

The Sarasota Jungle Gardens is located nearby. It has a large pond, with swans, and all kinds of exotic birds and vegetation. There, we could sketch the wild life, or paint water colors of the scenery.

So many of our classes were held outdoors. The school bus loaded us up in the morning, and off we would be taken on a day's adventure, to some exciting location: the waterfront docks, the keys, the beach, "colored town," even downtown to Main Street and the theaters. That's the way to run a school!

The best was yet to come. Sarasota, at that time, was the Winter Quarters of the Ringling Bros. Barnum and Bailey Circus. The show would tour "under

111

the big top" all year, but for the winter months, they "pitched their tents" in Sarasota. When they arrived, we would have many of our classes at "The Quarters," as well.

Marie invited me to her new Hendricks Island home, for the Christmas Holidays. The school would be closed, so why not? This time, I took one bus all the way, no more trains.

The builders did an amazing job in completing the house. They had barely broken ground in August, but now it was finished.

The house was built on only one of the two lots that Marie had purchased; the other lot was loaded with vegetation and critters, where the boys loved to play.

The garage was in front of the house, then the guest room/servant's entrance to the left, and the doorway to the kitchen, to the right. Beyond that was a huge living room and sun porch, that overlooked the waterway. Her bedroom was on the canal, as well. Then, between her bedroom and the guest room, down the hall, was Duane and Butchie's room. Each bedroom had it's own private bath. The entire floor was done in terrazzo. No air conditioning, but there were many windows with cross ventilation.

The cocoa brown living room was beautifully furnished with Florida rattan furniture. Her portrait was hung in the perfect spot, over the fireplace, at the far end of the living room. In her house in Knoxville, the painting had been hung on one side of the small fire-place, with a copy of The Laughing Cavalier on the other, not the best aesthetic arrangement. Here, it found its perfect niche, and looked spectacular. There she was, in that low-cut gown, with bared shoulders, sitting on her throne, holding court, and looking down upon all her subjects. Breathtaking!

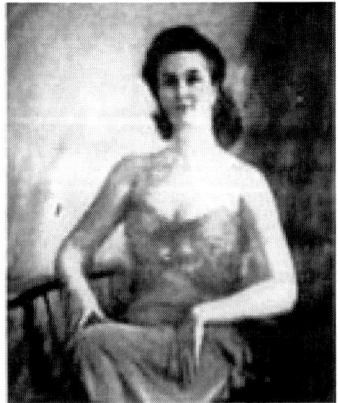

I hadn't been the first member of the family to visit Marie in her new house. Several weeks earlier, at her urging, Sam had paid a visit. She wanted him to look the town over, to see if he wouldn't like to move there. Even though she was such a "woman of the world," she preferred having a family member nearby. Within a year, he did move there.

On this visit, Marie couldn't have been nicer. She more than made up for the shabby treatment given me when I first arrived, No one was more charm-

112

ing than Marie when she wanted to be, which truly, was most of the time.

Duane was five and a half, and Butch just turned three. They were rambunctious, hard to control, but cute as hell. This time, we had the opportunity to become pals, spending much time in the "jungle," among the flora and fauna.

Marie made an elaborate Christmas dinner, "with all the trimmings." She was a marvelous cook, and enjoyed preparing food for company. Even though rambunctious Marino was there, a good time was had by all.

The Circus People returned to Sarasota. Little by little, the railway cars, the animals, the roustabouts, and all the performers came back to the Winter Quarters. We Ringling students were permitted to go there for animal drawing classes and landscape painting classes.

We had complete, and free, access to the entire place. There, we could draw all the creatures: King the ancient, blind lion, with a black mane, that extended the length of his underbelly; the wild tigers; the stately giraffes; the graceful horses; Chester the gape-mouthed hippopotamus; and Ruth, Minyak, Jewel and Ruby, the talented elephants.

It was fun drawing the beasts, but the performers were much more interesting: there was Madamoiselle Fifi, the chimpanzee lady, a tall, attractive blond who wore very skimpy clothes, and always walked hand in hand with one of her chimps; little Cucciola, the spoiled brat midget, of twenty, who was learning how to ride a horse, bareback, while honing his skills doing flips, and other acrobatics; then, there were the tight rope walkers, the animal trainers, the roustabouts, and the acrobats.

The best acrobat, in my opinion, was Signor Truzzi. On an eight foot

high wire, he balanced himself on one foot, while the other foot spun three hoops in different directions. On his forehead, he balanced a floor lamp, while he spun three balls, one on his shoulder, one on his forearm, and one on a finger of his left hand. With his right hand, he juggled three loops. Such concentration!

Truzzi, and his entire family, rented a small house a block away from the school. Every day, morning, noon and night, when he wasn't at the Quarters, you would find Truzzi practicing, in his yard. Later that year, Francis Braun joined the circus, and was billed as the world's greatest juggler, but I think it was Truzzi.

The chorus girl/dancers were the most fascinating performers, as well as the "web" girls, who climbed the ropes, and did acrobatic tricks. Each had her own story about why she joined the circus. One, in particular, was an aspiring actress from New York City, Mary Tahmin.

She had acted in some off Broadway shows, and had danced in some musicals. Before, "running away to join the circus," she had been dating Marlon Brando, while he was on Broadway, performing in "A Streetcar Named Desire."

According to her, he was terribly possessive. During his performances, he would lock her in his dressing room, until the show was over. To get away from this abusive treatment, she joined The Circus. Immediately, I became infatuated.

In that January of 1949, rehearsals began under the direction of John Murray Anderson, the well-known Broadway stage director. He could never remember the names of the girls, so he made up names for them all. Mary Tahmin became known as "Streak," because she had bleached the front part of her dark brown hair blonde. One red-head became Rita Hayworth, and a girl with high plucked eyebrows turned into "Eyebrows."

The "chorus girl/dancers" wore big, full skirts, from a previous show, for rehearsal. Anderson choreographed their various numbers, and had them dancing and prancing, all around the three rings of the main tent.

Then there were the "web girls." Most had been with the circus for several years as dancers, and to make more money, they would learn how to climb the "spider" web. The web consisted of dozens of long ropes, dropped from the rigging above, that encircled the entire three rings of the Big Top.

These girls had to learn how to, gracefully, climb up those ropes, where they had to perform synchronized acrobatics, while the "web boys," from below, steadied the ropes, and spun them around, and around, to the music. It was quite spectacular, seeing all those ropes, with all those girls, spinning at the same time.

Suzie, Beverly, Kenny, and I spent many happy times with Mary, and her fellow dancers and acrobats, when they were on their breaks.

One of her dancer friends was Ica (Eetzah) Szabo, *another* beautiful, blonde Hungarian, who really *was* from Hungary. Ica

was an exquisitely trained dancer, who worked with her acrobat husband, Jorge. Together, they were a striking team.

Instead of sketching the animals, many of us spent much of our time watching the rehearsals. Occasionally, we would sketch or paint the artistes rehearsing. By the end of the season, I had quite a collection of "circus life" water colors. Years later, in Hollywood, a lady friend of mine produced a musical called, "The Ringlings." She asked to borrow them, to hang in the theatre lobby, during the run of the show. The display of framed paintings was impressive. Unfortunately, I never got them back. Sad!

Many of the "web boys" were roustabouts, or elephant boys, or part time clowns. In the circus, everybody doubled up, and did many jobs. I made it a point to get to know some of the elephant boys, because soon, I was planning on joining them. Mary was checking on the particulars of my joining.

The elephant boys loved their charges so much that they slept with them, giving them twenty-four hour attention. Most were learning to become clowns, and some wanted to be acrobats, or tight rope walkers. In the circus, if you were willing to try, you could always work your way up the ladder, both figuratively and literally.

Everyone has heard the joke about the elephant boy shoveling up the elephants' dung, sweating and grunting away. When asked by a passerby, "Why do you keep shoveling shit, why don't you do something else?"

The elephant boy's retort was, "What? And give up Show Business?"

The interior of the Big Top was used mostly to rehearse the numbers of the dancers, and the web-girls.

Outside was a reproduction of the interior space of the tent, with its three rings, and oval path around them. It had bleachers and chairs, set beside it, for the tourists, to watch the rehearsals.

On March 1st, Monty Woolley, the bearded character actor, known for playing Sheridan Whiteside in "The Man Who Came to Dinner," attended a rehearsal, enjoying every moment. I snapped his photo and got his autograph on my sketch pad paper. He had always played such strident characters in the movies; it was nice to see that he was kinder in person.

The first week the Winter Quarters reopened, a group of us students were standing in The Big Top observing the rehearsals. From behind, unknown to us, a photographer from *Life Magazine* took our picture. When the magazine hit the newsstands, the caption read, "Tourists Observing

Circus Rehearsal."

How could they? It was us! So, we had our picture taken in front of the school, and sent it, along with a letter, to the magazine that said, "We object! We're not tourists, we're art students."

They not only published a retraction, they printed the snapshot we sent, and mailed us a check for five dollars. The photo was of me, Mary Alice Bunch, "Moe," Sue Gressing, Eva Bessemer, Beverly Bradley, "Goldie," and Alton Rape. Yes, that's Rape. During roll call, the various teachers would call out, "Rap pay," no answer. "Rope." Nope! "It's Rape," he would smirk, enjoying the embarrassment of the teachers.

Soon, he and Eva became a hot combination. She was *another* Hungarian girl, with an impossible to pronounce Hungarian name, so it was changed to Bessemer. She, and her girlfriend Hildy, were bleached blonde models, from Connecticut.

One weekend, the two of them were in the Music Room, touching up their dark roots with peroxide. Jim "de South Carolina" and I wandered into the room, while they were playing beauty parlor. Eva asked us, "Why don't you let us do your hair, too?"

Jim was very amenable, and agreed right away. When they were done with him, Eva said, "Come on, Bill We have just enough solution left to do your hair."

No way! Then, thinking of Mary, I thought, maybe just a little streak in the front, like hers. The girls agreed, but reneged. Hildy poured the remaining solution all over my entire head. What to do? It was too late. Jim and I became blonds, well not really blonds, copper heads. Ugly, ugly! Jim loved it, I hated it.

In that same music room, Suzie Gressing often played the piano for us to sing-along. When we were finished singing, to end a perfect afternoon, she'd play "Reverie" and "Claire de Lune," both by Claude de Bussy. She was not only beautiful, sexy, sweet, and kind, she also performed, impressively, on the piano. Every man's dream!

The John Ringling Hotel was the place that many of the Circus folk would frequent in the evening, for a drink, and to dance. Mary enjoyed its ambiance, as well. She was twenty-one, and I was only eighteen, but that didn't stop me from pursuing her. Being such a nice, sweet person, she did not rebuff me.

One day, after rehearsal, she described what a beautifully exotic, tropical hotel The Ringling was, and mentioned that she would be going there that evening. I took it to mean that she was inviting me on a date.

For the first time, I went there that night. It was jammed with Circus people, looking quite elegant, so different from their daytime appearance.

Immediately, I was fascinated by the place. It had such a warm atmosphere, both literally and figuratively; there were only fans, no air conditioning.

The ground floor had many rooms to roam around in, which everyone seemed to do. The dance band that night was Xavier Cugat's, so it must have been February 7, 1949, because that's the night I obtained his autograph. Yeah, that book was filling up with lots of celebrities.

When Mary arrived, I followed her around like a puppy dog. She was never condescending, nor did she ever treat me badly, but I could see that she was being held back from really enjoying herself with her friends. It was getting late, and never staying out past eleven or twelve, I thanked her for such a nice time, told her how much I loved The Ringling Hotel, and hitch-hiked back to the school.

BETTE DAVIS

There was something magical about the John Ringling Hotel. I dropped by as often as I could, and never spend a penny. What a cheapie! I didn't drink, so I just roamed around, watching all the fascinating people having a good time.

One night, Bette Davis, and her artist husband, William Grant Sherry, were having a party in the main dining room. The second story, had a walkway that encircled the dining room, so I stationed myself up there, gazing down on the gathering below.

There was a large, round table, with many guests seated around it, and a small table abutting it, where Bette and Sherry sat. They were not only a part of the group, they were alone at their own table, sitting close to each other, and bumping noses.

It did seem that, perhaps, they had a little too much to drink. Bette sat there looking rather bored, resting her chin on the back of her hand. Occasionally, it would slip off, she'd react with a slight surprise, then put her fist back under her chin, and take another swig of her drink.

William Grant Sherry was an aspiring artist, who was having an exhibit of his paintings at the Ringling Museum of Art, two miles up the highway. The exhibit was to run for a few more days, so perhaps I could catch Miss Davis at the exhibit, and get her autograph

Several days later, on March 13, 1949, at 10:05 p.m., I entrapped them in the parking lot of the Ringling Museum, as they were leaving. It didn't frighten her, at all, that she was being accosted in this dark, deserted parking lot, but it did gave him a start.

"Excuse me, Mrs. Sherry. May I have your autograph, please?" I didn't ask for his.

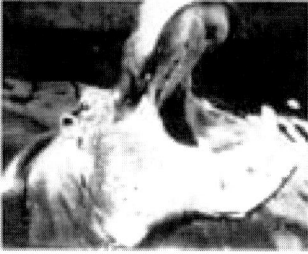

Without missing a beat in their conversation, she took the book and signed it, Bette Davis. For a minute, I was afraid that she would write Bette Grant Sherry. Whew!

Two days later, she was playing tourist at The Quarters, with her little daughter, B.D. It was great fun for them to observe all the animals. When I spotted them, they were walking right by my buddy, Chester, the hippopotamus.

Whenever his caretakers came to feed him, they'd say, "Open Up, Chester," and he'd open his mouth wide, ready to accept the cabbages or other vegetables that were thrown into it.

I had observed this many times, so when Miss Davis and B.D. came by, I ordered, "Open up, Chester," which he did.

The two B.D.s giggled, thoroughly enjoying the experience, as I threw part of my sandwich into his mouth.

Just then, Mary Alice Bunch, the Bette Davis look-alike, came by. I shoved her in front of the happy mother, and introduced them, saying how much I thought they looked alike.

Bette retorted, "Well, my dear, I certainly pity you if you look anything like *me*."

In her demure, polite Southern manner, Mayralice charmed them both.

Later, B.D. and B.D. sat in the stands, watching the outdoor rehearsals of the animal acts. B.D. Sr., carried with her a metal packet of "extra long" Phillip Morris Cigarettes, which she smoked incessantly, without inhaling. Such long cigarettes they were, and in a tin container no less.

After the "show," I went up to where she sat, and picked up one of her butts. It is still pasted in my autograph book, next to her signature.

LIDO BEACH

Once spring arrived, and it got warmer, Bev, Ken, Suzie, and I, often, went to Lido Beach, which was one of the best beaches in the land. It was set

in an inlet, and its white sand was as soft as powder.

To get there, we'd take the bus across the rickety Ringling Bridge, over the causeway, around St. Armand's Circle, and to Lido Beach. It not only had a sump-tuous, sun dren-ched strand, but it had a large swim-ming pool, and a glorious pavilion.

During the Second World War, it was an exciting place for the servicemen to swim, dance, sunbathe and meet pretty, young girls. There were always plenty of them on the beach, and in the dance hall, to entertain them.

For many years, Lido Beach was the sight of many beauty pageants, that were held around the pool and in the pavilion.

The main pavilion was deco-rated with seven foot sea horses, all around the structure, that glis-tened in the sun. Naturally, we kids would climb up on them, to have our pictures taken. Suzie, Bev, Ken and I were no exception.

Often, we stayed until sun-down. That was the best time to be on the beach. The cooling breeze would refresh us, and by being on the West Coast of Florida, we could observe the magnificent sunsets, any and every night, watching the sun disappear into the Gulf of Mexico.

On one of our sojourns to the beach, Suzie talked Mr. Blake into accompanying us. He had a splendid time with Sue snuggling and huggling him.

The Pavilion was torn down in the '60's, leaving only the pool and the beach. The local citizens, to this day still miss it, and every now and then, solicit City Hall to have it rebuilt. So far, no go!

PICNICS, PARTIES AND BALLS!

Many social events were held at Ringling: The Beaux Arts Ball; Sadie Hawkins' Day Picnic; The Halloween Eve Party; etc., etc., any excuse for merrymaking.

Whenever the Circus was in town, we students had *carte blanche* to the huge costume building, and were allowed to borrow any of the costumes from previous seasons. They were beautifully cared for extravaganzas of spangles, bangles, baubles, beads and feathers, impressively tailored, and of all genres and description.

The first party was at Halloween. The Circus had not yet come to town, so we all had to improvise our costumes. The students had no problem creating their own works of art.

Some creative guys decorated the entire lobby into an eerie phantasmagoria. They had taken the human skeleton, from the Anatomy classroom, and tied it to the springs of an old, metal bed. They posed "her" into a reclining position, with one hand behind her head, and the other in a "come hither" position, with the forefinger crooked.

She wore a black brassiere and panties, with sunglasses, sunhat, and a make-shift wig made out of straw. That was funny enough, but those cleaver artists took it a step further. They hung the entire "work of art" upside down, from the ceiling, where it gently spun around like a mobile.

The Beaux Arts Ball was the first party were everyone got dressed up in the circus costumes. Artists being artists, all improved on their individual costumes, creating something uniquely personal for each student.

Entertainment was needed, so I volunteered. Hugo Winterhalter had recently recorded "Blue Violins," which I thought would be a great number to do as an Apache Dance; it was already being worked out in

120

my head.

Chunky Toby "Big-Bum," begged to be my partner. She was not particularly beautiful, but desperately wanted to do it. After much deliberation, I thought, why not? Instead of doing it as a serious number, we would do it as a farce. That's not how it turned out.

The lights came up on me, standing under a street lamp, sneering nastily, wearing the garb of a French Apache, with beret and neckerchief, while reading a comic book. Then Toby made her entrance, wearing a skin tight, slit-up the side skirt, mesh hose, a low cut, off the shoulder busty blouse and swinging a small, beaded hand bag, on a long, thin strap. Suddenly, she sees me and stops. Then she slithers up to me trying to seduce me.

I appear to give in, dance with her a few steps, then throw her to the ground. She doesn't learn her lesson, so slowly, and painfully, she gets up and starts to seductively stroke my face. We dance and I throw her to the deck, again. The rest of the choreography was more of the same, the typical Apache Dance.

The ending was different. The last time I throw her to the floor, she angrily gets up, takes a knife, that was strapped to her thigh, and "stabs" me. I fall backward to stage left; she backs up in horror to stage right. I pull out my gun, and shoot her, all this in time to the music, of course.

We both collapse to the floor. Then, suddenly realizing that we love each other, slowly and painfully, we drag ourselves across the stage to each other, kiss passionately, and die in each others arms. The whole ending was stolen from "Duel in the Sun." That's how Jennifer Jones and Gregory Peck died in that movie.

Instead of the people laughing, they really got caught up in the drama of the dance, and despite Toby's lack of beauty, and my scrawny body, they took it all very seriously. So, Toby and I both became minor celebrities.

Sadie Hawkins' Day was fun, too. Everyone really dressed and looked like they were from Dogpatch. There were several Daisy Maes, a Moonbeam McSwine, Marryin' Sam, Sadie Hawkins herself, and all the rest.

There was a phony race, as well, with most couples joining in. Of course, the girls all "caught" their own steadies and had Sam

"marry" them.

There was a Southern guy attending the school, named "Marion," who was supposed to be a hypnotist. He didn't walk, he sashayed with his arms straight down at his sides. Mary Alice Bunch, dressed as Elizabeth I, came as his date for The Beaux Arts Ball.

Before he hypnotized anyone, he would perform various tests on them, to see if they were susceptible. The first time he did a test on one of the girls, I was doubtful that he could do what he said he could do. I was wrong.

The first test consisted of holding his subjects behind the neck, lowering them, as low as he could, then pushing them back to an erect position. Then, he would "talk" them into falling backward, into his arms.

The second test involved him "hypnotizing" his subject's arm. He would run his hands up and down the subject's arm, without touching it, talking it into rising up to the level of the shoulder. Then, he would stick a pin in the arm, or burn it with a match. Quite a feat! Once he made the tests, then he was ready to do the actual hypnotizing. After putting his volunteers under, he did all kinds of amusing tricks with them.

His popularity grew, and he was constantly being asked to hypnotize someone. Every chance I had, I watched him, studying, studying. Soon, I told myself that I would be able to do that, and soon, I could.

The Florida Theater, downtown Sarasota, needed part time ushers. I was available, and got a job working weekends. Now, I could see all the movies free, not only at the Florida, but at the two other theaters, as well.

Originally, the theater opened in 1926 as the A. B. Edwards Theater. A huge pipe organ was installed in it, which was later destroyed by a hurricane.

Sally Rand had danced there, Will Rogers joked there, The Ziegfeld Follies Played there, and, later, even a young Elvis Presley sang in that theater.

When the building became The Florida Theater in 1928, a theater marquee

122

was added for the Title displays. It's gone now.

In 1952, Cecil B. DeMille's "The Greatest Show on Earth," which had been shot in Sarasota, with Charlton Heston, Betty Hutton, Cornel Wilde and Gloria Graham, had its world premiere there.

What appealed to me most about The Florida Theater, in 1949, was the smell of fresh popcorn being popped. What an enticing smell! So few Cinemas do that today.

Even after a big meal, I just had to get my popcorn "fix." Jean, the girl who worked at the concession stand, and did the popping, always allowed me to eat as much as I wanted. The only caveat was that she could not give me a container, the containers were all accounted for. Therefore, by rolling up the weekly program into a cone, any time I wanted popcorn, she'd fill it up. Nice kid.

In 1979, the building was taken over by a fledgling opera company. It was completely renovated and, is now, The Sarasota Opera House, where world class singers perform each winter.

The Ringling Art School did not serve evening meals on Sundays, so we had to fend for ourselves. Usually, I went downtown to get a bite to eat at Kress's Five and Dime. They had a large lunch counter, in the front of the store, and the food was pretty good, and cheap.

I had a crush on Wanda Barton, one of the waitresses there. She looked like Snow White, with coal black hair, bangs, snow white skin, and ruby red lips. Wanda was friendly, but not overly solicitous. There was something otherworldly about her, which seemed to make her more appealing.

Somehow, I did manage to get her to go on a triple date with me, along with Suzie and Doug (a new boyfriend), and Bev and Kenny. We went to the beach for our own private beach blanket Babylon party. She wasn't too receptive, at first, but managed to warm up, but just a little.

At the Winter Quarters, Wanda worked out on the trampoline, and low trapeze, with some of the acrobats. She was hoping to join them in their act when they went on the road. All winter long, she got more and more proficient, and was looking forward to joining them on the tour. They left town without her.

Mary had talked to the Circus management about getting me a job, as an elephant boy. That sounded good to me, because I knew I'd be able to work myself up to being a clown, and then an acrobat, and who knows where I could have gone from there. Watch out Burt Lancaster! At last, I was going to be in Show Business! Shoveling shit.

While, working at the Florida Theater, I often collected tickets at the door for the evening show. After the customers bought their tickets, they would present them to me, to be torn in half, depositing one half into the ticket box, and returning the stub to the customer.

Many of the theater-goers were the Circus folk, whom I recognized. The Eck midget family usually came as a group, except for the "tall" one; she dated normal sized guys. Standing at the entrance, observing the customers, and collecting tickets was one of the things I enjoyed most about being an usher there.

One evening, some filthy guy, and his buddy, came into the theater, carrying his ticket between his slimy, green teeth. He was trying to put his money away, while he was entering with his popcorn. Instead of handing me the ticket, he grunted, and motioned for me to take it from his mouth. Disgusting!

I grimaced, and shook my head, "I'm not going to take that ticket from your slobbering mouth."

He became furious, removed it himself, and handed it to me. I wouldn't accept it.

"*You* tear it, and put the stub in this box. Do you want me to get sick?"

He was ready to slug me, but luckily, his companion held him back. Then he obeyed my order, tore the ticket in two, and stormed into the theater.

One of the other circus performers, who had observed this little drama, told me that if I were going to join them, I had better be careful, because that guy would certainly get his revenge on me. That didn't worry me a bit, I'd avoid him.

"You won't be able to do that," he warned, "That guy's the head cook!"

Then and there, I decided *not* to join the circus. There is no way in Hell I'd be able to eat that slob's cooking. Alas, a burgeoning circus career was nipped in the bud.

In late spring, the circus left Sarasota to go on its annual tour. Classes at school would soon be over. Spring fever hit many of us, school just wasn't as much fun without the Circus. Nevertheless, classes continued.

Often, I would model in portraiture class. Many charcoals were done, and given to me. Kenny Trimble was one of the best artists, who did my portrait. It was interesting to see that each artist's portrait resembled me, but also looked a little like the artist, as well. What a

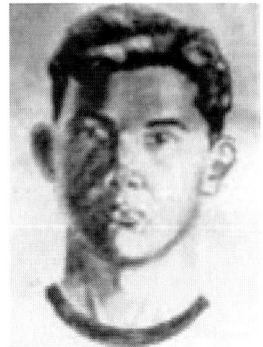

strange phenomenon.

One day, an artist named Whiteside set up easel and canvas, and decided to paint me in oils. I think he had been studying with Robert Brackman, the noted portrait artist who had recently finished painting Jennifer Jones' portrait for the movie "A Portrait of Jennie." Or was it portrait artist John Farnsworth, with whom he studied? I'm not sure, but it was one or the other.

Whiteside was an outstanding artisan. He did my entire portrait in just three sittings. Quite impressive! After finishing my portrait, he started asking all the good looking girls to pose for him. Most reciprocated, including Bev.

If you wanted to purchase your portrait, all it cost was seven dollars, the price of his art supplies. Somehow, some way, I scraped up the seven dollars and purchased mine. I especially liked it, because he made me look so rugged and masculine, despite my baby face looks. It still hangs in my living room.

Sue Gressing did an oil painting of me, also, which I didn't pose for. She had been doing it from memory, and would give it to me on the last day of school. It was amazing what she had done, without the benefit of my posing.

It looked very much like me, but like the artist, she made me look pretty. I must admit that I did like the Whiteside portrait better, but Sue's was done with so much love and caring.

She inscribed the portrait with the following inscription:

"To Bill, In memory of all the happy times we knew. May you paint my portrait in your heart as I have painted one of you. Love, Sue."

On our last day of school, she presented the portrait to me, in front of my rooming house.

The next day, she left for Cleveland. I never saw her again.

PITTSBURGH

I Grow Up?

CHAPTER EIGHT

When I got back to Brevard Avenue, in late May, 1949, only Sam and Pearl remained there. Sam was contemplating moving to Ft. Lauderdale. Papa was planning on getting married, and had already moved into his apartment building at 504 West Seventh Avenue, in West Homestead.

From the time Papa moved the family to Homestead in 1917, he not only purchased the house we lived in, he also bought two cheaper houses, several miles down the road, in the side of a cliff (naturally), in cheaper West Homestead.

We lost the first house during the depression, but somehow, by hook or by crook, Papa had managed to save his West Homestead properties. With the aid of Clarence and Kay, he had turned them into four rental units.

Joe's Lewis-Sheppard franchise must have been doing pretty well, because he moved his office to Swissvale Avenue in Wilkinsburg, a much more business oriented district than Brentwood. Martha found a nice, two story, brick house, within walking distance, in the adjacent residential town of Edgewood. For the first time in their marriage, the Jogeeses were going to live in their own house.

For Easter, Marilyn got a pet rabbit, that she kept caged in the yard. Joe was able to pursue his hobby of train making, in the cellar, where he created a virtual, miniature city, for his handmade train to traverse.

Clarence had been working for Sears-Roebuck, as an appliance repairman. He could do almost anything mechanical. By diligently studying the manuals of the various products, he became an expert.

Kay worked as a waitress/sandwich maker at a Woolworth's lunch counter. Sue finished tenth grade, and would continue going to school at West Wood High.

Ruth and Sol were getting ready for the summer season at Fascination, in Atlantic City. Mischievous Brucie would "help" by giving out prizes throughout the season. Ruth liked keeping him near.

126

They were tired of living in their little hovel of an apartment on Congress Avenue, and would soon move into their first house at 371 North Richmond Avenue, in Romantic, Enchantic you know where.

As soon as I got resettled, my first ordeal was to telephone Shirley Jordan. My vanity expected that she would have waited for me to return. She hadn't. Upon answering the phone, she seemed panicky and tongue-tied.

Apologetically, she confessed that she had become engaged. In a way, I was relieved.

Being the friendly, manipulative kind of guy I was, I suggested that we all get together. That didn't particularly appeal to her, but I talked her into it.

It was an uncomfortable reunion. Her fiance' Bill hadn't as yet arrived. Poor Shirl, she was a nervous wreck, but I was determined to meet my competition. Her parents and sisters were a bit apprehensive, too, but I was completely oblivious to their feelings, and went blathering on and on about my time in Sarasota, and how I had become a hypnotist.

When Bill arrived, you could tell that he was not happy to meet me. Nevertheless, everyone was as nice as could be, considering the circumstances. He was a pleasant enough guy, very ordinary, and down to earth. The important thing was, and it was quite obvious, that he was nuts about her. That's all that really mattered.

Soon, we ran out of conversation, so I suggested that I hypnotize Shirley. Figuring that she would be an easy subject, I did the two tests on her: pinching her elevated, hypnotized arm; and making her fall backward into my arms, without touching her. After passing those two tests, it was a snap getting her into the hypnotic state.

Under hypnosis, people cannot lie. How could Shirley be giving *me* up for that shit-kicker? After doing all the fun gags one does while under, innocently I asked her who she loved. She stiffened and looked distraught. Taking a long time to answer, she simply said, "Bill."

Which Bill? You could see her visibly struggling. "Which Bill?" I urged. Still, she only answered, "Bill."

Everyone was uncomfortable, especially the other Bill, so I stopped.

Upon awakening, as is customary, she was elated and in a very good mood. I wished the couple the best of luck, they thanked me, and I left. We never saw each other, or heard from each other, again. I wasn't even invited to the wedding!

Papa got remarried in the summer of 1949. He became a June groom on, or around, his sixtieth birthday.

His shy, blushing bride was Margit (Margaret), an American/Hungarian woman, who was in her forties.

She had been working, all her life, dipping chocolates in a candy factory, long before Lucille Ball had ever thought of it.

She had lived a very sheltered life, and had never been married, just what Papa had been looking for, a forty-five year old virgin!

Margit was little, probably about five feet tall, had short arms, her upper lip had a small mole with hair growing out of it, and even though she was born in America, she spoke English with a Hungarian accent.

And, to top that off, the poor soul was almost stone deaf, and wouldn't wear her hearing aid; she was afraid of getting electrocuted.

Sue, Kay and I went to the wedding. This was the first opportunity I had to wear my new, light blue gabardine suit that had belonged to Emmett; it looked great. and I felt quite grown up wearing it. Sue looked nice wearing a skirt, blouse and Mama's pearls.

Most of the guests were Hungarian, or German, or Slavic of some kind. They served kummel, a caraway liqueur, mixed with orange soda pop. What a combination!

The kummel was tasty and sweet poured over ice, it didn't need any soft drink to spoil its taste. Even then, I knew that sweet soda was not a good mix for hard liquor. All the Hunkies, except me, got falling down drunk, just like the Irish at a wake. A great time was had by all.

Now that Papa had married, again, he and Margit moved into the lower apartment, in the lower building, in West Homestead.

As before, he remodeled the front of the building, moved his shoe repair equipment down from Amity Street, and opened his new Sam Bordy Shoe Repair Shop.

He was living the way he liked most: his shop downstairs on the main street, and his living quarters upstairs. And, the most important thing, he had a new wife to wait on him hand and foot. She did, too. But it was her joy; she loved taking care of her new husband. No, she wasn't pretty, and talked funny, but she loved Papa, and took care of him, for the rest of his life.

Sam decided it was time to turn the upstairs of our house into a rental unit. The rent would be enough to pay our mortgage payment. After having a kitchen put into Papa's old sleeping quarters, Mama's bedroom set was relocated to the dining room, and the twin beds were taken to the cellar, thereby emptying the upstairs rooms. Those of us who were remaining moved downstairs.

The new apartment was rented to a good looking blonde, named June Potts, and her husband, Art. He drove for the Brentwood Bus Line, and was the uncle of the kid who called me Dumbo and crushed my foot, several winters before.

She looked terrific, when she got all dolled-up, just to go to work selling perfume at Kaufmann's Department Store. She tried to look like Fay Emerson, the movie star.

June was Sam's age, and she developed a terrific crush on him. It was sad. A few years earlier, she must have been breathtaking, but now, her looks were beginning to fade. Water did not touch her lips, just coca-cola, and, boy did she gripe! But we got along fine.

A month or so after the Pottses moved in, Sam quit his job at Bel-Air Cleaners, and took off for Ft. Lauderdale to stay with Marie. When Marie beckoned, Sam responded.

To avoid all of June's complaining, Art seldom came directly home after work; he preferred drinking with the "boys." As a result, she and I spent much time together, cooking for each other and "visiting." She would have preferred Sam, but I was a fair substitute.

Now that Pearl could pass for twenty-one, she started working in various nightclubs and restaurants where she could make more money. She never did stay in one place for long, so it's difficult remembering exactly where she worked, and when. Her Hungarian Gypsy blood kept her going from one place to another.

It was time for me to go to work, too, now that I was back home. Taking the easy route, I returned to toil for Old Man Davis, in Knoxville. Davis Drug Store did not change, neither did I. Once I got back, it was like never leaving, except that I was older, and wouldn't be taken advantage of anymore. This time, I demanded a dollar an hour, and actually *took* my half hour off for lunch.

When that respite came around, after making myself a milkshake, I'd take it, along with my sandwich, to the back booth. There, I turned my back to the store, and ignored the customers who came in. I let Arnie "Italiano," or Mr. Davis, attend to them.

After finishing eating, I'd spend the remainder of my half hour in the phone booth, talking to Anne Leone, a telephone operator friend of mine who worked for the drug distribution company, where Davis bought his supplies.

Before, whenever a customer came in while eating lunch, I'd have to get up and wait on them, but no longer. No longer. Rebellion was sweet!

Sam arrived in Ft. Lauderdale, and moved in with Marie, at the end of the summer of 1949. Almost immediately, he got himself a job as a spotter at Peerless Dry Cleaners, 110 North Andrews Avenue, where he stayed for many years.

His first week there, he took Butch and Duane to the beach, and met an eighteen year old Georgia Peach, named Betty Seyden. She was tiny, less than one hundred pounds in weight, and ten years his junior. He was twenty-eight and she was eighteen, soon to be nineteen.

They started dating right away. She was too young to drink, but that didn't stop them. All Southern girls always seemed to look older, and most had phony Identity Cards.

On the beach, the new couple would frequent the Elbow Room, which was made famous, a decade later, in the movie, "Where the Boys Are."

Another of their favorite hangouts was Freddy's Anchor Inn, way out on route A1A.

Betty had a curfew and was required to be home by midnight, just like Cinderella. Sam was not accustomed to the necessity of bringing his girlfriends home by a certain time. When he confronted Betty's dad about being able to keep her out to a later hour, Val gave Sam the age old ultimatum, "As long as she's living under my roof, she'll be home when I say!"

Once he left the Marine Corps, no one gave Sam orders! So, he married her. That's right! They borrowed Marie's car, drove up to Georgia, and were married on September 10th. Talk about a whirlwind courtship!

Betty's mother owned some property in downtown Ft. Lauderdale, and, as a wedding present, gave the new couple a year's free rent to one of her rental units, at 700 S.E. Sixth Court. When the year was over, and with the aid of a G.I. loan, Sam bought his first house at 1514 N.W. 11th Street, for seven thousand dollars.

Kay, Clarence and Sue made a standing invitation to me that, anytime I wanted a home cooked meal, which was often, "to come on by." Many Sunday mornings, I took the streetcar to West View Park, and climbed the steep hill, to visit them in the "Honeymoon Cottage."

Like Mama, Kay always had the big Sunday dinner around noon, right after church. All four of us would squeeze around that tiny table, in that tiny kitchen, in than tiny house. A good time was always had by all.

Sue was learning how to cook, in her home economics' class, in high school. One day, she made stuffed pork chops for me. My mouth still waters thinking of that delectable dish. She would make it for me any time I asked, which was often.

I missed Sarasota, and my art classes, so I enrolled at the Art Institute of Pittsburgh, to continue my artistic studies. Classes were twice a week.

That's when I started going to bars. After classes, some of us students would go to a bar for a "cocktail." Even though I didn't really drink alcohol, it was such a grown-up thing to do. So, I started to imbibe. Now, I was really beginning to feel like a man of the world.

Getting bored rather quickly with my art school acquaintances, I began going out on my own; it was much more adventuresome that way. After classes, I would tryout different clubs. The lounges were much nicer, and "smarter," than the bars. They probably weren't, but to me, at that time, they were the epitome of chic. I'd order rye and ginger ale, and sip the one drink, as long as I possibly could.

One of my favorite places, to carouse, was The Cork and Bottle, on Smithfield Street. They had a piano player there, and crowds hung around the piano singing, my second favorite pastime, after going to the movies. I was not quite nineteen, still had a baby face, but "acted older." Somehow, I got away with it, and was soon recognized by the bartenders as one of the "regulars."

Drinking booze was not particularly to my liking, neither was smoking. All through High School my friends smoked, but I would not; I thought it was stupid. It is. But to fit in, I had to learn to smoke and drink. Soon, it all became such a natural part of me.

Even though he had just gotten out of high school, one night, I dragged Bill Weinhaus to a seedy nightclub in North Side, to see a tacky floor show. He was impressed and couldn't wait until he was old enough to play in such an "impressive" establishment.

Besides going to Jaffe's

Casino to see the strippers, Ray Harmoning and I went out drinking, occasionally, too. The places that we went were usually kind of run down, cheap dumps, with cheap women. We slowly drifted apart, especially after he moved away from Carrick. Then, we lost all contact with each other.

Along with the new suit, that I had "inherited" from Emmett, Marie included his new, camel hair coat. At first, I wouldn't wear it, because I didn't want to wear anything worn by a dead man. But, as the weather got colder, necessity won out.

I must say, that coat was the finishing touch to my new found sophistication. Whenever I wore it (over it didn't matter what), with a white, silk scarf, I automatically stood taller, and became that "man about town."

At that time, camel hair coats were the epitome of chic, and very expensive, as well. Usually, I kept the coat on, because I didn't have that many dress clothes to where, underneath. When I walked into a bar in that coat, sexily smoking a cigarette, I felt invincible. And, I was.

The drudge of working at Davis Drug Store went on. Even though I got a little bored with the job, it did pay for my tuition to the Art Institute, and gave me enough spending money to support my new found lifestyle.

The evenings that I didn't go to school, my usual routine consisted of taking a streetcar to Brownsville Road, in Mount Oliver, getting a transfer, for later, and stopping off for something to eat. I discovered Chinese cooking, and had a favorite, second story restaurant, where I could enjoy my plate of chop suey, on a table with a linen tablecloth, no less.

My other favorite spot was less classy, but they served the best hot roast beef sandwiches, loaded with mashed potatoes and gravy. There, I could sit at the counter, look out the window, and wait for my streetcar to arrive for my trip back to Brentwood.

Other times, I'd take the streetcar to Maytide Street, walk back past the bowling alley, to McCann's Restaurant. There was a bar in the front, with a nice dining room in the back. When the fancy struck me, this is where I would splurge on a satisfying, ritzy dinner.

McCann's had one other feature that made it fairly exclusive: it had a television set! That strange new device was catching on, slowly, but surely. Heretofore, the only way to see television was by standing in front of an electronics store, in order to watch the few shows that were telecast. At that time, the only one I had ever seen was "Kukla, Fran and Ollie," while eating dinner at McCann's.

It was fascinating, at first, but soon, I tired of it. No one I knew could afford a TV set. Movies were still my joy and passion. Television just didn't entice me and, certainly, was "*not* here to stay!"

Other evenings, June Potts and I would take turns cooking for each other. She was alone, often, so the two of us looked forward to employing our culinary skills. When it was my turn to cook, I'd cook up a prepackaged Chef Boy-ar-dee Spaghetti Dinner. Hmm, hmm, good!

The winter in Pittsburgh was delightful. It was nice to return to the cold weather after the hot climate in Sarasota. I didn't realize how much I missed the cold. It was fun bundling up in warm clothing, playing in the snow, and sliding down the hills at the Honeymoon Cottage. Unfortunately, Kay could not join in because she was pregnant.

That nice camel hair coat that Marie gave me, sure came in handy. On Friday nights, often, Marilyn and I went ice skating. She was getting taller now, and really thought of me as her date, rather than her uncle, showing me off to her girlfriends.

After skating, we'd get back to the house, in Edgewood where Martha would have a big pot of her Chili ready for us to gorge ourselves on.

Usually I'd sleep over in Martha's sewing room, right across from hers and Joe's bedroom. I never got much sleep, because of the "racket" coming from it. Joe was *very* slow and methodical.

Now that Joe was really ensconced in his offices, in Wilkinsburg, he offered a job to Clarence to service his customers' equipment. Clarence studied the manuals for all the Lewis-Sheppard equipment, figured he could do the job, and accepted Joe's offer.

Martha and Katy had been continuing their little "feud," that had started at Mama's funeral. Clarence wanted the job, and figured that if he kept his wife away from Joe, all would be well. Besides, he was going to make a lot more money. That appealed to Kay, so she gave in, and they accepted.

Once Sam got married, and moved out of Marie's house, she was, again, in need of a family member to "help her" with the boys. Pearl had enjoyed her previous stay with Marie, in St. Petersburg, so she accepted the new invitation without hesitation. It took Pearl a week or so to clear up loose ends in Pittsburgh, but by the end of October, she left, and arrived at Hendricks Island, to assist Marie. Surprisingly, she stayed there until September of the following year.

Marie had a full time maid to keep an eye on the boys during the day, so Pearl had much free time to herself. She did sit with the boys, most evenings, while Marie and Marino went out to dinner, or when she had "business" meetings.

On Pearl's free evenings, she attended a young adult club, on the beach, where she met many nice guys. But, being a Bordy, Pearl needed other work to earn money. Somehow, she managed to get a job for a major league baseball team, as a secretary. How she managed that, God only knows; she was not the secretary type, nor was she interested in sports. The name of the team escapes her, but she remembers it to be something with the word

"Athletics" in it, or "The something-or-other A's."

Her office was next to the men's dressing room where she heard the most atrocious, vulgar language, from the players. They deliberately used the foulest language they could think of, only to embarrass her.

When she complained to the manager, he took her by the hand and stormed into the dressing room, proceeding to chew out the team, using the *same* kind of repugnant language. Pearl developed a tougher skin.

When the team went on the road, Marie and Marino got her a job, as a hostess, at a very exclusive restaurant in downtown Ft. Lauderdale, where she worked the ten to three shift. That allowed her to sleep in late in the morning, and be available to watch the boys at night.

For Butch's fourth birthday, on November 13th, Pearl bought him a cowboy outfit, and a gun. Duane already had an Indian outfit, so the two of them created chaos playing Cowboy and Indian. Marie was not too happy with all the racket, but the boys had fun. Getting Butch out of that suit proved to be next to impossible. He actually slept in it.

The winter came and went, and then it was spring. One afternoon, while walking downtown on Smithfield street, I ran into Helen McKibben. She was that beautiful redhead who lived next to the convent, on Churchview Avenue. We hadn't seen each other in a while, so I asked her if she wanted to go into the Cork and Bottle for a drink. Willingly, she agreed, because she was now "legal;" she had just turned twenty one.

We went into the bar and I ordered us drinks, and took them to her at the piano. The bartender motioned for me to come back. He asked how old the young lady was, that I had with me.

"You, I'm not worried about. I know you from coming in here, but she looks a little young to me."

You could have knocked me over with a feather; I was only nineteen, but he was convinced that I was an "adult." I assured him that she had just turned twenty one, and that I would vouch for her. Nevertheless, the bartender had me sign a paper, swearing that she was of age, which I did. I signed it W. Bordy, but slanted the W so that it could be mistaken for an E, as in Edward.

On May 12, 1950, Kay gave birth to the prettiest baby I had ever seen. Linna was named after her grandmother Lina. With this increase in the size of her family, it was time for them to move elsewhere.

When I went to the hospital, I expected to see the usual squint faced infant. What a surprise! Her face was tranquil, and she purred like a kitten. The only thing that amazed me was that Kay still looked pregnant. It took a

while for the "swelling" to go down.

Now that Clarence was making good money working for Joe, by servicing the Lewis-Sheppard line of trucks, and with the use of his G.I. Bill, they would soon be able to purchase a "log cabin," with several acres of wooded land, in Wexford, which is located about twenty miles north of Pittsburgh, on route 19, way out in the boondocks.

The Schotter "estate" was located deep in a wooded area, and half way up a steep hill, naturally. They were fortunate in that they had their own well that pumped delicious, fresh water into the house.

The big living room was, actually, at one time, a log cabin. The walls were about twelve inches thick. The house had a small kitchen and dining room on the first floor, with two bedrooms and a bath, on the second. At last, privacy!

Once they moved in, Clarence, over several years, completely renovated the house, while Kay and Sue worked on clearing up the two acre yard that was thoroughly overgrown with vegetation. Kay could hardly wait to get her hands into those bushes and briars, to make the yard presentable enough for entertaining. She was anxious to bring out her Salvation Army Senior Citizens, who were called "Golden Agers." She would feed them, and entertain them, about once a month.

Ruth invited Suzie to spend the summer with her in Atlantic City. Even though Kay just had her new baby, she encouraged Sue to go.

The Mintz's had bought their new house at 371 North Richmond Avenue, over the bridge from the isle, and on the mainland. They had much more space there than their tiny apartment on Congress Avenue.

The first floor had a large living room, kitchen and two bedrooms. Ruth and Sol shared the one; Sue and two year old Brucie shared the other. The upstairs was divided into three unfinished rooms, not yet ready for habitation.

Sue helped out at Fascination, giving out prizes, and occasionally, tending to Brucie by taking him to the beach. Ruth preferred watching him, herself, by bringing him to work with her. After a while, Sue got bored.

There was, perhaps, too much spare time for her to enjoy the beach, and the city. Soon, she made "friends," who would take her into bars and nightclubs. She wasn't quite fifteen, but was encouraged by her new "friends," to start wearing makeup to look older. Unknown to Ruth, she was developing

135

these objectionable relationships.

Not being there, at that time, I can't speak from actual experience, but several years later, she told me all about her adventures in Atlantic City, claiming that they were really quite innocent. Like her big brother, Bill, she was always sympathetic, and empathetic, to all the odd-balls in the barrooms.

Ben Coty, who dressed like Buffalo Bill, ran a nightclub right on the beach, only a few blocks from Fascination, called The Dude Ranch. Many stars, over the years, played there, including Sarah Vaughn and Christine Jorgenson.

He was a would-be actor, and quite personable. Sue did frequent his reputable place, but with some of her dubious friends.

Now that Sam and Pearl had moved to Florida, I had the entire first floor and basement, of Brevard Avenue, to myself. After the cold weather, what was a young, red-blooded American boy to do, all alone in that big house?

On weekends, I started having friends in for little "get-togethers." It was a cheap Friday night date for my buddies to bring their girlfriends over, and to hang out at my place. Generally, they brought their own refreshments, and we would just sit around, listen to music, dance and visit.

Once in a while, even June Potts would join us. At first, she declined saying that she didn't want to hang out with a bunch of kids, but after a time, she really started enjoying herself, especially, one night, when someone brought a record album of "Carmen."

She got so carried away, when The Toreador Song played, that she got up and started to dance around like a Gypsy, accidentally stomping on, and breaking, one of the records. 78 rpm records broke easily. She apologized profusely to its owner, and ordered a replacement for him.

One night, June asked my small group of friends up to her apartment. It was a strange, quiet, melancholic evening. Everyone sat around her living room, on the floor, quietly conversing.

Someone asked "Rick" to sing. He obliged. Somehow, I remember all of the lyrics: "*Circus, life was a circus a hectic thing. The moon was a toy balloon we held on a string. Gay banners unfurled, lovely confusion. We were in another world, the world of illusion. And as in a circus, daring young love on a high trapeze, we suddenly flew threw the air with the greatest of ease. We painted the town, did it up brown, I was your down. You were the laughter, echoing after. Yesterday, the circus left town."*

We cheered, and asked him to sing it, again. He did. It was just as compelling and wistful the second time. To this day, I don't know who the guy was, and where the music came from. It just happened!

These little parties started out innocent enough, but soon, word got out about the fun everyone was having, and guys, I barely knew, started attending. Little by little, these simple little *soirees* grew, and grew, into big, bad bashes.

Some of the fellows started bringing "loose women" to these nice, little, polite parties. After several weeks, the "nice girls" would no longer attend. That suited most of us guys fine. We were having the time of our lives with the other ones, and it didn't cost me a dime. To get in the front door, you either had to bring food, booze, or a "young lady," who "put out."

Nancy was one of our favorite party-girls. She lived in Mount Oliver, and was most receptive to most of the guys, but only if I approved. Whenever someone wanted to be "alone" with Nancy, he'd ask me if it was okay to go to the cellar to play on my "antique." That was the old player piano, which was next to one of the beds. The piano would tinkle a bit, then silence. Bordy's Bawdy House was in business!

Pearl was getting tired of Florida and wanted to return to Pittsburgh. Marie asked if I would take her place. I said, yes. It was time to put the Brevard Avenue house up for sale, anyway. That way, the money gotten from the sale could be put in the bank, and earn interest, for Suzie and me. So, with Martha and Joe's help, we put the house on the market.

My debauched way of living was catching up to me, regardless, so the invitation to go to Florida was a life saver. I quit working at Davis Drugs because I didn't need the money. I was living quite well on my savings, and on the rent that was being collected from June. After paying the mortgage and utilities, there was enough left over for my needs, 'til the house was sold.

Bill Weinhaus and I still got together, once in awhile, to gallivant all around downtown, or see a movie. Or, I'd stop by to see him and his sister Shirley, at their house in Mount Oliver.

He was getting to be pretty good on the piano, and was anxious to get a job as a professional.

Gloria and Ruth Conn, two very good looking sisters, had placed an ad in the newspaper, looking for a piano player/accordionist, to complete their Trio. One played the bass fiddle, and the other played the guitar. Most of

their repertoire was country/western, but that didn't stop Bill.

They commenced rehearsals, and learned from each other. The best thing they had going for them, at that time, was that the two blondes were appealing, had flashy costumes, and were very good looking. They liked Bill because his piano playing was very "classical," their word for classy.

The girls made an appointment for Bill, with the manager of a night club. They thought it would be best if he did the interview; that way he could sell the Trio, by showing the girls' photos and clippings. They were smart hillbillies, straight from the West Virginia Hills.

Bill was afraid to go alone, and asked if I would accompany him. Why not? I agreed. It took us two streetcar changes to get there, arriving late in the afternoon. The Nightclub was quite nice, with a plush restaurant, a "classical" cocktail lounge, and a dance floor with one of those new fangled revolving, mirrored globes, hanging from the ceiling.

When the manager came to meet us, I recognized his name immediately. It was Bob Albright. Yes, Bob Albright, the boy who attended the same Hungarian Church as I, when we were kids. After all those years, we remembered each other. Bill and the girls got the job. He was ecstatic to get his first professional gig.

They called themselves The Sentimental Three, and they soon managed to get a long engagement at the impressive Rose Room, of the William Penn Hotel.

From there, they played at many Ethnic Clubs on Carson Street, in Pittsburgh's South Side. For those gigs, Bill had to learn to play the accordion. Soon, the girls got a better offer in Las Vegas, and left.

Bill was devastated. He had been able to work with the girls because, technically, the "clubs," where they played, were restaurants. Working solo in Cocktail Lounges was out of the question, until he was twenty-one. So, he went to work for a plumbing supply company. Gotta eat!

The old homestead sold easily, almost too soon. Everything had to be put in order by the end of August. Kay and Clarence picked up Mama's elegant Art-nouveau living room set, the bedroom set, and some other odds and ends, for their new house. The other furniture, was in the process of being sold, or given away.

For my final week of residency, we had one last celebration. Word went out, far and wide, about Bawdy Bordy's Ultimate Bash. Even though there was very little furniture left, we expected to break all records in attendance.

A bunch of guys showed up, but only one girl attended: good old reliable Nancy. The booze flowed heavier than usual, and we all got stupid drunk. Nancy became uncomfortable, and got more and more nervous, as the guys began "coming on," a little too strong. She saw the writing on the wall, and became apprehensive.

"I ain't gonna ball all these guys!" she confided in me. Then she wished me well in Florida, kissed me good-bye, and left.

What were we to do without Nancy, or Helen, or Dolly, or any of the other girls? We played Buck-Buck. That's a game beween two teams, that is usually played outdoors. The first player, of the first team, hugs a tree, while each guy hugs the team member in front of him, forming a hunched over column.

Then, each member of the opposing team, runs, and jumps on top of the first team, trying to knock them over. The rest of the team follows suit, all piling on top of each other, until either the lower team collapses, or the upper team falls off.

A wild and crazy time was had by all. But, after hearing the beams, that were holding up the dining room floor, crunch, I called an end to "the game." I still wonder if that cracked beam ever created any problems for the new owner.

Leaving Brentwood behind was an emotional time. This time, I *really* was going off into the big, wide world, perhaps, never to return. Again, whither bound? There wasn't too much time to ponder that question, so much resolving had yet to be accomplished.

Luckily Martha and Joe took control of the escrow, which closed on September 8, 1950, after I left for Florida. On that date, Martha sent a check to brother Sam for $6,123.25. She made it out to read: "Pay to the order of Samuel Bordy, Jr., Trustee for William J. and Suzanne E. Bordy, Miners (sic)." Sue and I were to get a nice little bundle, when we became adults.

Suzie returned from Atlantic City, and her new found status as an "heiress" made her very happy. She was looking forward to attending Veterinarian college, when she graduated high school, in 1952. There was a weight restriction to get into the school, so she had two years to get rid of the excess bulk.

Sam returned to Marie the money she had advanced for my schooling at Ringling. Once he gave her that money, from the "estate," the pump was primed. Whenever, she need extra money, she demanded that Sam "loan" it to her. He kept making her "loans," until it was all gone.

When the time came for Sue to attend Veterinarian school, the news was sprung on her that there was no money left. Marie hadn't paid any of it back, and never would. After all, she *"needed* it to pay bills." Her sense of entitlement was astonishing. Sue never forgave her.

Would I ever see Pittsburgh, again? It was time to start the next adventure. Papa, Martha, Kay, and Sue continued living there, so I was sure that, somewhere along the line, I would come back. When? I did not know. Goodbye Brevard Avenue, and to all the kids I grew up with.

RETURN TO PARADISE?

HENDRICKS ISLAND

CHAPTER NINE

In the first week of September, 1950, I arrived in Ft. Lauderdale to relieve Pearl of her duties, in the Carmalt household.

Marie, Duane and Butch picked me up at the train station, and seemed genuinely glad to see me. The boys were excited, jumping all over me, and asking all kinds of questions.

We left the station, and drove east on Las Olas Boulevard, toward the beach for a mile and a half, to the double entrance bridge of Hendricks Island. After crossing over the bridge, the house was only about a hundred yards away.

The yard was in full bloom, with all its greenery, and palm trees. Quite a difference from when I was there, the year before.

Even the boy's "jungle," in the lot next door, seemed more lush and verdant.

Pearl was at the house to greet me, and was anxious to leave. Her bags were already packed for her journey home. I thought she would stay around a little while to indoctrinate me, but she was leaving the next day. That evening, though, she would show me around the town.

After a quick dinner, she was prepared to show me the night spots. Pearl couldn't drive, so she called Joe "Blowhard" to chauffeur us around. He was an obnoxious, would-be ladies man, who thought no woman could resist his charm. Well, Pearl sure as Hell did, but we needed transportation.

He came to pick us up, with an attractive brunette he thought was his girlfriend, Joan Erbig. Joe was nuts about her, but like Pearl, she only used him to get around town. She and I were immediately drawn to each other.

Joan had freckles, and wore pancake makeup to cover them. She had

long, straight hair and was a little on the skinny side, but very attractive.

Marie called her "Rag Mop," which was the name of a popular song, at the time. Thus, to Marie, she was "that skinny, scraggly, boney Rag Mop."

Our first stop was a beer bar called The Shamrock. There, you could buy ten cent beers and drink all night, for a dollar or two. I explained to Pearl that I didn't drink beer.

"You better start drinking it," she told me, "liquor's too expensive in Florida." So, I learned to drink beer.

Next door to The Shamrock was The Aloha Club, that presented a floor show of strippers. They were all "B" girls, who got a commission on every drink they could hustle from a customer. The week I arrived, they not only had two girls stripping, but they had a drag Queen doing an exotic dance, as well. The combo consisted of a lesbian drummer, a bass player and a piano player. The show was vulgar, but fun.

When the performance ended, Pearl and I returned to the Shamrock to visit with Mae, the bartender/owner. She and her husband Pete were a nice couple who lived in a trailer behind the bar. Their work was never done. They serviced the bar morning, noon and night. Not much of a life, but necessary when your profit on ten cent beers is so small.

Not long, after consuming a few drinks of her own, Joan began cozying up to me, right in front of Joe. He was furious. Ignoring him, she continued to nuzzle me. I, too, thought he was a jerk, but figured that we'd better cool it. We did need him to drive us home. Joan and I made arrangements to meet the next night, which we continued to do for many months to come.

The next morning, bright and early, I was awakened by having my face licked by some grotesque animal. It was Timmy, the boys' English boxer. They had shoved his face into mine, because they wanted me to wake up, and play with them.

Marie was in the kitchen, making breakfast for all of us. Pearl was dressed for her trip back to Pittsburgh. She didn't have time to eat, because Tom Marino was coming to take her to the train station.

While waiting for Marino to arrive, Sam and his new, pregnant bride, Betty, stopped by. So this was my new sister-in-law, that ninety-eight pound Georgia gal. She wasn't quite what I expected. All the other southern girls I had met talked very leisurely, and with a southern drawl.

Betty was quite the opposite. She was very animated, vivacious and talkative. We yakked away as if we had know each other all our lives. Sam could hardly get a word in, edgewise.

Then Marino arrived, and off he and Pearl

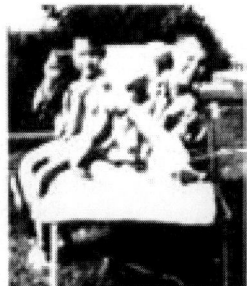

went to the train station. Sam and Betty invited me to visit them, in their downtown apartment, as soon as I got settled. They wouldn't be there long because, with the baby coming, they were hoping to buy their first house. We said goodbye, and they left.

The move was complete; I was officially a Florida resident. Eva, Marie's maid, arrived shortly after everyone's departure. The boys had been getting too rambunctious for her to continue as baby sitter. She and Marie had made an agreement, that after her brother Bill arrived, he would look after the boys, and she would only have to tend to the laundry and cleaning. That made her happy.

When Pearl got back to Pittsburgh, she moved in, temporarily, with a girlfriend until she could find a room of her own. She found one near a lovely cocktail lounge/dining room, that had just opened in Whitehall Center. A new song, sung by Nat King Cole, was becoming very popular. Both the song and the restaurant were called "Mona Lisa." This is where she would go to work.

Business must have been pretty good at the Lewis-Sheppard franchise, because, Martha and Joe sent Marilyn to a Catholic boarding school. None of us were really Catholic, but that didn't stop Martha. She rationalized that Mame would get a better education, there.

In reality, she wanted a little more "alone" time with Joe. It paid off, because ten years after giving birth to Marilyn, she became pregnant, insisting that it was planned.

Kay was busy at home, in Wexford, enjoying their beautiful new baby, Linna. Clarence continued working for Joe, and on weekends and evenings, he was busy remodeling the Log Cabin. Sue started her Junior year at West Wood High.

Ed's auto repair business in California was thriving.

As well as her real estate interests, Marie worked part time with two wheeler-dealer real estate brokers, Thurman "Bud" Starr and Arthur Dixon. Several years before, the two men had purchased the Clyde Beatty Jungle Zoo, at Sunrise Blvd. and N.E. 19th Ave. They were in the process of developing it into Ft. Lauderdale's first major shopping center, and had already begun building it, when Marie went to work for them.

She didn't take a salary, but instead, the partners gave her "one sixth of one sixth per cent ownership" of their new Gateway Realty Company. That wasn't much, but it was a start. She could see what a profitable concern this could be. At first, she was little more than their secretary and bookkeeper, but Marie was willing to work hard for a future payoff. After all, she was a Bordy.

Even though she had been building, and acquiring, real estate on her own, she had not yet become a licensed broker. That was high on her list of priorities. After I arrived, she began attending real estate school.

By going to work at the Gateway office each day, attending real estate classes, and socializing at the Coral Ridge Yacht Club, she didn't spend much time at home. There wasn't much time left for me to socialize but, somehow or other, Joan and I did manage to go out once or twice a week.

Because I was working "full time" for Marie, I didn't have time to look for another job for myself, and soon I began running out of money. Occasionally, she would give me two dollars for my dates with Joan. Actually, at the Shamrock that two dollars lasted most of the night. The regulars often bought us a few beers, too, especially the guys who yearned for Joan. She was very popular, but she was mine.

DUANE AND BUTCH

Marie's maid loved having me share her duties. It cut her work load in half by my tending to "the boys." Duane usually played explorer in the "jungle," next door, toying with the land crabs, and wading in the smelly bayou water. He could stay there, with the critters, for hours on end, and never tire of them. Butch kept him company most of the time, but he was more spirited and adventurous than "Dee."

Duane was the curious one who, one day while prying through my belongings, discovered "The Giant," my zombie-like marionette. He was immediately intrigued by this strange discovery. Butch was fascinated, too. What was it?

I demonstrated by hanging a towel across the doorway of their room, and hiding behind a chair, that I used as a make-shift backdrop. Then, I dangled the Giant in front of them. He talked to them, calling each by name. They were absolutely enthralled. It was fun for me, too. They couldn't see me, but I could observe them through the towel.

The "Mummy" movies, from Universal Studios, were very popular, at the time. I was a Nefertiti nut, too, having scrutinizing her replica, so often, in Pittsburgh's Carnegie Museum. So, with a little imagination, I stole the stories from the movies, added in a dose of Nefertiti, and with my imagination, created some exciting adventures to relate to the boys, about dead mummies that came to life. They were both petrified and exhilarated. The Giant became my Sheherazade, telling tales to the boys on an almost daily basis.

Television was just beginning to come to Florida, but until the Carmalts got theirs, the boys made due with their many story books and children's records. In particular, they loved "Mickey and the Beanstalk," and "Tubby the Tuba," which were most entertaining. I think I enjoyed them as much as they did.

Duane had learned a little trick at school, and shared it with Butch. He took him around the back side of the house, and started to pee against the wall, trying to write his name. Butch was anxious to try his skill, as well. Soon they had a contest going, as to who could pee the highest, and who could pee the farthest. They did love their water sports!

Butch was a little more daring than Duane. One day, when Betty's little sisters were visiting, Butch took Carolyn around the side of the house (where they played their peeing game), laid her on the ground, and got on top of her, kissing her "passionately."

I observed all this through my bedroom window. After tapping on it, they guiltily jumped up, and ran around to the other side of the house. Secretly, I was very impressed with his audaciousness.

The boys took most of their meals in the kitchen, sitting in a circular breakfast nook. For the evening meal, Marie would often make bacon, French toast and toast. I could never see the logic of so much bread, but the boys relished it, I didn't. It was quick and easy for Marie to prepare, before gallivanting off to the Coral Ridge Yacht Club. She did tend to get lax with her motherly duties when she had a *rendezvous*.

Whenever other meals were prepared, especially those with vegetables, the food took longer for them to ingest. Usually, Marie would put their food on the table, with the explicit instructions that they were "*not* to leave the table, until they ate *everything* off their plates." I took her literally.

Sometimes, it would take hours for them to finish. Being a Taurus, Duane was the most stubborn. He would put the food in his mouth, chew it a bit, then stow it in his jaw. He absolutely would *not* swallow. Butch was easier; he enjoyed and ate most of the food, with no trouble. But, wanting to ingratiate himself with Duane, he would play the same game.

This became a battle of wills. When I got tired of their little game, I would leave the kitchen, giving them the opportunity to throw away what they hadn't eaten. It usually worked, but I could never figure out what they did with the food.

One day, a foul, rancid odor permeated the air. The stench seemed to materialize from the breakfast nook. Marie sniffed, and picked up the seat pad. Aha! There was the evidence! The boys had hidden their uneaten food under the cushions. There must have been food there from months before. After that incident, I became a little more lenient. Even so, occasionally, I checked under the pads to see if any relics were left behind.

Dr. Robert Grigsby, M.D., said that he had won the Nobel Peace Prize for his cure for burns, and had been married to a very famous Hollywood Movie Star, named Ann. He would never say who she was, because he didn't want us to become disillusioned by learning what a horrid person she actually was.

He was in love with Olivia de Havilland. They were friends and saw a lot of each other, but she did not love him. Her sister, Joan Fontaine, according to Bob, was not as nice. She liked him, but he did not care for her. How much of any of this is true, only Heaven knows!

His medical practice had been in New York City, and after an embarrassing situation, whereby he impregnated a teenage girl, he was forced to pack up his few belongings and leave; his wife was insistent upon that. With "Rosa," his beautiful, pregnant, eighteen year old girlfriend, they fled to Ft. Lauderdale to begin a new life, together. Shortly after their arrival, Rosa gave birth to Robert Grigsby, Jr.

By this time, Marie had finished her real estate studies, took the test and got her Florida license. She continued to work each day at Gateway. Much of the shopping center itself had been complete. The principal building of the theater project was yet to begin. After the ground-breaking ceremony, the construction of the new, state of the art Gateway Theater was launched.

One day, quite by chance, Doctor Grigsby wandered into the Gateway Realty office, was greeted by Marie, and was immediately smitten. Marie picked up on his "message," and encouraged him. She did like to charm men. Besides, she needed a break from all the work that Art Dixon and Bud Starr had unloaded on her.

Grigsby related to her his story of woe, how he couldn't work as a doctor in Florida until he met the state residential requirements, and took its tests. To earn money, he had become a kind of entrepreneur, using the Gateway Center as his stomping grounds.

Since there were so many new businesses opening, he commenced to design store facades for the various new enterprises. His hope was to sell his designs, create the signage, and take care of the installations.

Marie could tell by looking at his examples that he was not really a very good artist, and suggested that her brother, who had gone to the Ringling School of Art and The Art Institute of Pittsburgh, go to work for him. What a great idea! That night, she brought him back to the Hendricks Island house to meet me.

We sat around the kitchen table exchanging ideas. I could see, too, that his artistic talent was limited, although his ideas weren't bad. After all, he was a doctor not a trained artist. He was very proud of the rendering he did for a new store called "Lampshades Galore." It consisted of a window display of a revolving Ferris wheel, with lampshades as the cars. He designed the signage for the parapet, as well.

This was the only thing he had sold, so far. He was using this art work as a means for getting new customers. When he did get them, he would act as the contractor, by subcontracting with a Neon guy, a Metal guy, and a Plastic guy, whatever was needed to complete a project.

There would be no pay for me, at first. Would I be willing to work on speculation? Sure, why not? By this time, I was just glad to get away from the house, in the daytime. The next day, we formed The Bel Art Sign Design Company. Hey, I was in business, and with a partner no less!

Bob had taken an office in a building, right next to the Gateway Center, but still on Sunrise Blvd. The only piece of furniture in the office was a huge, architect's drawing table, that the previous tenant had left behind. At first, I would sit at that table, all day long, trying to look busy. Occasionally, Bob would get an order for a sign, that I would design and render.

Often times, I accompanied him to meet a prospective customer. He always made a terrific impression, but then he would talk, and talk, and talk himself right out of the job. He just didn't know when to stop schmoozing, and how to close a deal. Necessity is the best teacher, so to survive, I started jumping in to conclude the transaction. Then, I'd try to sell the new customer a logo, that I would render in pen and ink, for them to use on their stationery. That was a little extra money for me.

After working for a few months designing and constructing the signs in the Gateway Center, Bob pulled off a coup by getting us the contract for the marquees, and window signs, for the Smith Drug Store chain. This was a big job, and would keep our sub-contractors busy for quite awhile.

Even though there was plenty of activity, there was very little money left over for me, after Grigsby paid all the bills. He really wasn't a very good businessman, and I desperately needed money.

About a half a mile away from our office was Swenson's Drive-in Restaurant. They only hired boys as car hops, so my career as a car hop began. By working there, from nine to five, that allowed me time to continue working with Bob on weekends, and for Marie whenever she needed me at night, or on my days off.

Getting around without a car became more and more difficult, so Dr. Grigsby taught me to drive. Automatic transmissions were just starting to be built into the newer cars, so if you drove an older car, you had to learn to use a clutch. After grinding and groaning the gears on his car, I finally learned how to shift.

Somehow, I passed my driver's test, so Bob helped me to buy a car. It was an old wreck of an Oldsmobile, that clanged and growled when I drove it, but it was mine. As soon as I received my license, my first solo trip was from Gateway Center to Pompano Beach, six miles north. It was great to have that sense of freedom, even though this piece of junk, and the drive itself, scared the crap out of me.

Bel Art's biggest job was for the Ft. Lauderdale Drive-in Theater. They had a triangular marquee sign, about ten feet off the ground, that could only be seen when you neared it. They wanted a "tower" built, that reached into the sky, and that could be seen from miles away. So, I designed the tower. Years later, I went to see if it was still standing. It wasn't. A hurricane, surely, must have blown it away.

The job we really wanted was to create the marquee of the Gateway Theater. Even with my contacts, no luck. The architect of the building had already taken care of the design part. We didn't get the job at the theater, but we did create the signage of many of the shops, and stores, surrounding it.

It took him over a year to get his Florida medical license. His divorce had come through, so he married Rosa. When his certification materialized, he packed up his pretty little wife, and ancient looking child, and moved elsewhere in Florida to set up practice. Or did he return to New York? Who knows? It was just as well, because The Bel Art Sign Design Company had "done the town," and I was ready to move on.

On November 18, 1950, Betty gave birth to "my niece Denise." By now, Sam and Betty were ensconced in their new house at 1514 N.W. 11th Street. It was a very nice house, built for ex-servicemen and their families, in one of those new developments, way out of town.

Betty was alone, and happy as could be, when I got to the hospital to see her. Beaming broadly, she showed me her new creation, as she talked on, and on, explaining, in precise detail, the entire birthing process.

I don't know if it was from the "gory" details of the birth, or from the smell of the hospital itself, but I fainted. Yeah, right down on the terrazzo floor I went. How embarrassing. Betty had just given birth, and I was the one who needed medical attention. A nurse put cold compresses on my forehead, until I could get up. They both had a good laugh. Once I got back into the fresh air, all was well.

Betty was ecstatic. All she ever wanted in life was a husband who loved her, and a family. These were the most important things in her life, all her life.

LILLIAN SHELL

Bored to death, one day, with nothing to do, I was sitting in my office at The Bel Art Sign Design Company, when this dowdy, fortyish blonde matron came in, to enquire about having a sign made for her new store.

She was a no-nonsense lady, and knew exactly what she wanted: that was to open a new dress shop in Gateway Center, to be called Lillian Shell

Fashions. This frumpy lady was going to go into the fashion business? Good luck!

Appearances can be deceiving. Lillian was very well organized and knew exactly what kind of sign she wanted, and what kind of merchandise she was going to stock, when the shop opened. Every detail had been thought out. She had a budget of two hundred dollars for the sign, and that's what she was prepared to pay. For what she wanted, her price was exactly right.

My ears really perked up when she informed me that she had just purchased the two most "sluttish looking" mannequins ever created. They would be displayed in her storefront window, to entice customers into her establishment. Was I hearing correctly? Did she say "sluttish?" Ladies just did not use that kind of language. She smirked, knowing that she had finally gotten a reaction out of me. We became instant best friends.

She may have appeared dowdy, but she had lived a glamorous life as a dancer with the Ballet Russe de Monte Carlo. Her real name was Lillian Scheldorfer, who was divorced, with a gorgeous thirteen year old daughter, named Jill. When walking, she still glided, even with the added *avoirdupois* around her hips.

Since her name was "Shell," she wanted a shell to be used in her design. So I designed a sign with a shell that looked remarkably like that other Shell logo, except that ours was pink. Her name was spelled out in long, elegant letters that traversed it. And, of course, I rendered the logo in pink and black, which she used on all of her stationery.

After a month of waiting, Lil became impatient for her sign to be completed. Everything else was on schedule for her grand opening: the merchandise was pouring in, and the "sluts" were in her window, but no signage.

Our plastic fabricator had been swamped with work, and was unable to get to our project. I went to Grigsby and volunteered to go into the plastic shop and make the sign, myself. Why not? I was always good at making things with my hands.

Dick Bradley had a small factory, downtown, called Luminous Plastics, where he manufactured anything, and everything out of Plexiglass. Plexiglass was a new plastic that had been used by the Air Force, during the war, for its fighter airplane domes.

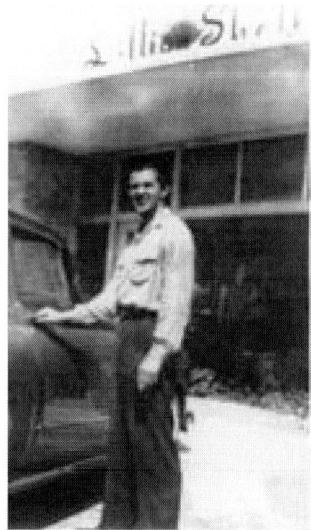

148

It is quite a versatile plastic that can be sawed like wood, or be molded into any shape with heat. Another unique quality is that the edges of the yellow and pink sheets actually glowed brightly, in the daylight. This new "daytime neon" is what we made many of our signs from.

Dick's father had a gift shop on the main street, that sold the items created in the backroom workshop. The most popular items they sold were the individual glowing letters that could easily be made into desk plates, or door signs. Because these items were in great demand, the Bradley's were kept very busy.

Lil's job needed no molding in the ovens; it was just a simple jigsaw cutout job. I went in, drew up the plans for the individual letters and the shell, transferred them to the plastic, and cut them out on the jigsaw, myself. Then it was done, except for the installation and the pink shading of the shell, which I did, also. She was very happy with the final result.

Dick Bradley was happy with the results, as well, and offered me a full time job. There was a very friendly ambience in his shop. Being occupied with Grigsby, I had to decline. If ever he got swamped with work, I'd be glad to help out, if I was available. Usually, when he needed me, I found the time, because the work was enjoyable, and the extra money was always welcome.

Now that the "slutty models" were on display in Lil's window, dressed in her latest fashions, she was open for business. Wearing her store fashions herself, and with a blonde touchup of her dark roots, and with a new pulled back hairdo, she was quite lovely.

Word of her styles, and her friendliness, spread. She was a warm and gracious business lady, and soon, her little shop was doing exceptional business. Everything was done by her, including the altering and shipping, if need be. If she didn't have the style, or size, in stock, she took the order, and mailed it to the customer.

Often, when I got bored sitting in my little cubicle, I'd walk down the stairs, and over to her shop, for a visit. We would sit, sometimes, for hours, while she told stories of her days as a ballet dancer, and her life in New York. She claimed that she had a beautiful figure, then, and wasn't "hippy," either, and that her stomach was so firm, that it was actually convex, not just flat. There were photos to prove it.

After we got to know each other well, she asked me if I would show her around the town. Since arriving, the poor soul had done nothing but work. Now that business was going so well, and she was making a comfortable living, Lil was in dire need of a nights entertainment. I was happy to help out. We went out and had a grand old time, the first of many more excursions.

Things were tough for Pearl that winter of 1950. She lost her job at the Mona Lisa. Things were bad all over, and she needed work, badly. She moved to North Side, across the Allegheny River from downtown, where she got a job at a screw factory. North Side was that shabby neighborhood where Ray Harmoning went on those Saturday morning "adventures."

After leaving the screw factory, she worked at the Clark Candy Bar Company, where she didn't make much money, but was allowed to eat all that she could consume. And consume, she did. Zagnut bars and Clark bars, so often, became her main source of sustenance.

Things got so bad that she couldn't pay her rent, so sister Katy came to the rescue, paid her rent and fed her. I think she actually stayed with Kay for a while, until she got her next job, and moved out.

That beautiful redhead, Helen McKibben, and she shared a room for a while. When they were hungry, they would go to the garden, at the convent, that her father cared for, to reap supplies. What her next job was, even Pearl doesn't remember, but she always worked somewhere, somehow.

For the rest of the winter, Joan and I continued dating. She was living with her mother Evelyn, who had divorced her husband before coming to Florida. She got tired of sitting around the apartment, moping, and decided to get out, and join the world. And boy, did she!

She started dressing like a teenager, bought an old, beat up car, and went "Jukin'" with Joan and me. In the south, jukin' meant going from one "Juke Box" joint to another.

This was before I got my car, so it was great having transportation.

"Evvy" did go overboard with her new found freedom, which made Joan terribly embarrassed by her actions. Then we both learned to overlook them. What the heck, we had our own chauffer.

Joan was a terrible flirt. It never bothered me, because I knew she didn't mean anything by it, and that she always came back to me. Evvy thought it was reprehensible, and that I should do something about it.

One night, after leaving the Shamrock, we drove up the road to the Banyan Club, named for the huge banyan tree in its front yard. Immediately, after sitting down at our table, Joan walked up to the bar, and started tantalizing some guy.

"You better do something about that, Bill," Evvy demanded.

So, calmly, I called Joan back to the table, and told her I wanted to show her a little trick. Curiosity won out. She

came back to the table. I told her to stand by my right knee. She obeyed. Then I instructed her to cross her arms in front, and to bend over. She bent over. With a gentle push, I put her over my lap, and began paddling her.

Because her arms were crossed in front, she couldn't get up. When it was over, I helped her to her feet. Tears came to her eyes, not from pain, but from embarrassment. She stopped flirting.

Evvy was so pleased, that she became my immediate confederate. It wasn't long before my almost-future-mother-in-law thought it was time for Joan and me to get married. That became her foremost aspiration.

One night, she started buying Joan and me Rum and Coca Colas, at Freddie's Anchor Inn. I never drank sweet drinks, but that was all she would buy us. So, what were we to do? We drank rum.

There was an ulterior motive to her madness. She was going to get us drunk, and drive us to a justice of the peace, to get married. Where the Hell she was going to find a justice of the peace, in Florida, at one o'clock in the morning, Heaven only knew. We all got so drunk, it didn't matter. We were going to elope. Thank God, we got a flat tire, and by the time I finished changing it, Joan and I sobered up. The next day I got my first hangover, and was miserable. Rum has not touched my lips since.

Several weeks later, Mr. Erbig summoned Joan and Evvy back to New Jersey. Evvy was ecstatic, but Joan didn't want to go. She cried, and cried, but to no avail. I would miss her. She said she loved me, and promised to return. She didn't.

Marie continued working at Gateway Realty. Her partners, Art Dixon and Bud Starr, treated her more like a secretary/bookkeeper rather than as a partner who owned one sixth of a sixth of the corporation. Like all Bordys, she was a worker, and did what was necessary for the company to be successful. She was meeting all kinds of people there and, occasionally, was able to use her newly gotten realtor's license to sell a property.

One day, she came home furious, carrying piles of papers, folders and books. She slammed them down on the kitchen table, while she vented. When she finished ranting, she enlightened me on what had happened.

Art and Bud were trying to pull some kind of *coup*, to take complete control, and ownership, of the corporation. Why should they have to share their wealth with a secretary? Wow!

She calmed down, and began to smirk, appearing quite pleased with herself. It seems that they had been keeping two sets of books for the corporation, and that is exactly what she brought home with her.

"I'll show those bastards who their dealing with!"

When the partners found out what she had done,

they panicked. Sweet, devoted Marie had outsmarted them, and threatened to go to the authorities. She hid the documents away, in the trunk of her car, and invited the two culprits to her house, to talk things over. I think that was the first time they ever, actually, visited Marie in her home.

Don't ask me how she did it, but before they left, she had negotiated herself into owning a full sixth of the corporation. She did not turn over the books until the new stock certificates were in her hand. Marie could be very shrewd and powerful when she wanted to be.

Now that Joan was gone, I started driving myself out to the old Shamrock to visit Mae, and the old gang. Then, usually I'd stop next door at the Aloha Club to have a drink, and catch the show, tacky as it was.

The first time I sat at the bar, alone, Sherry, a new stripper at the club, tried hustling me for a drink. She tripped over her feet, as she tried to seductively slither up to me.

"Hey, good-lookin,' how about a drink?" she asked.

My answer was, "Why, thank you very much. I'd love a drink."

At first she wasn't quite sure that she heard me correctly, then burst into laughter. That was the funniest thing she ever heard. Even though she was a lush, we became buddies. She actually ordered me a drink, and "paid" for it. Her husband, Artie, was the bartender, and he only pretended to take her money.

Sherry had been stripping for over twenty years, and had a twenty year old daughter who did the same thing; they both danced with boa constrictors, to an exotic jungle number called Tabu. Her snake was named after the music. The dance consisted of her holding Tabu up in the air with both hands, while undulating, then letting him slither down her body. As it encircled her, she let it climb up around her neck, so she could kiss it. Its tongue would flutter around her face, as the audience gasped. Boa's are not venomous, so the audience really had nothing to gasp about.

The dangerous part of the dance was imperceptible, to the audience. She had to be careful of the snake's tail, making sure it was kept away from her torso. While she danced, gently she would push Tabu's tail away from her. If it grabbed hold of her waist, it could wrap itself around her, and crush the life out of her.

Mickey was the other "B" girl/stripper. After meeting me the first time, and realizing she couldn't hustle me, either, we became friendly, too. The winter tourist season was over, so we'd sit around the bar drinking, until a "live one" came in.

In Florida, when a "B" girl hustles a customer, she must be seated at a table with him. There, she orders a bourbon and coke. The waitress brings a shot of whiskey, with a small glass of coke. The girl gulps the shot, and quickly, surreptitiously, spits it into the coke. The waitress immediately comes by, picks up the glasses, and asks "the young lady" if she would like another. Of course, she does. Half the price of the drink was hers. Cherie didn't spit; she swallowed, with gusto.

The Aloha Club, it seemed, always had difficulty keeping their piano player. Usually, a clash would transpire between the pianist and Skippy, the drummer. Skip was a demanding bull dyke, who had been working so long at the club, she thought she owned the place. There was *no* contradicting her!

If they were having trouble keeping piano players, perhaps my friend Bill Weinhaus, back in Pittsburgh, could get a job there. He wouldn't particularly care for Skip, or playing in a strip club, but so long as I forewarned him, he would know what to expect. So I wrote to him, dangling the job carrot in front of him, and awaited his answer.

Marie loved giving little parties. She would spend hours making hors d'oeuvres for her guests, using Philadelphia Cream Cheese for the basis of her works of art.

Whenever she got ready for her party, or a date, she had a ritual. After drying off from her shower, and powdering herself, she would come to me for help in stuffing herself into her brassiere. It wasn't a standard bra that "little" women wore; it was more like a half-corset. There were no straps, and it had to be hooked up from the waist, all the way up the back.

She would come to me, holding the "long-line bra" in front of her, while I hooked the bottom hook. Then, she would bend over, putting everything where it belonged. She would stand up straight, while I pulled, and squeezed, to get her into that contraption. The result was extraordinary. She was not only beautifully shaped, but she had perfect posture, with boobs that made their own entrance when she walked into a room.

Marino had given up on ever marrying her and went back to his jewelry business in New York, so Marie was in the market for a new guy. Dr. Jack Fassinger, D.D.S., rented one of her units, across the street at Bexley Hall, for the entire season. Marie thought he would make an ideal husband, but he was not interested. All he wanted to do was bask in the sun, on the beach, and visit with the young people. He was forty-eight, and still a teen-ager at heart.

The fact that he was a confirmed bachelor didn't deter Marie. Despite the fact that he was a complainer, who moaned and groaned about everything, he was invited to all of her parties. After all, if he could vacation for the entire winter, he must have had money. Most of the other men, who came to her soirees, were either married, or rather effete businessmen, not really interested in marriage.

Her partners, Bud Starr, with his sweet wife Nellie, and Art Dixon, with his wife, were usually guests, too. Then, of course, Bob Grigsby was an eager invitee, who always came, leaving his "wife" and baby at home. The women were charmed by him, and his stories of Hollywood.

For her gatherings, Marie always bought two fifths of Old Heaven Hill bourbon, set them on the sink in the kitchen, where everyone helped themselves. When the bourbon was finished, the party was over.

Often, I would act as bartender, by mixing drinks for the guests, and flirting with all the old broads, while Marie flirted with all the old guys. Between us, we kept them all happy. My favorite guest was sweet Nellie Starr, Bud's wife, who came to be Marie's best friend for many, many years to come.

Keeping good background music going, during the evening, was my duty, also. I had just purchased a beautiful, melodious recording, that featured the theremin. It was called "Jet," and was written by Harry Revel. Toward the end of one evening, I placed it on the phonograph and the entire party came to a standstill. Everybody sat on the floor, in front of the phonograph, raptly listening to the eerie sounds. When it was over, they all cheered and applauded. Everyone insisted that it be played, again, and again.

After one of these parties, probably because she had a few drinks too many, Marie got a bee in her bonnet about something or other. She bombarded me with accusations of being a free-loader, and sponging off of her. That really came as a surprise. I didn't pay her rent, but by being available for her, at her beck and call, and with all my duties around the house, I certainly more than paid for the value of my room. Whatever I said that night made no difference, she was pissed.

She accused me of being lazy. That really got to me. I was juggling Grigsby, Swenson's, Bradley's, and her children, all at the same time. She ordered me to get out of *her* house, *that* night. I advised her that I'd leave in the morning. That was not good enough.

Then, she got dramatic, and said something to the effect of, "Get out of here right now, and never darken my door again!" Too many old time melodramas!

When she threatened to throw my clothes in the canal, I remembered that old Rita Hayward/Victor Mature, movie "My Gal Sal," where he ripped up her gowns with a knife. That's exactly what I threatened to do.

"Go ahead! If you touch my stuff, I'll cut up your gowns, and throw *them* into the canal! They're a lot more expensive than my stuff."

That calmed her down, and she went to bed.

The next morning, I drove downtown to Luminous Plastics. By then, I was almost a full time employee. Chris, one of my fellow workers, had mentioned that there was a room available in his rooming house. Was it still available? Yes, it was.

I went back to Hendricks Island, picked up my belongings, and moved into my new quarters at 495 S.E. Third Avenue, a few blocks from the plastic shop. I quit Swenson's, and went to work, full time, for Dick Bradley.

Dian Gittins had been one of my customers at Swenson's. When we weren't busy, she often came by, in her big convertible, to buy a cup of black coffee, and to flirt to me.

"Oh, Willy, Willy, Willy. Taste this black coffee, it's heavenly." The coffee didn't turn me on, but I did like her calling me Willy.

Soon, we were dating, mostly beach dates, at first. The two of us never really committed to each other, but we liked each other, and passed a nice summer together, until we each went our separate ways. Her father owned the Blue Water Hotel, a lovely little hotel on the Inter-Coastal Waterway, a block from the ocean.

During the summer, she, and her sister Sue, lived in one of the penthouses. On the roof of the Blue Water were two small houses, that rented for a small fortune, during the season. The girls felt very grown-up living there on their own. And, of course, we had many nice little get-togethers there, that summer. I didn't know it then, but in October, with Dian's help, I would be working at the hotel as a bell hop.

There was another Dianne, I met on the beach, that summer. She was about seventeen years old, under five feet tall, and cute as a button, who dreamed of a show business career.

Many boys bustled and tussled with her in the ocean, while she giggled delightedly. She was in her sweet bloom of youth, and Mama Leone kept an eagle's eye on her; nobody was going to get fresh with her little bambina.

On one of our get-togethers, I played her that exquisite, instrumental recording of "Jet." She was so captivated by it, that she decided to choose Jet, as her stage name. When she got older, I promised her, we would do some kind of show together, where she could use that name. In a few months, we did.

Back in Pittsburgh, Martha gave birth to her new daughter, Lizabeth, in March of 1951. Now, instead of devoting her time to her rabbit, and reading, Marilyn spent the summer helping her mother with the new baby. Joe kept on keeping on at the Lewis-Sheppard franchise.

Clarence continued working for Joe, and remodeling the Wexford property. Sue got herself a part time job in a dairy, and Kay obtained a position for herself as a saleswoman in Horne's Department Store.

Pearl was offered a job by Sol and Ruth Mintz, to work in Atlantic City for the summer. She was to work with them at Fascination, as a "checker,"

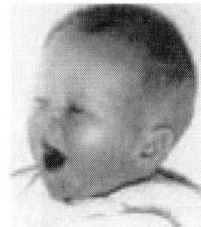

155

counting the heads of the players.

After her terrible winter of near starvation and poverty, it would be nice to have a buck in her pocket, have family around, and get better acquainted with her three year old nephew, Bruce.

In California, Ed was prospering at his auto repair business, Liberty Motors, while Helen and baby Jayne stayed at home, playing house.

PARADISE LOST

SHOW BIZ REGAINED

CHAPTER TEN

The West Hollywood Drive-in Theater hired me to produce, stage, and emcee a variety show on Saturday nights. West Hollywood was about twenty miles south of Ft. Lauderdale, a long distance for this novice driver to drive, but I wanted the gig.

"Johnny Reb" was the owner, who built a huge outdoor stage in front of his movie screen. Opposite the stage, he erected about six rows of seats, so his customers wouldn't have to watch the performances form their cars.

Most of the local acts, we got for nothing. I only made a few bucks, but that was fine. After all, I was back in "Show Business!" Each Saturday afternoon, after arriving, and depending on the available talent, I created a new show.

The shows were a hit, and to drum up more business, he decided to add strippers to the already established variety shows. So each week, Johnny brought in a "star attraction." To publicize the upcoming show, on Saturday afternoons, he drove his sexily clad star of the week all over town, in his big convertible, while he barked the particulars of the show into a loud speaker. It seemed to work, because we got huge crowds, mostly men.

Two of my favorite strippers were Mona, the Monkey Woman, and Mademoiselle Carmen. Mona was good looking and demure, and did a strip with a monkey. It consisted of the beast pulling off her clothes, piece by piece, but who was not always accommodating. Often, Mona had to "pretend" her clothes were being ripped off, by putting the monkey's paw on an item of her clothing, and ripping it off herself. She was a school teacher, who stripped to make a little extra money. What would her students have thought? Tsk, tsk.

Carmen was one of the homeliest women I had ever seen in my life. She was very tall and skinny, with no waist, who wore a diaphanous blue, Harem costume. Her frizzy, black hair was wild, and her nose was monumental, with a huge bump on it. She had enormous, protruding ears, with hoop earrings, three times the size of her ears, hanging from them. Two huge, pendulous breasts, the size and shape of two watermelons, hung from her chest.

Yes, she was not pretty, but like all French women (and Southern women for that matter), the fact that they were women was enough to be considered sexy and desirable. No matter how unattractive any of them may have actually appeared, each was "beautiful," in her own mind, in her own unique way.

157

Before each show, Carmen had a ritual. She'd pin me against the wall, rub her body against mine, speak French into my ear, then ask me to pin a huge, fake orchid over her G-string. *"Attachez-la, mon amour."* Very delicately, I would oblige.

Mademoiselle Carmen brought the proverbial house down. The men hooted and howled, demanding more, especially when she shook those melons and bumped that orchid. You know what? She actually did look pretty in the ethereal, blue light.

While emceeing, I usually did some shtick with one of the girls. Dianne "Jet" Leone was to make her stage debut. Wearing mirrored sunglasses, a full gold lame skirt, a busty, white angora sweater, big loop earrings, and carrying a long cigarette holder, I had her sing/talk to "The Sheik of Araby."

Naturally, I was the Sheik, turban and all. After each line of the song, I stated or asked, "Without no pants on?" The final line of the song, I sang, "You'll rule this land with me. I'm the Sheik of Araby." To which Jet innocently asked, "Without no pants on?" as I dropped my pants. Blackout. The squares loved it.

Often times, I would bring up a couple of shy guys from the audience for Jet to fawn over, doing some kind of shtick. On one occasion, I went into the audience and heard a woman's voice calling out, "Bill, Bill." Why was someone calling me Bill? My stage name was Tino Valen, not to be confused with Valen-tino.

I glanced over, and there, seated in the first row, were Betty and Sam Bordy. I tripped over my feet, almost fell over, but recovered. It made me very nervous having family members watch me "perform." Nevertheless, Jet and I finished the show. Betty loved the whole performance. She was always such a marvelous audience.

BILL WEINHAUS

After working a year in that plumbing office in Pittsburgh, my buddy Bill Weinhaus was getting ready to quit. That new fangled ladies' urinal, that you "just sneak up on from behind," did not interest him. It sounded like a good idea to me. I think women, today, would like such a contraption, especially during intermission in the theaters.

After much floundering, he decided to accept my invitation for his adventure in Florida. Before he arrived, I rented a small furnished duplex apartment for us at 1468 N. W. Eighth Avenue, in

158

Wilton Manors.

I picked him up at the bus station, giving him a quick tour of the town, before going to our new quarters. Because it was so close to the bus station, our first stop was at Luminous Plastics to meet my boss, Dick Bradley, and my coworkers, Edna and Chris. Then we drove to Gateway Center to meet Lillian Shell at her dress shop. As was inevitable, Bill was captivated with both Lil and the "slutty" mannequins in the window.

From there, driving across the Center, we stopped by the Gateway Realty to meet Marie. She couldn't have been nicer, and invited us to dinner, after Bill got "settled in." Even though we no longer lived together, it was impossible for the two of us to stay angry. After all, we were family. By the time Bill came to town, we were on friendly terms, again. Occasionally, I'd still sit with the boys, and of course, always, go to her soirees. Later on, even Bill would sit for her, from time to time.

The first thing he really wanted to do was to go shopping for a piano. He wasn't in town for more than two hours and wanted to start hunting for a piano. Better to wait until he got a job, and settled in, before making such a major investment.

He had arrived on a Saturday morning. I had a show to emcee, that night, at the West Hollywood Drive-in. After unpacking and showering, off we went to the "Theater." He had a grand time meeting Jet, and all the other performers. How fascinated he was to see that outdoor stage, in front of the screen. Why couldn't *he* play the piano for the show? Because he needed a full time job if he was going to be able to buy, or rent, that piano. Have a little patience. Besides, we only used prerecorded music.

When my show was over, we drove the twenty miles back up A1A to the Aloha Club. He was very anxious to see it; I had given him such detailed information on all the people who worked there. So, on his very first night in Ft. Lauderdale, we went to the Aloha Club. And guess what!

The piano player had just quit. How propitious! That night, the girls had to dance to just a bass fiddle and Skippy's drums. It was easy for Sherry, because she did a "jungle" dance number with Tabu, her boa constrictor.

Mickey had a more difficult time, so she reverted to her old routine of tap dancing. How novel: a tap dancing strip! Bill had arrived in the proverbial nick of time. The girls liked him, immediately, Mickey especially. She was fascinated by his innocence. Skippy was the one who was not amiable, and kept her distance. The "girls" told Bill not to take any guff from her, that they would protect him from her.

He had to audition for the boss, first. After the last show, when the club was fairly empty, Bill was asked to play. Skippy smugly sat at her drums, waiting for the new kid to play, expecting the worst. She was impressed. Mickey got up and did an impromptu dance, while Skip and Bill improvised.

Sherry brought tears to our eyes when she sang an emotional song called, "So Many Memories." She was amazed that he knew it. The boss liked him, the girls liked him, and even Skip liked him, so he was hired.

159

Fortunately, no one asked him his age; he was only nineteen.

For the first week, until he was really comfortable, I drove him back and forth to work. After that, he took a bus and, usually, someone from the club would drive him home. Skippy came more, and more, under his spell. My goodness, she had a feminine side! Bill could be charming and endearing. At last, he had a steady job in a nightclub. It wasn't his dream of playing in a nice, refined cocktail lounge, but the Aloha was a great deal more audacious and exciting.

Several weeks after Bill started work, he rented a new spinet piano, which he polished to a high luster every day. It was his pride and joy. Now, he could play music at home, as well as at work. He did love to play the piano.

In no time at all, he became acclimatized to Florida, and enjoyed all it had to offer. Sometimes, we'd go to the beach, although that was not one of his favorite places because he was so fair and afraid of sunburn. Most of the time we just enjoyed our Show Biz lives.

We got friendly with Dick Bradley, my boss from Luminous Plastics, and his girl-friend, Edna. By using his father's membership in the Pittsburgh Club, at the Escape Hotel, we were often invited to join them for a swim.

All of us, including Lillian, enjoyed the ambiance there. Playing cards and using its facilities became a welcome diversion for us.

Edna was a beauty operator by trade, and to me, she looked just like a more fleshy Rita Hayworth, red hair and all. One day, after her shift at the beauty parlor, when Dick had a busy spell at the shop, Edna volunteered her services. She was so good, and liked it so much, Dick hired her as a fulltime employee. As a matter of fact, it was she who taught me the ropes when I went to work there.

Johnny Reb didn't have a star stripper lined up for his extravaganza, one week, so I suggested Mickey or Sherry, from the Aloha Club. Once he saw the pictures of Sherry, with her snake, he jumped at the chance to hire her.

As was my habit, on the way back from the "theater," I stopped by the Aloha for a drink, and to give Bill a ride home. Sherry and Artie agreed to the job offer, on the condition that I would pick her up at the Aloha, and return her there. Artie thought it was hysterical that Sherry was going to do her dance at an outdoor drive-in movie theater. Why not? They'd played worse places.

About an hour or two after Bill and I got home, there was hysterical crying and rapping on our apartment door. Who the Hell was coming to visit us, so late? It was Sherry, covered with blood, and carrying a large wicker basket, with Tabu inside.

Artie had beaten the Hell out of her. They had brought Bill home a few times, so she knew where we lived. Where was she to go? What was she to do? Kindly, sympathetic Bill Weinhaus invited her to stay with us. That's all we needed. Two guys, a drunken stripper, and a snake in a basket, all living under the same roof.

Wasn't that going to be difficult? This was not the time to worry about it, Sherry had to be cleaned up, and "nurtured" with another drink, first. That woman could surely could put away the booze. Luckily, we just happened to have a bottle of Old Heaven Hill bourbon. What the Hell, let's all have another drink.

Sherry took a shower and Bill gave her a pair of his pajamas to wear. What had happened? Apparently, this kind of "little spat" occurred all the time. Was this how they showed their love for each other? How bizarre!

After several drinks, we all began to relax. Then Bill panicked. He realized how scared he was of snakes. How was he going to sleep with a boa constrictor in his apartment? What if it got out of its basket? Then, he became belligerent, and demanded, "Either that snake goes or I go!" Hell, he's the one who asked her to stay in the first place. The bourbon must have given him some *cajones*.

"Don't worry about Tabu. We'll keep him in his basket and put him in the cabinet under the sink. He won't be able to get at you from there."

That sounded like a plausible solution. Bill breathed easily, again. Sherry began to worry that Tabu might be lonely under the sink. He normally slept in the same bed with Artie and her, usually curling up on his chest. Well, he was going to have to sleep alone, tonight!

The next night, somehow, she pulled herself together, and cheerfully went to work. All seemed to go well for the rest of the week. To divert suspicion, she and Bill, went to work at different times.

All seemed fairly normal when I dropped by the bar on Friday, supposedly to remind Sherry of her gig at the drive-in, the following night. Artie was as nice as could be. No one could tell that there was anything wrong between them. They hugged and kissed, as usual. He did, however, confide in me about the little trouble they were having, and was wondering who was taking care of her. I surely couldn't tell him, but I did sympathize with him on his tale of woe.

"If I ever find out who she's shackin' up with, I'll kill the son of a bitch!"

A vestige of apprehension entered my being, but not for long. When I got home, Sherry, Bill and I had a couple of drinks, and sat around the piano, singing and joking, having a merry old time.

When Sherry was three sheets to the wind, her favorite expression was, "God have mercy on my poor crazy ass hole!" I'm embarrassed to write it, but that *is* what she said. Such charm, such elegance, such grace!

We were a little more boisterous, than usual, having a jolly good time. Suddenly, there was a loud banging on the front door. Who the Hell was that, and at such a late hour? Who? It was Artie. Bang, bang, bang!

"I know you're in there, Sherry. Open up, or I'll break this God damned door down!"

He almost did. Oh, my God! It was the big bad wolf! Trying to gain some kind of composure, I opened the door. Artie gave it a good shove, toppling me to the floor. He grabbed Sherry by the hair and whacked her across the face, knocking her off her feet. Blood poured from her nose as she screamed, hysterically. So did Bill.

"My piano," Bill panicked. "There's blood on my piano!"

He stood in front of it, like a brave parent protecting his child. Artie slugged him, too. Blood started running down his face. He didn't feel a thing; he was too concerned for his "baby."

"What do I give a crap for your piece of shit piano? You're the one Sherry's been shackin' up with, you dirty son of a bitch! Coming into the club each night and acting like nothing's wrong. I thought you guys were my friends."

I almost felt sorry for him, but not quite. He was drunker than we thought, and pulled out a gun, threatening us. Sherry screamed, again, even louder than before. Once again, he whacked her.

"Get your stuff together," he ordered. "We're getting the Hell out of here."

Sherry quickly grabbed her belongings and took Tabu's basket from under the sink. Artie slugged her one more time, knocking the basket to the floor.

Mrs. McGilligan, the landlady, who lived next door, heard the ruckus and came over to investigate. When she peered in through the open door, and saw a six foot boa constrictor slithering on the terrazzo floor, and a drunken woman all covered in blood, she let out a scream, too, slammed the door, and ran for her life.

Artie put Tabu back into the basket, then flourishing the gun at Bill and me, he warned, "I'm not done with you two bastards. I'll take care of you, later."

We took that to mean that he would be coming back to shoot us. Cherie continued shrieking, at the top of her lungs, as Artie dragged her, and the snake basket, down the long pathway to his car. Then, the love birds drove away.

In the calm that followed that storm, we collapsed a few moments to pull ourselves together. Artie's threat had unnerved us, so we thought we had better get out of there. After cleaning up, and getting dressed, we headed for the beach.

When we got there, I began to laugh, perhaps a bit uncontrollably. The humor of the whole incident began to register, so I laughed louder, and harder.

"Why are you laughing?" Bill demanded.

"When we get old, we're going to look back at this as a very funny incident." He did not agree. We waited for the sun to rise. Then, we drove to Lil's dress shop to tell her what had happened. She was aghast, but sympathetic. Would Artie really return to shoot us? Certainly not. She told us to go home and get some rest. When we arrived there, Sam and Betty were waiting for me. Oh, oh!

"What the Hell went on here last night?" he demanded.

How the heck could he have learned about our debacle, of the night before? Easy. He had called our landlady to talk to me; we didn't have a phone. She told him what had transpired

"You crazy kid! What's wrong with you, having some screaming women over here, in the middle of the night? You shouldn't be living on your own, you're still a minor. Go pack up your stuff, you're coming to live with me!"

In a way, I was relieved, but what was going to happen to Bill? No need to worry about him; he did well by continuing to work at the Aloha Club, for a short while, even though Artie still intimidated him. Quite fortuitously, he managed to get an engagement in The Tropical Club, on Wilton Drive, only two or three blocks from where we had been living. Goodbye Aloha Club, for good!

Fifty years later, after I had retired to Sarasota, we met again. Did half a century really pass? Our friendship picked up where it had left off. To us, it was a momentary glitch, but "life" did happen. His sister, Shirley, had moved to Florida, also. She had become Shirley Arce, had two sons, and divorced. Bill had gone into the army, married, divorced and returned to Ft. Lauderdale, then to Deerfield Beach, where he is still active with his Senior Choral Group. Each summer, he visits his cute, French/Canadian girlfriend, Jeannine LaVerdure, in Montreal.

For twenty five years, he was the "star" at a piano bar, in an elegant cocktail lounge, overlooking the ocean, in Pompano Beach, called The Sea Garden. How fortunate he was. He got exactly what he wanted out of life: to play the piano in a beautiful, "classical" cocktail lounge.

There was still a show to do, that final evening of my "freedom," before moving in with Sam and Betty. I agreed to make the move the following day, on the condition that I could come and go, as I pleased. After all, I was nearly twenty-one, and had been taking care of myself since High School. Sam agreed, and as a man of his word, he never questioned my activities. Often, I would be returning home at eight in the morning, as he was going to work. He never asked where I was, or what I was doing, or whom I was with.

On my final afternoon of independence, I drove to the Drive-in Theater, alone. When I got there, Johnny Reb wanted to know why Sherry was not with me. He needed her to parade around the town to advertise the evening's show. She was supposed to perform that night, and he had spent a lot of money advertising her upcoming performance. And, If I knew what was good for me, I had better go back to Ft. Lauderdale to get her. Off, he fumed.

Time was running out. After the first run through, of the evening's show, the problem of getting Sherry there remained. I telephoned the Aloha Club and talked to the owner. The girls weren't due to arrive for a couple of hours. When Sherry got there, would he please give her the message to call me?

Perhaps, he would call her at home? She hadn't been there in a week, he informed me and had no idea where she was staying. I assured him that she was back home, with Artie, and would he please call her for me? After we hung up, I had no idea what to do. If worse came to worse, I would have Jet do an impromptu dance, in her place.

Dianne was scared to death about going on. What was she going to wear? The mirrored sun glasses, cigarette holder, stiletto heels and gold lame skirt would suffice.

What was she to dance to? To the recording of "Jet," of course. No time to waste, we put on the music and had her improvise to the music.

How much was she to "take off?" Nothing. That would be the gimmick. All the men would think she was going to disrobe, and she doesn't. Besides, she was still barely eighteen. What would Mama Leone have thought?

That important phone call did come through. Sherry was on the line, in very good spirits, as though nothing had happened. Not to worry about Artie, everything was "fine" with them, and they were back to "normal." Yikes!

Was he going to "get even" with Bill and me? Don't be silly, of course not. She told me to pick her up, in front of the Aloha, at six o'clock. She'd be waiting out front for me. That was fine, I was not quite ready to confront Artie, yet.

The show went off without a hitch. Even though our star showed up, I decided to let Jet make her dancing debut, anyway. She tripped once or twice, but didn't do badly, for a first try. The dancing was adequate, but the music is really what carried her through. After the show, she was ecstatic with all the attention she got, from the shit-kickers, at the concession stand. A star was born!

The next day, 1514 N.W. 11th Street became my new home. Betty welcomed me with open arms, and treated me like an honored guest. She liked having me around, to have someone to chatter with. Sam often turned his deaf ear, but I enjoyed schmoozing with her.

My niece Denise, and I became fast friends. She was at that adorably cute and happy stage, always with a big smile on her face.

Sam had purchased a child's table for her, with a suspended seat, right in the middle of it. While seated, she was always "at the ready" to eat, and with the aid of the table, was able to, easily, wander around the house. She was adventurous, and kept exploring all the time.

After several weeks of living with Sam and

Betty, I felt right at home. She loved taking care of her expanded family and made me feel very comfortable.

Sam worked long hours at Peerless Cleaners so, more and more, when I wasn't working, I'd take his little family shopping, or to the beach, or to do other errands. That made him happy, less for him to do.

Before I knew it, Betty introduced me to many of her neighbors. Most of them were, like her, newly married. Most mornings, the neighboring "girls" would stop by at Betty's for coffee, and for whatever else any of them brought. They would sit around and visit most of the day, munching and smoking.

Some would leave, and others would arrive at the Bordy Brunch. Everyone was welcome, and all enjoyed the gab fest. Betty did like to chitchat. Around four in the afternoon, she'd realize that Sam would be home, soon, and she hadn't even fixed the beds, yet. Like a tornado, she whirled around the house, straightening it up, before starting dinner.

When Sam got home, Betty was usually collapsed on the couch, complaining about how tired she was from all the work she had done that day. I'd chuckle, knowing the real truth. The sympathy she expected from Sam, never came; he wasn't stupid.

The bathroom was directly across the hall from my room. Betty kept a container of dusting powder on the back of the toilet tank. One day, I had a bit of prickly heat and thought I would use some of her powder to relieve the itch. Upon picking up the powder puff, that was inside the box, I discovered what I thought was the biggest condom I had ever seen. My god! Was Sam that big?

I picked it up and showed it to Betty. What the Hell was it? She got quite embarrassed, and told me that it was a diaphragm. Don't be silly, a diaphragm is that part of the body, located right under the rib cage. Then she told me what it was used for and, perhaps, gave me too much information. Oh, I see.

Work was pretty steady at the plastic shop, so I got rid of my old beat-up Oldsmobile and purchased an English Austin. Sam and Betty drove around in a Crosley, which was one step down from a golf cart, but it got them where they wanted to go. Whenever they needed a larger vehicle to go to a drive-in movie, they would borrow my "big" Austin, which was only one step up from a golf cart.

Betty had two cute little sisters, Valerie and Carolyn, who were about eight and six, at the time. They loved my big, little car, and were delighted when I took them for a ride in it.

One evening, I had a date with Dian Gittins, and we had to use Sam's Crosley because he was borrowing my "sedan" for a date of his own, at the Drive-in Movie.

Sam had removed the passenger seat of the Crosley to make room for Denise's table. They used it, whenever they took her anywhere. Without a passenger seat, Dian, dressed to the nines, had to sit in the back seat, with her legs straight out in front of her, while I drove that dingy heap. She was accustomed to being chauffeured in luxurious cars, not mini-piles of nuts and bolts. She loved it, and thought it was hysterically funny, having the time of her life!

Ruth, Sol and Brucie came to visit. It must have been in October of 1951, after the summer season of Atlantic City, and before the winter season of Florida. Several years before, Sol had worked at the Fountainebleu Hotel, in Miami Beach, as a bellhop.

He wanted to return there to play "big shot," by showing off his beautiful wife, and spending a lot of money, and to show how successful he had become in Atlantic City.

This was the first time Sam and I had seen our nephew, Bruce. What an imp, he was! After Sol and Ruth left him behind, he spit at Sam, and tore the place apart: up one wall and down the other. He never stopped moving, or talking. After a good whack from Sam, he calmed down.

The next day, we took him to meet his cousins, Butch and Dee, and to play in their "jungle." Playing in dirt was a new treat for Bruce; he was more accustomed to dressing nicely and playing on the Boardwalk, among the bright lights, the noise, and the bustling people.

By the time Ruth and Sol returned from Miami Beach, several days later, Bruce had had such a good time, he wanted to stay longer. After they left, the Bordy house was calm, again.

Betty loved having visitors. Sam's old buddy Jack Smith came for a visit, as well as his old girlfriend, Annie, at different times, of course.

Even though she had recently gotten married, Annie was still in love with Sam, and confessed it to Betty, while crying on her shoulder. Dear, sweet Betty was sympathetic, and held Annie's hand, while she wept.

Jack missed Sam, too, and when he visited, he wanted to take us all out for the evening. Sam declined, he didn't go out drinking, anymore. He was a married man, and had settled down. So, Betty and I accompanied him. He got a little drunk, and kept calling me Sam; he missed the "good old days," when the two of them hit all the joints in Pittsburgh.

166

The Blue Water Hotel beckoned.

Dick Bradley had moved the plastic workshop, way out in the boondocks, to his brother's airport. It was too far away for me to travel each day, so with the help of Dian Gittins, I got a job as a bell-hop in her father's Blue Water Hotel.

It was a nice, little "boutique" hotel with a pleasant, sunny dining room, a quiet, intimate bar, and situated right on the Inter-coastal waterway. For convenience, the beach was only two blocks away.

For several weeks, in October, I along with the housekeeper, and her lazy husband, the custodian, scrubbed every room in the hotel. Thank goodness, I had experience! It was learned when I scoured Bexley Hall, for Marie, several years before. Before the hotel, officially, opened for its season, I turned twenty-one on November 2nd, and could, now, legally serve alcohol.

After I got my first paycheck, one of the first things I did was to learn how to water ski. Being naturally agile, it came easily for me. The guy who gave me the lessons took my picture skiing, in front of the Blue Water. He was a better instructor than he was a photographer.

Most of the staff were pleasant, especially the Italian chef. For some reason or other, he always fed me better than the rest of the help. The salad lady, Angelina, made me a special salads, of whatever I wanted. She and Gianni, the chef, kind of adopted me. It wasn't unusual for me to get prime rib of beef for dinner. For the rest of the employees, he made a standard dish for all, usually some kind of stew, or hash from the leftovers.

The only person I really disliked was the hotel's assistant manager, Miss Ready. She had no sense of humor, and insisted we pronounce her name "Reedy," not "ready." She was a dour, old maid with pursed lips. For weeks, I tried to get her to smile, or to get a civil word out of her. That was never to be. She detested me, and really treated me quite shabbily; I just couldn't understand why.

To the hotel guests, she was remarkably civil, even friendly, especially to returning clients. She would actually smile at them, and when she did, she was almost pretty, even with her irregular features.

Not only was she rude, and abusive, she insulted me whenever she had the opportunity; that was whenever she thought the manager wasn't around, observing her actions. Her treatment of me did *not* go unnoticed, by him.

After a month or so, I could take her insults no longer, and asked her why she was treating me so shabbily. She finally told me. When I was working as a car hop, she had come into Swenson's for a bite to eat, and I waited on her. After I delivered her order, I said what I said to most of the single girls: "If you want me, just honk. You know how to honk don't you baby? Just put your hand on the horn, and push."

Most girls got a big laugh out of that, but *not* Miss Ready. She was insulted, and apparently carried that grudge all through our time at the Blue Water.

Her harassment didn't cease, it got worse. I never said anything, but the manager had quietly been observing her, all along. He couldn't abide the bad treatment any longer, either, and, finally, fired her. What a relief!

There was a plethora of ugly, single girls staying at the hotel, that season, who were desperately looking for "romance." Most were pretty persistent, and wouldn't take no for an answer.

I owed the manager a favor for getting rid of Ready. One of his best clients had a repulsive daughter who wanted to date me. He even offered to pay me to take her out. She was not very subtle, her lascivious leering at me had been very apparent. My debt had to be paid, so I was impelled to reciprocate.

She was taller than I, but had a good figure, even though it was trussed into very tight undergarments; I don't know how she sat down. She had a bad nose job, overly coiffed hair, and was practically illiterate. Making small talk was next to impossible, and she had a constant sniffle.

Nevertheless, I took her out to dinner (with her Dad's money), then drove her back to the hotel parking lot in my little Austin. We were very cramped, but I felt I had to make the obligatory "pass" at her, which I had put off as long as I could. Finally, I gave her a little peck, and stroked her boob. She panicked, and dashed out of the car, into the back door of the hotel. Whew! It was over. Never again. I had learned my lesson: no more favors!

For the rest of the season, my dates were only with those I wanted to be with. And, there were quite a few, Dian not being among them. She occasionally came into the hotel with her parents for dinner, but we had officially stopped dating.

The Torch Club had opened, almost next door to The Aloha Club. It was much nicer, and more plush, than my old hangout. It also had a better class of strippers. There, I met Toni Turner, a gorgeous brunette with long tumbling hair, and an incredible figure. We become "friendly."

Nothing much, really exciting, happened at the hotel for the rest of the winter, just that which one would expect during the season at a resort: cheating spouses having trysts; priests taking off their collars and raising havoc; the French courtesan of *une certaine age*, who was looking for a rich husband. Nothing extraordinary!

TWO WEDDINGS AND A CONFLICT

The season was just about over when I got the surprise of my life. Dian Gittins was about to get married, on March 22nd, and had invited me to the wedding. I didn't even know she was dating anybody. We had seen each other, only occasionally, at the hotel. I figured that after the season, we'd pick up where we left off. That wasn't to be.

Betty agreed to accompany me to the ceremony. She wanted to get a new hairdo for the occasion, so I took her to meet my ex-associate from the plastic factory, Edna, who had returned to the beauty business. Betty and she chatted animatedly, while her hair was being styled.

The design was some grandiose construction that Betty loved. But how could she keep in tact? The wedding wasn't until the next day. Edna instructed her to wrap her hair up in toilet paper, and to sleep on her back, and not to take a shower in the morning, just a sponge bath. Betty obeyed, and looked terrific at the wedding.

Marie was about to get married, too, to a Curtis Straker from Virginia, a very polite, southern gentleman who looked every inch the part. It must have been a whirlwind courtship because everyone was surprised.

The actual date of the wedding slips my mind, but the reception was held at Marie's house. As usual, she had prepared all the hors d'oeuvres herself, and had a ham baking in the oven. Betty and I helped serve up the food.

The Strakers were going to spend their first night of wedded bliss, together, in Marie's bedroom, on Hendricks Island.

Betty and I thought we'd play a little trick on them. During the party, we went into the bedroom, carefully folded back the sheets, and on the pillows, we placed a red maraschino cherry on one, and a green maraschino cherry on the other. We thought that was funny. Neither Marie nor Straker commented.

At the end of April, I got drafted. The first week in May, I was to report to a facility in Pittsburgh for my physical. The Korean Conflict (not War) was being waged. Most guys were drafted when they reached eighteen; I thought the government must have forgotten about me. After all, I was an old man of twenty-one.

Denise was now a year and a half. I would miss my brother's little family, as well as Duane and Butch.

U.S.M.C.

FROM THE HALLS OF MONTEZUMA

CHAPTER ELEVEN

The bus trip back to Pittsburgh was the most miserable trip I had ever taken. It took three days of changing and missing buses, over hilly, twisted roads. No more long bus trips!

It was good to be back. I stayed with Martha, in Edgewood, and managed to see all the family who were still in the old Smoky City.

Papa, and his new wife, Margit, were nicely ensconced in their West Homestead apartment. Pearl was getting ready to go to work, again, at Fascination, in Atlantic City. Clarence was still remodeling the house, while Sue and Kay got ready to celebrate Linna's second birthday, on May 12th.

On May 8, 1952, at 8:00 a.m., I reported to the 2nd Floor Assembly Room, of the Old Post Office Building, at 4th Avenue and Smithfield Street. From there, we draftees were transported to "the induction station" for our physical examinations. The physical examination was nothing like what you saw in the movies. We were given lockers, then told to strip completely naked for the entire examination. That's how we were escorted around the facility. Quite embarrassing!

The examination took most of the day. When I passed, they asked which branch of the service I would prefer: the Army, or the Marine Corps. I asked for the Army; they put me in the Marine Corps. Actually, I was glad they did. "The Corps" was known for being the toughest branch of the service, and that appealed to my vanity. After all, If brother Sam could be a Marine, so could I.

After being sworn in, we had a few hours, before being shipped off to Parris Island, South Carolina. So what did I do in those couple of ours? You guessed it. I went to the movies, and saw "Singin' in the Rain," my last film as a civilian.

The busload of raw recruits arrived in Parris Island, early in the morning, of May 9th. We were greeted by the guy, who was to be our D.I. (Drill Instructor), Sergeant W.H. Bodaford. He was rather diminutive, and slightly built.

Getting off the bus, he sized us up, while we new recruits did the same with him. Then he herded us, as best he could, into some kind of order, and told us to stand at attention. A dismal failure. Then he tried to get us to march while he called cadence, "Hut, two. three, four . . . "

We were a sorry assortment of humanity, most of us had long hair (for the time), some were bearded, and all dressed slovenly, after the all night bus ride.

Sgt. Bodaford sashayed as he marched. "Hut, two, three, four . . . " Is this the guy who's going to make us Marines? I couldn't believe it. With my hands in my pocket, and smirking at his graceful gait, I ambled along, contemplating what was to come next.

Then, out of nowhere, came this booming voice, shouting at me, "Get your hands out of your pockets, you cotton pickin' f#%ker! Hut, two, three, four . . ."

This guy meant business. Maybe he was tougher than he looked. We "marched" to the indoctrination center, where we were, again, told to strip. It wasn't any easier the second time.

"Take all your personal belonging, and wrap them up," was our next instruction. "You're going to be sending everything home."

No personal possessions were to be kept, by any of us. Everyone followed the instructions. When you're naked it's pretty hard to hide anything.

The next stop was for a haircut, well, really a scalping. Each guy had to sit on a metal chair, while the "barber" sheared each of us completely bald. Watching our locks fall into our naked laps was a sure lesson in humility. Some of the guys actually cried. After a shower, to wash off any residual hair, we were issued our clothing and toiletries.

Our new home, for the next ten weeks, was the next stop. We were to live in what was called a Quanset hut: a "glorified," arched cabin, made out of corrugated metal. Two of them were needed for the fifty two guys in Platoon 407.

After stowing our newly issued gear into our locker boxes, we were taught the proper way to make our bunks, before we got in them for the night. Taps was at 10:00 p.m., Reveille was at 4:00 a.m.

Basic training began the next day, and lasted for the full ten weeks. It was going to be a tough job, but Sgt. Bodaford was up to it. Just like all those Gung Ho movies, the training was exhausting, miserable and exhilarating. We were kept too busy to think about anything but the training.

One of the first things we were taught was how to curse. In the mess hall, you were not permitted to say, "Pass the salt, please." You had to say, "Pass the f#%kin' salt you mothah f#%ker!"

Hell, I never used that word even when I was doing it. Everyone else could cuss, but not I. Mama taught us better.

It was like learning a whole new language: the men's room was the head, who knows why; the wall was the bulkhead; the bed was a rack; the water fountain, or a rumor, was the scuttlebutt; underwear was skivvies; etc., etc.

You were required to wear only government issued clothing. That included the baggy, white boxer-type skivvies. One of the guys had complained to his mother about having to where those terribly uncomfortable under pants. So, being a good mother, she sent him a half dozen jockey shorts, in the mail. That was a no, no. All packages had to be unwrapped in front of the D.I.

When his package was opened, the D.I.s made great fun of the "girly panties." They made him strip, and put on all six pair. That wasn't bad enough, he had to strut around the camp, shouting at the top of his lungs, "I'm the sexiest Marine in Parris Island. I'm the sexiest Marine in Parris Island." And in the rain, no less.

We were instructed to never call a rifle a "gun." A rifle was to be respected and cared for. The first time this happened, the guilty party was ordered to learn a little poem and recite it to the platoon: "This is my rifle (holding out the weapon), this is my gun (grasping his crotch). This is for killing, this is for fun (again, the crotch)."

When you go through boot camp, you are isolated from the rest of the world. There were to be no visitors. Somehow, that didn't apply to my family. Martha, Joe, Marilyn and Marie were driving to Florida, from Pittsburgh, and thought they would pay me a visit. Somehow, these two Bordy girls charmed the Commanding Officer into allowing a visit.

It was around six in the evening, during letter writing time, when I was ushered to a parking lot, and lo and behold, there they were. I didn't realize how much I had missed civilization — well, our kind of civilization, anyway. Martha insisted I take the box of See's candy she had brought for me, as well as a camera with film. She had a bottle of whiskey for me to take back, too. That, I declined.

Marie noticed that I was limping, and wanted to know what happened. I showed them the wound on my shin where some lousy corporal, from another unit, kicked me because I didn't stand at attention when he asked me a question. They couldn't believe the "brutality." How good it was to have family around to gripe about the Corp to.

172

When I got back to the hut, my hungry buddies smelled the candy, and it was gone in five minutes. Everyone enjoyed that little taste of "home," and were doubly excited about having a camera. Those, who had to return theirs, were hoping to borrow mine.

For some reason, Sgt. Bodaford allowed me to keep the camera, and everyone had a grand old time mugging for it. Some guys managed to get film for their own mementos.

Everyone looked forward to Sunday, the only day where we could have a little R & R (Rest and Relaxation). We could play a little soft ball, or just lounge around, doing nothing except shining our shoes and cleaning our rifles.

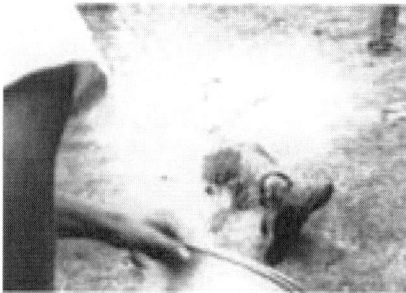

The "Smoking Lamp" was, also, lit all afternoon. That meant, you could smoke any time you wanted. During the week, it was only "lit" occasionally, at the whim of the D.I.

One strict no, no was, No Napping! If anyone fell asleep, a bucket of water was thrown on him. That was great fun for a few masochists who kept their buckets full, patiently waiting for the next snoozer.

One of my favorite pictures was taken in front of our hut after an extra long hike. When we returned to the base, everyone collapsed from fatigue.

In that photo, you can see one of the guys sitting with his feet in a big puddle of water, too tired to get out of it.

One of the other guys seems to be saying, "Whew!" And the third, for some reason or other, looks elated, probably because the

hike was over.

We had several assistant D.I.s who took over when Sgt. Bodaford was away. One was a pot bellied, booze guzzling weirdo, named Sgt. "Zero." One Saturday night, he was gulping whiskey out of a bottle, and insisted that this young, eighteen year old kid drink with him. The kid never had a drink in his life. Nevertheless, Zero forced him to imbibe. Soon, he was falling down drunk, and the sergeant ordered him to take off his clothes. Then he made the kid lay naked on the top of a table, while he attempted to shove ice cubes up his rear. This was funny?

That was all I could take. I got off my locker box, stood right in his face, and convincingly said, "Knock it off! Knock it off right now, or I'll report your ass to the commanding officer."

We had been required to study the U.C.M.J. (Universal Code of Military Justice), and I knew what our rights were. He knew I was serious, and backed down, trying to laugh it off as a big joke. I was not amused.

The smoking lamp was not lit, but I took out a cigarette, anyway, lit it, and blew smoke in his face. And there were no cameras running. Damn!

Then, I stomped back to my rack, and stretched out on my back, enjoying my fag. It was strictly forbidden to sit or lay on your cot until you went to sleep for the night, but that didn't phase me in the least. I never felt so in control.

Toward the end of training, we all had to go to the rifle range to "qualify." That meant, you had to reach a certain score to graduate boot camp. I loved the range. The only miserable part was the weather. All heat records had been broken that year. Several recruits, from other platoons, had already dropped dead from the high temperature.

It was so hot, that when I laid on my belly in the prone position, to shoot at the target, I'd sweat so profusely, that when I got up, I'd be covered in mud. Hard to believe, but true.

What I really loved about shooting was that I was good at it. I was actually the highest shooter in our group, and was awarded a certificate that says that I was "the outstanding Marksman of his platoon." Not only did I receive the certificate, I was given a new fangled steam iron. Sgt. Zero tried to con me out of it, but I sold it to him instead. Who needed to lug that heavy thing around, anyways?

Platoon 407 graduated, as an "honor platoon," on July 16th, 1952. Sgt. Bodaford was happy to win the award. He was really a very conscientious Marine, and did his utmost to make us into the best that we could be. All of us raw recruits were awarded our P.F.C. (Private First Class) stripes, that we had to sew on our sleeves, immediately.

Most of the guys were transferred to Camp LeJeune, and boy, were they worried. From there, they would receive further battle training, and be shipped to Korea.

I was one of the lucky ones to be transferred to Cherry Point, North Carolina, into something called The Marine Air Wing. That's the Marine Air Force, but don't let any jarhead hear you call it that.

Sue graduated from Wexford High School that June of 1952. She had lost all of her baby fat and looked quite glamorous at her graduation. She was getting herself ready to attend Veterinary College in the fall.

When autumn came around, there was no money for her schooling. Marie had borrowed it all from Sam, and had returned none of it.

College was cancelled. Sue never, *ever* forgave Marie for the slight.

At home, with Kay, Clarence and Linna, you'd never think anything was wrong. On the surface, she appeared her usual happy, jovial self. There was always time to play with her favorite niece. And, of course, she helped Kay feed and entertain those "Golden Agers," at their picnics.

Resigned to the fact that she would never be a Vet, she started to drink. Almost every day, after she finished work at The Otto Milk Company, she would meet her coterie of friends at the various bars. All her cohorts loved and adored her, but she never recovered from not being that "heiress," she thought she was.

P.F.C. William James Bordy was shipped to The Second Marine Air Wing (MAW), Marine Air Maintenance Squadron (MAMS) 14 at Cherry Point, North Carolina. Here, the quanset huts were only used as offices. We lived in big, two story, red brick barracks, with a modicum of privacy.

There were four guys to a cubicle. Each cubicle consisted of two double deck racks, leaning against two double door lockers, where you could actually hang up your clothes. Under each rack was our trusty, locker boxes. These cubicles ran the entire length of the barracks, on both sides.

My three bunk mates were: a lovelorn Jewish

butcher, from Chicago, Harvey Wexler; an old Sergeant, who had been in the Corps for about fifteen years, and was "busted" to P.F.C., called Pappy; and under me, a quiet, introverted Southern boy, from Mobile, called Deigo. Harvey was the talkative one; you couldn't get much conversation out of the other two.

We all worked in Aviation Ordnance. I still don't know what that means, except that it has something to do with weapons, and the air field, and the jet airplanes that flew in and out, each day. That was exciting only because Captain Ted Williams, the baseball star, flew his jet for the 2nd MAW. Most of the time, we just hung around, all day, inside our quonset hut office, twiddling our thumbs.

After all that hard work, toward the end of the year, I was given a ten day leave. The great thing about being in the Marine Air Wing was that you got free flights to wherever you wanted to go, if there was one scheduled. As luck would have it, I got a flight into Pittsburgh.

Kay, Clarence and Linna picked me up at the airport, and drove me back to their house, in Wexford. Most of the renovation had been completed, and there were rooms for all. Every thing was warm and cozy, and all decked out for my homecoming.

Making cottage cheese at the Dairy must have been paying well, because Sue bought herself a yellow Chevrolet Coupe, to drive to work each day. She couldn't wait to introduce me to some of her friends, and to "make the rounds" of the bars, with her.

We had a good time. I had done my own share of drinking in my time, and couldn't really condemn her for doing exactly what I did. We both loved the *camaraderie* of visiting, and actually "ministering" to our bar-fly friends, while imbibing.

After a few drinks, that's when the anger and frustration of Marie "stealing her inheritance" came up. It was difficult trying to calm her. But, after a few more drinks, she'd returned to her old fun-loving self.

A couple of nights, Sue allowed me to borrow her Chevrolet to drive myself into Pittsburgh, to see some of my old friends. That was difficult, because I had never driven in Pittsburgh before. The buses and streetcars always sufficed for me. Manipulating those hills, and cobble stone streets, and streetcar tracks was very difficult for a novice driver, but I managed.

A buddy took me to West Homestead to see Papa and Margit. She had made a very nice, comfortable home for Papa, with all new living room furniture. They seemed contented with their married life. For the first time, Papa seemed old. Margit had aged a bit, too.

Papa reminisced by telling me, again, the story of how he met Mae West, and how much he loved California. He wanted The Dummy (Margit) to go there with him. He did talk her into driving there, a year earlier, but she hated it, and refused to live there, just like Mama. So, they returned to West Homestead.

Martha, of course, was a little upset that I didn't come and stay with her. She really didn't have much room, now that she had both Marilyn, and nine month old Lizabeth, to contend with. I did stop by to see them, though. How and when, I can't remember. And, perhaps, Mame and I even went ice skating.

After the ten days vacation, it was time to return to Cherry Point. Before going on leave, there had been the "scuttlebutt" that we would be "shipping out," overseas. Those ominous words did make us all a bit uneasy. Were we going to be sent to Korea?

The rumor was true. We were about to be shipped overseas, but luckily, not to Korea. We were going to be dispatched to Puerto Rico, for "Maneuvers." For the next few weeks the base became an anthill of activity: packing, loading, and stowing all the equipment to be used in the maneuvers on the cargo ships, in Moorhead City. No more sitting around in our quanset hut, twiddling our thumbs.

Once the supply ships were laden, then we shit-birds were loaded on a troop ship, ironically called the *USS Sarasota,* and set sail for the Isle of Vieques, Puerto Rico.

It was going to be a pleasant cruise through the Caribbean Sea, with nothing to do until we got there. Not true for me. I was immediately "chosen" to be put on Mess Duty. That's the Marine equivalent of K.P.

First we had to be assigned our sleeping quarters, which were five decks below, in the aft of the ship. The racks were about two feet wide, attached to supporting poles, and stacked four high. During the day, they were folded against the poles to make more walking space. It was claustrophobic and smelly trying to sleep on those shelves at night.

After one evening in the netherworld, many of us took our slim mattresses topside and slept on deck. My friend, Tony Alderette, and I found a great spot under a life boat. Sleeping outside, with the tropical breezes blowing, was delightful.

177

Being aboard a troop ship, did have it's inconveniences. Our "head" was down in the hold, were we slept. There were no toilets, per se. Instead, there was a long trough, with five toilet seats attached. The cold sea water gushed through the conduit, while you tried to do what Nature intended. Defecating became most difficult, for most of us.

Not only did you not have any privacy, but the damned water sprayed up against your rear end, while someone's turd shot by. And, to make things more difficult, by being in the aft part of the ship, it kept rising and sinking, rising and sinking. Just when you were ready to drop "one," the ship would rise up, making it next to impossible to "drop" it down. There were scores of constipated guys aboard that ship, until we reached shore, and disembarked.

After landing, and after unloading, and setting up camp, I was, again, conscripted to be on Mess Duty. This time, I didn't mind. My group was busy unloading and belting ammunition, and making napalm bombs. That's what we were there for: pretend war games.

It was difficult getting any time off. I did manage to get one afternoon off, and went into the nearby town of Fajardo. Considering we were blowing up their entire island, the townsfolk were all very nice and friendly. Of course, we were spending the good old "Yankee dollar."

For the first time, I grew a moustache, fitting right in with all the Latinos. The black guys, in particular, loved Puerto Rico. There was no color delineation.

Some of my buddies, and I, got a daytime flight to a nearby isle, Charlotte Amalie, one of The Virgin Islands. No jokes!

While there, it was very frightening driving on the "wrong" side of the road. We took a taxi up a steep hill, to the Virgin Isle Hotel. The driver scared the Hell out of us, speeding up that mountain road, and around its treacherous bends.

When a car came in the opposite direction, we nearly had heart attacks. By driving on the left side of the road, it looked like we were about to crash into each vehicle, as it came toward us.

They treated us royally at the Virgin Isle, offering us the use of all it's facilities. They even gave us a room to change our clothes in, at no charge. What a nice day we had, acting like tourists and lolling around the pool, most of day.

When Maneuvers were over, we left Puerto Rico, and docked in Port Everglades, Florida, in May of 1953. The port was only a few miles from all the juke joints I used to frequent, while living in Ft. Lauderdale.

One of the first things I did, after getting shore leave, was to call Marie and some of my old friends: Dianne "Jet" Leone, my old cohort at the Drive-in Theater, in particular. She was, now, living with a sexy (how redundant!) French girl, named Yvette. The two of them would be my dates for the evening. Boy, was I going to strut my stuff in front of my mates.

Dianne drove me to Hendricks Island to see the family. Marie was upset, that I wasn't going to spend my first night in town with her. She was pregnant, and hadn't been getting out much, lately. I assured her that we would go clubbing the following night.

Curtis was settling in, quite nicely, in Marie's house, and taking over the disciplining of Duane and Butch. Whenever he wanted the boys, all he had to do was blow his whistle, once for Duane, twice for Butch and three times for both of them. They obeyed. I was *not* amused! Those kids were not dogs. The pregnancy had made Marie too complacent to say anything; she liked the peace and quiet, without the hassle.

The boys were a little rambunctious with me, but Curtis didn't butt in. He let them play. They wanted to know what happened to The Giant. He was back in Pittsburgh, stored in a trunk.

Dianne drove us back to her apartment and made dinner. Then, she and Yvette got all dolled up, to meet the troops. There were so many bars near Port Everglades, that no matter where we went, we'd run into my shipmates.

The first place we went to was Freddie's Anchor Inn. Corporal Nussbaum, a fat. Jovial guy, who spoke with a Yiddish accent, was there. He was inherently one of the funniest people I ever encountered. As soon as he met the girls, his eyes lit up as he grabbed the duo, to introduce to the other guys.

He asked them, in his Yiddish dialect, "Have you met Yvette and Jet, yet?"

That became the joke of the evening. We couldn't get rid of him. He followed us wherever we went, asking each guy the same thing, "Have you met Yvette and Jet, yet?"

My shipmates were amused, and amazed, at the good looking babes I was out with. The girls enjoyed the attention, too.

The next night, true to my word, hugely pregnant Marie, Curtis and I went out clubbing. Marie wanted to see all the strip joints that I used to frequent. We stopped at the Aloha Club first. They no longer did floor shows, it was now just a bar with a few "B" girls. It appeared that the Torch Club, two doors down, had almost put them out of business. That's where we went, next.

To my surprise, Mickey, the old hoofer from the Aloha, was now working at the Torch Club, as a waitress. Once in awhile, when a girl didn't show up, she'd "take 'em off," but not as often. Waiting tables was easier. She didn't have to worry about her figure so much, and made more money serving drinks.

Whatever happened to Cherie? Oh, she was working there, doing a strip, later on that evening. She was no longer with Tabu, nor Artie, for that matter. We were looking forward to seeing her. Toni Turner was still working there, and made it a point to come by to say hello, before the show. She still looked ravishing.

Being seven and a half months pregnant, Marie really should not have been drinking alcohol, but, in those days, women drank when they were expecting, no big deal. By the time the show began, she was three sheets to the wind. And, of course, when Marie got drunk. she got very demanding, and slightly obnoxious. During the first few numbers, she was fairly quiet, then all Hell broke loose.

The final dancer of the evening was Cherie. As usual, she was stoned out of her mind, only now, even worse than before. She no longer shimmied with a snake, but was doing a "comic" striptease, wearing shabby streetwalker clothes. Her makeup was clown-like, and smeared all over her face.

As her clothes came of, garment by garment, she could barely stand up. When she saw me, delightedly, she came over to our table, to dance for us. By now, she was down to two metal funnels, used as a brassiere, and big, fake cherries undulating from her crotch. Before I could stop it, she had climbed up on our table, and started to bump and grind her cherries in my face. Marie was very indignant.

"Get this creature off our table. How dare she? Who does she think she is?"

In her inebriated stupor, she pushed Cherie off the table. Luckily, I caught her before she hit the ground. It didn't phase her a bit. She thought it was hysterically funny, snickering throughout the rest of the "act."

"God have mercy on my poor crazy ass hole," she laughed. The mind and body were gone, but her sense of humor was in tact.

Marie and Straker made it to the ship, the following day, for a private tour by the Captain. She wanted me to be there, but I had had enough. I just wanted to get away from it all, so I took a bus into Miami, to spend the day there, alone.

On May 28, 1953, Betty gave birth to Samuel Bordy III in, of all places, Pittsburgh, Pennsylvania. She, Sam and Denise had temporarily moved there to manage an apartment complex that Marie had purchased. *Noblesse oblige!*

Then, on July 2, 1953, Marie gave birth to her third son, James Straker. Apparently the booze and the "gallivanting" didn't harm him, although, I wouldn't know. After all these years, I still have not met him.

Cherry Point looked the same that summer of 1953. It was like we had never left. To preserve my sanity, I had to find something else to do with my spare time. Trying to date the local girls was useless. The Marine base had been around too long, and the town's people were all leery of us.

Harvey Wexler was smart. Each Saturday, he went to the Synagogue for services and the great food that was served, afterwards. There he met some nice Jewish girls, and was, often, invited home by their families, for dinner. That pleased him. He had a nice time, and was still true to his beautiful finance, Reva.

Around this same time I had heard about a guy, living in the other wing of my barracks, they called Shakespeare. He was an actor, from Boston, who got into some kind of a trouble, for allegedly being anti-Semitic.

Captain Shapiro was not pleased, and called the actor before him. It seems that "Shakespeare" was only reciting Shylock's speech from "The Merchant of Venice:" "If you prick us, do we not bleed? . . "

It seemed that this guy was such a good actor, he had convinced his barracks mates that he was a Jew hater. Had they listened to the speech, they would have found out the opposite to be true. This guy, I just had to meet.

His name was Donald Perkins, a very well trained actor, who had been attending Emerson College, in Boston, before he got drafted. At last, a personable guy I could "talk shop" with. We became fast friends.

Don and I started running around together. He couldn't stand being cooped up in the barracks. When he was required to stay on the base, he would pace up and down the barracks and scream out, "I can't take it anymore!"

He scared the Hell out of everybody. That gave him a thrill, he loved "acting" the schizophrenic. Besides, it kept his voice, and "acting chops," in good shape.

Anytime he had liberty, out of the barracks, and out to "freedom," he would go. There really wasn't much to do outside the gates in town, other than drink beer at the one and only beer joint. At least, we were free of the confines of the base. On the base, we only had the slop-chute (tavern) to drink in. Drinks were cheap, but you were still on the base, with the M.P.s standing by.

Don had attended Emerson College for a semester and a half, before being drafted. He chattered about the wonderful times he had there, and of the exciting professors who taught there, and of the rich beautiful girls who went there.

After my release from the Corps, I had been planning on attending U.C.L.A., because they had an excellent drama department. The best part about going there was its proximity to Hollywood. There, I would be able to make the rounds, and try to get into the movies. Don insisted that I give Emerson a chance; he did make it sound enticing. I would think it over.

Summer had arrived, and the seventy two hour pass had come into exis-

181

tence. That meant that, once a month, you could take an entire weekend off, away from the base. Guys with cars immediately started posting ads, looking for passengers to share expenses to various cities. There were always rides available to New York and Philadelphia.

Perk and I decided to take one of these trips to Philadelphia, and hitch-hike from there to Atlantic City. We stayed with Ruth, Sol and Bruce. Pearl had just arrived there for her annual job at Fascination. Perk was about 5' 8" and Pearl was 5' 10". That didn't stop Don, he became enamored with her, just the same. She was very nice to him, but definitely did not lead him on. We had a grand old time, anyway, roaming the Boardwalk, playing Fascination, and looking for "cute tomatoes," girls. Good luck!

Harvey was jealous that I had invited Perk to Atlantic City, and not him. After all, he was Jewish and my sister Ruth was Jewish, they certainly would have more in common. The next month, I took him. The only trouble was that we could only get a ride to Philly, one way. We'd have to hitchhike all the way back, because our driver had a longer liberty that us. That didn't deter us. It would be an adventure. And it was.

When we got there, we played tourist by going to the Steel Pier, roaming the Boardwalk, and eating all kinds of Jewish delicacies. Again, Ruth, Pearl and Sol were all good hosts, welcoming us with open arms.

Since we didn't have a ride in Philadelphia, by looking at the map of new Jersey, we figured we could save a lot of time by hitching a ride south, to Cape May. There, we would be able to take the ferry across the Delaware River, into Delaware. We set out bright and early, figuring it would only take a few hours to get to the Cape May Ferry.

Each lift was shorter than the previous one. At first, we figured we'd get a ride all the way to the cape, with no trouble. We were mistaken. On the last leg, into Cape May, we inquired of our driver, where the Cape May Ferry was located.

He asked, "What Ferry?" The one that crosses Delaware Bay. "Oh, that hasn't been built, yet." What?!

After looking at the map closer, it read, "Prop. Ferry," proposed ferry. Oh my God, what were we going to do? Hitch all the way back up to Atlantic City, then to Philadelphia, then south to Cherry Point? We'd never get back to the base in time, and we would certainly be A.W.O.L.

Our driver informed us that there was a small airport nearby; perhaps we could hire a plane, to fly us over the inlet. But, how were we going to pay for it? We'll figure something out. Sure enough, there was an airport that had rentals. One of the pilots saw how panicky Harvey and I were, so he offered to fly us across the bay for fifteen dollars, just enough to pay for his gasoline. Whew, what a relief!

We climbed aboard his Piper Cub, and off we *flew!* Oh my God! It felt like we were a kite, being blown by the wind, up and down, and so low I could swear the water splashed up on us. It was more fun, and frightening, than the wildest roller coaster. We happily paid the fifteen dollars, and the nice guy even got someone to drive us out to the highway, where we could get a ride. We made it back to the base in time for roll call.

When the summer season was over in Atlantic City, Pearl went to Chicago with a girlfriend, to work in a Country Club. "Julie's" boyfriend, Frank, was working there as a bartender. The other bartender was his long time buddy, Larry Frazier. The four of them got along well together, dated, and stayed at the Club for almost a year.

Rumors began to abound, about the fact, that gambling would soon become legal in Miami Beach. The four of them packed up and departed for those greener pastures; the money to be made there was going to be exceptional. Unfortunately, they were not the only people to hear the rumor. Hordes of would-be workers descended on Miami.

Back at Cherry Point, a former producer/director from Connecticut, Bill Scholes, was directing a production of "You Can't Take it with You," to be seen in a make-shift theatre he had created on the base. This guy could hustle up anything. It was too late for me to get in the play, but I was looking forward to his next production.

There was talk that he might direct a musical variety show. I definitely wanted to get involved, so I offered to be his stage manager, and possible assistant director for the Revue. After all, I had worked in Burlesque! He agreed readily.

The play went okay, but Bill had bigger dreams. He wanted to produce a show in the base's huge movie theater. Being such a pushy kind of guy, he managed to get permission to do a show there.

We had open auditions for any and all talent, for our big Extravaganza.

Joe Gargulio, the Catholic Church organist and alter boy, was set to do the music, Del Lozier, a woman marine I had seen dancing in the Woman Marines' slop-chute, was set to do the choreography, Bill was to direct, and I was to be the assistant director/stage manager.

The four of us got together to create what came to be known as "Can Can U," where we would glorify the cancan, and utilize any kind of talent we could dig up. A storyline, of sorts, was evolved for Joe and a chubby woman Marine soprano, as his love interest. Joe was a married man, but that didn't stop "Sally," she *wanted* him, badly.

Quite an assortment of people showed up to audition for the show. Among them, was an elegantly dressed lady, wearing a black cocktail dress, a mink stole, a little black hat and veil, spiked high heels, and much expensive jewelry. Wow, Mrs. Rockefeller!

She proved to be the most cooperative, and talented, performer in the group. Manya was married to a Master Sergeant, and probably about thirty, a little too old for the show, perhaps, but she looked great. The other girl dancers were all relatives, or wives, of guys stationed at The Point.

The production looked like it was going to be quite spectacular. There were many professional, ex-professional, and would-be professional singers, dancers and comics, Nussbaum among them. He had never been in front of an audience, but he was such a natural talent, surely he could do a comedy stint in the show. I was wrong. He bombed.   We even had an Indian Chief, who did a Rain Dance in his dazzling tribal regalia. He bombed, too, but the costume got rave revues.

Del got cold feet and dropped out. That left me to do the choreography. My bluffing with Scholes paid off. I had never actually choreographed dance steps before, even though I did help Jet, and some of the strippers, with their routines. Now, I had to "put up," and come through.

Bill concentrated mostly on the "dramatic" part of the show: the love story between Sally and Joe. That's what he lived to do, because he was a *"Director!"* Joe was not an actor, and had enough to do just playing all the music for the show. As a result, the brunt of the staging, and choreographing, fell into my lap. That didn't bother me; I liked being in charge.

Of course, I loved working with the chorus girls. At the very first rehearsal, I started them out with the big cancan routine.

I even created lyrics to *"Gaiete Parisienne"* for the girls to speak, before the big dance number. The lyrics were dumb, but they killed a little time before the girls actually danced:

"You cancan and I cancan. Can you cancan like I cancan. You cancan and I cancan. Can you cancan like I cancan?" Brilliant!

Manya, the elegant lady, turned out to be our star. Wanting to show as much flesh as possible for the troops (because I knew that's what they wanted), I had Manya do "The Ritual Fire Dance," in a very skimpy costume, a la what I would have done for the strippers back in Florida. It was more like Salome and her seven veils, that kept coming off. She was ecstatic; her long lost dream, of becoming a star, was coming to fruition.

The "story" part of the show was dragging everything down, so I kept

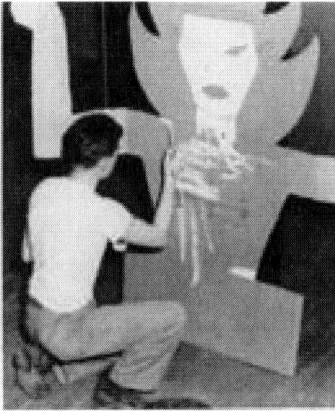

creating more and more risqué numbers. I had Manya do a jungle number, too, to "Tabu," the same music Cherie had danced to at the Aloha Club, without the boa constrictor. Finally, believe it or not, she and I did a reprise of the Apache Dance I did at Ringling Art School to "Blue Violins." She was better looking than Toby, so we played it straight.

Most of the scenery was constructed and painted by me, including a Parisian Café, and a "fire god" for Manya to dance around.

Scholes had contacts in New York and was able to procure professional costumes for the girls. The cancan costumes were the greatest! Unfortunately, the girls did not have them for the dress rehearsal; but they did arrived, just in time for the show. Luckily they fit perfectly, and our little moths turned into butterflies.

Watching the big cancan number from the wings, opening night, I was so proud of the girls. They did their little song, then went into the dance. The costumes really brought the number to life. Half way through the dance, when the girls were up stage in a line, they picked up their skirts over their heads, shook them back and forth, while they pranced all the way down stage, to the apron. The men hooted, and howled, and whistled, and stomped. What was happening? Uh, Oh!

The underwear, that the costumer sent, was made of cotton, and was a pale yellow color. The panties crept up, into the girls' private parts, as they danced. Shocking! I knew what the guys were howling at, but I didn't dare tell the girls, until after the final performance.

The first night's spectacle went very well, except for the little "acting bits." Joe was a terrible actor and knew it; he refused to "act" in the second

185

presentation. That was the best thing for the show. Without the maudlin story, the show was a smash, especially the cancan girls.

The Apache dance went exceedingly well. This time, I smoked a cigarette, under the streetlamp, before throwing my partner to the floor. After the final show, a bunch of Women Marines came backstage to tell me how sexy I was. One in particular caught my fancy. She looked like a chubby Betty Grable. It was very difficult getting a date with any of the W.M.s, but now I had an opening. "Betty" agreed to meet me the next night.

Don Perkins wouldn't be in the show because he and Scholes didn't get along. It was too bad, because I found out later what a talented singer and comic he was. From time to time, he did come to a few rehearsals and got to know the girls pretty well, so they invited him to the cast party at Manya's house.

He was short, but that didn't hinder him at all. With any girl, he was a giant! Actually, they liked to baby him because he was so "cute."

My chorus girls had a great laugh, when they learned about the revealing costumes. One or two of them couldn't quite understand, exactly, what it was that the guys were hooting about. It was just as well they remained naïve.

We danced the night away. Hostess Manya was in her glory, having done two solo dances, an Apache dance with me, and been a cancan girl. She was exhausted.

The next evening, I had my hot date with that Woman Marine who loved my Apache dance. We went to the W.M.'s slop-chute (canteen), to drink beer and dance. No man got into the women's slop-chute without a W.M. Del had invited me several times before, but this was my first actual date, there.

"Betty" was rather pretty, but not the brightest bulb on the tree. I flattered her, telling her how attractive I thought she was. After every compliment, she would say to me, "Oh, Bill, you're such a phony."

What the Hell was she talking about? Everything I said to her, I meant. The third time she called me a phony, I decided to *be* a phony, handing her the biggest rash of bullshit I could come up with. She melted.

The autumn air was turning chilly, so on our way back to the women's barracks, we snuggled close together. When we arrived at the entrance, she turned to me and said, "Bill, I take it all back. You're definitely not a phony, and if I wasn't getting a Bad Conduct Discharge tomorrow, I think we could make a go of it."

What? That floored me! She not only believed the crap I spewed, but she would have continued the relationship, had she not been getting a bad conduct discharge.

What had she done to be relieved of duty? She didn't tell me. In reality,

I was glad she was leaving the next day; who needed a nutcase like her?

After we arrived at her barracks, we kissed goodbye, and I tasted something salty on my lips. When I looked at her, snot was running out of her nose, down her lips. And, I had just gotten a mouthful. Ugh!

Christmas of 1953 was to be spent in Pittsburgh. It was great being home for the holidays. Kay had "decked her halls with ivy," and her house was, as usual, warm and cozy and welcoming to me.

More and more I started wearing civilian clothes that I had bought at the P.X. It really had quite an assortment of things to buy, and at reduced prices, so I brought my "civies" with me. My hair was a little longer than regulation, as well. I was getting ready for my release in five months.

Kay, and Clarence, and Sue pulled out all the stops for the Christmas feast. Sue (or was it Clarence) went to pick up Papa and Margit for the occasion. They enjoyed the holiday celebration, as well.

One night, Sue and I made the rounds of her bars, like we had done before. She was still angry about her inheritance. I let her drive, not being accustomed to the icy roads of Pittsburgh. With her behind the wheel, the car practically drove itself.

It was too cold to go anywhere, so much of my time was spent at Kay's, getting to know my little niece better. Linna was the perfect hostess, catering to my every wish and whim. Playing "little mother," cleaning and sewing, vacuuming, and taking care of her little "baby," was her joy. She was a mini Kay, keeping the house in order, and seeming to love it.

Martha was anxious to show off Liz. She had grown quite a bit since the year before, and was now walking and talking. Martha insisted that I spend half of my leave with them. Why not?

Even though it was still cramped, I stayed in her sewing room. This time, sleep came easier. She and Joe must have exhausted themselves caring for two girls, a rabbit, a cat, and a business.

187

There was to be a Christmas Day parade, up on Wilkinsburg Avenue, that Joe wanted Liz to see. She was as cute as a button in her little, red snow suit, with the pointed hood. Her cherubic, pouting lips, and chubby cheeks were cherry red, from the cold. Joe strutted up and down the sidewalk, showing off his petite pixie.

She turned many heads, of many people, who stopped to admire her, and tell her "grandfather" what a cute kid she was. Joe got a kick out of it, and proudly announced that he was not the grandfather, but the father! As he told many of them, "There may be snow on the roof, but there's still fire in the grates."

He, also, taught her how to swear. In front of people, he's nudge her, and she'd respond with, "Son-of-a-bitch" or "God damn it to Hell." She had no idea what she was saying, but Joe was extremely tickled, watching the reactions of the passersby.

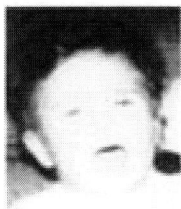

Marilyn no longer went to boarding school. She was a freshman at Edgewood High School. Most of her time was spent in her room, reading and rocking in her bed; she was so introverted, doing her living in her books. We didn't go ice skating this time; she thought that she had "outgrown" that pastime.

Back in Atlantic City, on January 7, 1954, Ruth gave birth to her second son, Robert. No one even knew that she was pregnant. Now, Bruce had a brother to take care of, and play with.

The days at Cherry Point were numbered. Almost immediately, M.A.M.S. 14 was transferred to the Auxiliary Landing Field in Edenton, North Carolina. No longer did I work in a quanset hut, they put me in an office building, with a lot of other "office pinkies," in something called Aviation Ordnance Group Supply. I came to be "handling" millions of dollars worth of government parts and equipments.

My commanding officer, Major Hughes, was in a turmoil, as were Captain Shapiro and all the other officers. No one new what the Hell they were doing. Whenever you asked a senior N.C.O. how to do something, the standard reply was to "fake it." So, I faked it, and apparently, I faked it well.

Soon, I was the "expert," that everyone came to rely on, when they needed an answer. Could I "fake it," until my release in May?

The only good thing, that came out of my new position was that I was finally promoted to the rank of Corporal, on November 1st, the day before my twenty-third birthday. After that, the Captain and the Major tried to get me promoted to Sergeant, but no dice! They recommended me for several "meritorious" promotions, but they were both turned down, even though I was doing the work of a Master Sergeant, a Buck Sergeant and a Private. Ranks had been "frozen." No one was getting promoted.

The gambling initiative in Florida did not pass. Work was next to impossible to get. Larry managed to get a job washing the windows of skyscrapers. Pearl succeeded in getting a job as a waitress, with no pay, only tips. Money was needed desperately, so she took the position. That's how tough it was to find work.

Frank and Julie skipped town, owing the hotel for back rent. The hotel owner was sympathetic and only charged Pearl and Larry for their half share, in each room. The two of them struggled to survive. When they had enough money, Larry returned to Chicago, then later Pearl. Apparently, the struggle only brought them closer together and, soon, they would marry.

M.A.M.S. 14 was transferred to the Edenton Auxiliary Landing Field, North Carolina. Our five months there went quickly. The Korean Conflict was over, so we no longer had to worry about fighting the war.

Edenton was a much smaller base than Cherry Point and there was much more to do in town. Elizabeth City was about twenty miles away, and Virginia Beach and Norfolk were only about an hour or so away, so there were plenty of places to go on liberty.

In downtown Edenton, there was a little café called The Busy Bee, where you could get a bite to eat and try to pick up a local girl. It was easier there, because the town had not been overrun by Marines.

One night, with the aid of my new North Carolina buddy, Joe Gamble, we picked up two girls, there. He had a car, and promised them we'd get a bottle of White Lightning, and go on a typical North Carolina date: that was drinking the bootleg whiskey, stopping to knock of a little, drive some more, drink some more, and knock off a little more. Oh, that's how they do it in the South.

Joe was smart. He didn't go for the young, cute things; he preferred something a little more "ripe," someone who would be a little more appreciative of his "charms." It worked for him. He got the action; I got the cute little thing, and *no* action!

It was from my "cute little thing" that I learned my two favorite southern phrases, spoken in a drawn out accent, of course: "Do Whaaaat" and "Waan'to?" To which I would respond, "three, four." It went right over her head. She was pretty, not clever.

On that particular date, Joe got pretty smashed and almost drove off the road, several times. It didn't phase him at all; he was having a blast. He noticed a group of our buddies, who needed a lift back to the base, so he picked them up and squeezed them all into the car. Finally, I got "Waan'to" to sit on my lap, while the five other guys squeezed in. We were all scared shitless with Joe's maniacal driving.

After dropping them off at the base, Joe, "The Ripe One," "Waan'to,"

189

and I drove back to town and dropped them off. By then it was daylight, so we hurriedly drove back to the base, hoping to make it in time for roll call. We made it.

Shortly, after we were transferred to Edenton, Don Perkins got his release, and made it back to Boston in time to attend the second semester, at Emerson College. He sent me all the information I would need to enroll, being that sure I would attend. He was right. In September of 1954, I became a student at Emerson, too.

On weekends, some of my buddies and I would go to Virginia Beach to bake in the sun, or to Norfolk to sweat in the bars. I met a sympathetic B-girl there; she liked me, and didn't hustle me for drinks. We made a date to do nice "normal" things, like taking her little boy out, for the day.

We even went to the movies to see "Miss Sadie Thompson." When the Reverend called Sadie a prostitute, we both cringed. It must of hit home, because she quit the B-girl business, that night.

Elizabeth City was the best place to go on liberty. There was an actual night club there that was frequented by local girls, and it had a dance floor. No alcohol was served, but you where allowed to bring in your own bottle of booze, set it on the table, and just pay for your "set-ups," which was the ice and chasers.

Another buddy, Bob Ennis, and I hitchhiked several times to the club, to dance with the girls. He was a rather hot tempered guy, whose attitude always got him into trouble. The last night we went out, he was wearing Sergeant stripes on his blouse and P.F.C. stripes on his shirt. He had actually been "busted" down to being a Private.

Desperately, he was trying to pick up one of the girls, who wanted nothing to do with him. The more he pursued her, and was rejected, the more he drank. At closing time, as we were getting ready to leave, he turned around and approached the girl, one last time. After her final turn down, he loudly barked, "Well, kiss my money making ass!"

The Shore Patrol guys approached him, and asked, "What did you say, Marine? What did you say?"

Bob hauled off and slugged the first guy. The other S.P. then hit him over the head with a club and arrested him. They dragged him out of the bar as he was screaming at the top of his lungs, "Let me go, you Mother F#%ers. Kiss my money makin' ass!"

When I went to visit him in the brig, he was not in the least repentant, just ecstatic about the "great time" we had that night. It seemed that he was actually happy being in the brig, but was anxious to get out so we could go out on the town, again. No way!

Upon my release on May 7, 1954, I went directly to Atlantic City. Pearl was not going to make it that season, because she and her new husband, Larry Frazier, were back working at the Country Club, in Chicago.

Marie's new baby turned out to be a blond. His brothers were as impish as ever, especially Butch, but that did not keep either him or Duane from responding to Curtis's bell ringing. Pavlov would have been proud.

Martha and Joe's business was beginning to flounder. Marilyn was now going to Edgewood High School. Liz was as spunky, and shocking, as ever. In California, Ed started to build his boat, L'il Toot. It would take a few years to complete.

FREEDOM
BY THE SEA AND IN BEACON HILL
CHAPTER TWELVE

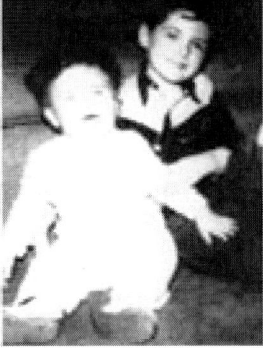

Returning to Atlantic City was a joy, especially as a civilian. When I visited there the previous summer, Sol had offered me "half a hundred" a week, to work for him at Fascination. He promised, that after I was broken in, I would become a Mike-Man, the guy who hustles customers into the store.

371 North Richmond was beginning to look like home, as it would for many summers to come. Brucie was as devilish as ever, but was enjoying his new brother, Bobby, who was just learning to sit up, with Brucie's help, of course. He was such a happy, cheerful baby.

After arriving, I was anxious to learn the workings of Fascination, so Sol took me up to the Boardwalk to show me the ropes. He introduced me to Joe "Smitty" Carceranno, the day manager, a very conscientious worker, who loved Fascination even more than his home. His only problem was that he was a terrible "Mike-Man." He screamed into the microphone, and his "pitch" was boring and unintelligible. But, he was reliable, and always showed up to open the place in the morning. Often, he even helped to close the place at night.

The Season hadn't quite begun, so Smitty handled the Mike and the "checking" by himself. I was to work with him as the checker, counting the heads of the players. That is what Pearl had done the previous two years, and I was to replace her.

As well as checking, I was to give breaks to the boys who collect the money. Then, whenever Smitty needed a break, I would be able to relieve him on the microphone. That is what I was looking forward to doing, "pitching" the game. The trouble was, he never took a break.

Toward the rear of "The Store," in the center, was the elevated Mike-Box where the Mike-Man spieled, and the checker added up the players, on

a specially made NCR cash register.

There were twenty four tables on each side of the store, with six behind the Mike-Box. That's where the players sat, and rolled their ball, trying to score a bingo.

It cost ten cents to play, and the winner of each game received a minimum of one dollar, in cash. That was exciting for the players, to be paid off in cash, not coupons. Of course, we also paid off the "powers that be," for that privilege.

Every now and then, the "heat" would be on, and we would have to pay the winners with coupons. For our steady customers, we would cash them in later for money. Many people did prefer to use their coupons for merchandise, instead. Ruth always did a great job of "flashing" the show cases, with expensive looking prizes.

Because Ruth worked the night shift, she had her days free to take care of the house, yard and kids. She was a dynamo, and never stopped moving, until her shift at "Fasc" was over.

That's when she and Sol, sometimes, found time to stop for a drink, or see a late show. Ruth had Sol take me around town to show me the local joints he used to hang out in, when he was single. Over the summer, they became my hangouts, as well.

Part of my new job was to stay at home with the boys, in the evening. They were fun, so I didn't mind. Beside, I had lots of experience taking care of little boys in Florida. So Brucie and Bobby became my surrogate Duane and Butch.

On the Fourth of July weekend, the season really got underway. Ruth worked full time on the night shift as the checker. Mike was our crackerjack Mike-Man, whom I would soon emulate. When he got on the microphone, he talked non stop, hustling in the customers.

That's what our owner, Herman Rapp, wanted. If anyone was sitting on the benches in front of the store, the constant nattering would either move them on their way, or they'd come in to see what all the excitement was about.

Mike made it sound terribly exciting with his enthusiastic patter. Here is part of the spiel, that he, and later I, pitched to the passersby:

*"This is it people. This is what you're looking for. This is Fascination! The fastest game on the Boardwalk. Walk right in. That's right lady, it's just like Bingo, Bango, Bongo, Lotto — all those other five in a row games, only no cards, no chips, no numbers — just lights and **balls**! All you do is grab a seat, sit down, put your money up on the glass in front of you (the boys behind the tables will make change for you) and pick up your ball, for the next game.*

"Now, when you hear the bell ring, this game ends, and we announce the winner. When the next bell rings, pick up your ball, roll it under the glass, over the hump and into the pockets. The corresponding light on the board will light, the ball returns to you, you pick it up and you roll it, again.

"Keep that ball rolling, until one of the players wins the game, by lighting five

193

lights in a row, any row, vertically, horizontally, or diagonally — that's top to bottom, side to side, or corner to corner, five lights in any straight line, and you win. Easy to play, easy to win, walk right in."

Business was slow my first month in Atlantic City, so I had lots of free time to roam up and down the Boardwalk. I enjoyed the other pitchmen and studied their technique. Ed McMahon was there, my first summer, and was very adept at pitching kitchen gadgets. Those slicers, dicers and juicers, are still being pitched on television.

Closer to Fasc, almost in front of the Steel Pier, was a lady named Josie, who pitched a lanolin product for the hair. Her son was a "mechanical man" who robotically performed in front of her portico, to entice the tourists into their store. They were both terrific entertainers.

In the shop, directly next door to Fasc, was a beautiful model named Virginia. She demonstrated her little tube-like blouse in the store window, by twisting and turning, and moving parts of that tube, into fabulous fashions.

She never ceased to fascinate me with her contortions. On all my breaks, I watched her, giving her the "eye." That made her very nervous, and she would falter in her pitch, blushing. Naturally, we began dating.

Even though I was making fairly good money, she was no "cheap" date. She drank Pinch Bottle scotch, probably the most expensive scotch there was. Luckily, she usually nursed one drink, all night.

During the day, I sat up on the Mike-Box, staring at the Atlantic Ocean and The Steel Pier, while "checking" and "pitching" the game whenever Smitty would let me. It was almost impossible to pry him away from that microphone. He was such Mike-Hog.

At least, the view was nice, watching the waves roll in and out, as well as the amusing assortment of sightseers.

Pearl had married Larry Frazier on July 10, 1954 but it didn't last long. Out of the blue, she returned to Atlantic City wanting her old job back. There had been a fight with Larry, so she packed up her belongings and left him at the Country Club, in Chicago. I was a little pissed because her job had become my job, and I was getting to be pretty proficient at it. Now, I was going to loose it.

Actually, it all worked out pretty well. By her working her old day shift with Smitty, my schedule could be flexible. I was able to work days or nights, whenever and wherever I was needed. Initially, that meant that, mostly, I would be working in the "pit." That was the space behind the tables where the boys ran in and out, down the line, collecting the money for the games.

Then, occasionally, I was allowed to talk on the microphone and operate the game. As the summer progressed, I got more and more adept at spieling, and everyone settled into their own work routine. I was back in Show Business, "Barking on the Boardwalk."

Mike, the Mike-Man, was a school teacher in Philadelphia, and wanted only to work weekends. That suited me fine. After not too long, I became the full time night Mike-Man, and a kind of minor celebrity. That's when lots of girls started to come in to play, and to flirt.

Connie Sax was a cute, fat blonde waitress who began stopping in every night after work. She would walk up to the Mike-Box, throw a white paper bag down in front of me, and sit at one of the tables to play and talk to me. The bag usually contained a ham and Swiss cheese sandwich, loaded with mayonnaise, and with a big Kosher pickle, on the side.

She wasn't really my type, but she was persistent in her pursuing. When she didn't bring a sandwich, we would go to Stanley's Restaurant, on Atlantic Avenue, for a nosh, even if I had a date with Joan de Windemere. She was a pushy broad! We became very good friends, and that friendship lasted all her life, until her death in 1998.

One afternoon, there was a knock at the front screen door. I was home alone with Bruce and Bobby. Standing there was this most forlorn guy, looking as if he had lost his best friend. He had. He was Pearl's husband, Larry Frazier. Hesitantly, he asked, "Is Pearl here?" Then he told me who he was.

Feeling so sorry for him, I asked him in, and called Pearl at work. She instructed me to entertain him until she got home, she would leave early. They kissed and made up, and he stayed. So, we had a built in baby sitter for the rest of the summer.

He thought nothing of changing Bobby's diapers, actually enjoying it after a while.

The Honeymoon continued. One night, the three of us went out to see Sarah Vaughn at Ben Coty's Dude Ranch Nightclub, on the Boardwalk. This was the same nightclub Suzie had visited with her "friends."

After the summer, Pearl and Larry went to California to seek their fortune. Once they saved up enough money, they were planning on opening up their own bar.

Sol was a compulsive gambler, so we seldom saw him at Fasc. He always seemed to be somewhere else, doing what gamblers do, in that *demi-monde* of wagering. At closing time, however, he always returned in time to count up the money. Ruth usually stayed with him, rolling up the coins, and helping him count.

Betting on the baseball games was one of his favorite pastimes, next to finding time to pitch the ball to Brucie while little Bobby gleefully looked on. The three of them seemed to enjoy that little amusement.

EMERSON COLLEGE

Don Perkins picked me up at the train station and invited me to spend that first night with his family, in Revere Beach. The next day, he personally took me to Emerson College. There it stood, at the corner of Berkeley and Beacon Streets. It consisted of three old, five story mansions, standing side by side. Like Ringling Art School, I was initially disappointed. Is that all there was?

The boys dormitory was directly across Beacon Street, which made it very convenient to get to classes. Because all Freshmen were required to live in the dorm, that is where I dropped off my bags. There were two double decked beds in my room, almost like my cubical in the Corps, except the room was much larger, and we had our own private bathroom, with a huge tub.

My new roommates hadn't arrived, so Don and I crossed the street and he gave me my initial tour of the campus. We walked up four flights of stairs, where he showed me the well-equipped WERS-FM Radio Studio. On the fifth floor, he showed me the library. On another floor was a meager, closed-circuit Television Studio.

We descended the stairs to the basement, where there was a small café and a book store. Then we walked through the labyrinth of corridors, past the makeup and dressing rooms, and onto a platform, that overlooked a fairly large room, filled with chairs.

"When are we going to see the theatre?" I asked.

"This is it. You're standing on the stage, right now."

This three foot elevation, that overlooked a roomful of chairs, was the stage? And, that room full of chairs was the theatre? Yes, it was. The auditorium was the old carriage house, located in the rear of 130 Beacon. Despite its size, the productions that were performed on that stage, were astonishing.

Don, later that year, would play Romeo on that platform, and the following year, Hamlet. I never knew what a great actor my old Marine Corps buddy really was until I saw him in action. He portrayed every kind of character you could think of, and excelled with all of them.

Even when he played a minor part in "Mourning Becomes Electra," he stole the show by singing the old folk song "Shenandoah." As a matter of fact, by the end of that year, he and I were chorus boys, singing and dancing, in "Finian's Rainbow."

Later, in his career, he made a good living playing Tevya in "Fiddler on the Roof," and John Adams in "1776," touring with many companies, across America.

Later that day, I met my new roommates, Ron Bagley, Bernie Gregoire and Ken Saunders. I felt like an old man next to these kids. Our room would become the meeting place for all the "adolescents" in the dorm. The bathroom had an entrance, from the back staircase. It seemed that, any time I took a bath, there was some kind of activity going on in our room. Naturally, everyone used the bathroom entrance, making snide remarks as they passed me, lounging in the tub.

During that first week of indoctrination, at Emerson, there was a special get together at the girls dormitory for the new students. Don introduced me around to all his girlfriends, ex-girlfriends, and wanna-be girlfriends. They all adored him.

At the top of the staircase, I espied a tall, beautiful blonde, with long, flowing hair, wearing a skin tight black dress, and showing much cleavage. She would have fit in perfectly as one of the performers at the Torch Club in Ft. Lauderdale. I gawked as she started to slink down the stairs.

Disbelieving what I was seeing, I said to Don, "Oh, my God! What in Hell is *that?*"

"Oh, that's Nan Hellegers. Do you want to meet her?" Of course, I did! She descended the staircase in front of us, in all her sensual glory. Perk winked at me and said to her, "Hey, Nannette, I want you to meet a buddy of mine from the Marine Corps." Before she had a chance to say a word, he continued with, "Oh Nan, by the way, my back is killing me, how about a massage?"

Instead of the caustic response I had expected from this explicit question, with great distress, she responded in the most angelic voice you could imagine, "Oh Don, I'd be happy to massage your back. Is it giving you trouble? Are you in much pain?"

She was genuinely concerned for his wellbeing, never picking up on his lewd intention. Was this girl for real? How could anyone look so blatantly sexual and act like the Virgin Mary?

This was no act. After all these years, we are still good friends. She remains the same person she was, those many years ago, almost *too* good for the world around her.

When I was still in the Corps, I told myself that when I got out, I would find myself a nice wife and settle down. During the second night's gathering, I thought I had found her. She was a thin, blonde wistful girl of eighteen, wearing a grey, full skirted jumper, with a demure white blouse.

Her name was Barbara Dow.

There was so much activity going on that evening, that every time I tried to get close enough to introduce myself, there was an interruption of some sort. I did, however, manage to observe her from across the crowded room. I felt like Emile de Becque in "South Pacific."

Because she lived in Newton, and had to take the subway to school each day, it took a few days before I actually tracked her down. When we finally met, she was as sweet as she looked. What a perfect wife she would make.

We were completely compatible. For our first year at Emerson, we had many of the same classes and were inseparable. We never tired of talking to each other, and visiting, every chance we could. Evenings, of course, she returned to her house in Newton, where she still lives.

The Drama teacher, Leo Nickole, noticed our blossoming friendship and cast the two of us as the lead characters in William Saroyan's one act play, "Hello Out There." She was exceptionally good, playing the lonely, scullery maid in a Salinas jail, while I played the inmate who tries to "con" her. We were a good team and acted well together.

Before the year was over, everyone started to ask when we were getting married. Our togetherness had been noticed by all. We were embarrassed and started seeing less of each other. For the following three years, we stayed friends, but went our own separate ways. Both of us had many other roads to traverse.

She was/is one of the sweetest and nicest people I had ever met, and as much as I loved her, that little "amorous spark" was missing. We are still friends.

That "amorous spark" came a week later. At a school luncheon, I met Helen Teitelbaum. She was quite voluptuous and wore a tight, black angora sweater, with skin tight, black toreador pants. Her coal black hair was pulled back into a pony tail.

I gawked as she went undulating around the room, greeting old friends and laughing irresistibly. I've never seen anyone move like her, except maybe, Marilyn Monroe. Bingo!

We had a tempestuous friendship during our time at Emerson. It was one of those can't live with, and can't live without relationships.

She was very popular and dated many guys, especially those rich ones from MIT, or Harvard, too much competition for me. However, any time there was a party that we both attended, we were immediately in each others arms. We started to look forward to the weekend parties, even though, we both remained "free agents."

Her talent was immense. She was not only an incomparable comedienne, she wrote comedic plays, as well. One of her short farces was called, "English, Sminglish," which I directed. Another was called "Run-ins to Oblivion," a satire on the Actors' Studio, in which I played the mad acting coach.

After seeing the movie, "The Barefoot Contessa," she imitated Ava Gardner doing her sensuous bolero. She did it satirically, but was actually very good and was very sexy, despite herself. That's when I gave her the nickname of Contessa. Once, I had told her that I was a Hungarian *Baro*, so she called me Baron. She still does.

Classes barely began when I got a call from Ruth. Sol was found dead, in his car, with a bullet in his head. She was distressed and begged me to come to her Mother-in-law's home in Seagate, New York, where she was staying. I arrived late that evening.

As is the Jewish tradition, all the mirrors were covered with sheets, no one wore shoes, and everyone was sitting on small, wooden stools, except for Minnie Mintz, Ruth's Mother-in-law. She didn't endure strife very well, so she sat on the sofa. Ruth was almost somnambulistic, but was glad to see me.

The funeral was to be held the next day, so I tried getting some sleep on a cot in the cellar. It was dark and creepy down there, and I swear, Sol's ghost was roaming around, trying to tell me what had happened to him. I was too scared to listen. His spirit hung around for years, before it left.

The next day, we went to the funeral home. Sol's dad, Irving Mintz, and his brother, Al, tried to console the inconsolable Minnie. When they took her to view the body, she broke down, crying about how could he do this terrible thing to her? Ruth and I avoided going to the coffin for as long as we could. Neither of us, really, wanted to look at a corpse.

Luckily, she was "out of it" during most of the afternoon. I sat with my arm around her the entire time, while people came up to her with their condolences, which she barely acknowledged.

Martha arrived, making a grand entrance. She was wearing a too tight, two piece turquoise suit, and a Peter Pan hat, with a long feather sprouting from it. All the men, young and old alike, gaped and gasped. Like Marie, she could captivate an entire room when she walked into it. She strode directly over to Ruth with her arm outstretched, "Oh, Ruthie, you poor baby. You look like shit. Let's get the Hell out of here and get a drink."

Ruth relaxed and almost laughed. "Oh, Martha, It's so good to see you."

Martha insisted on going for that drink, but Ruth explained it just wouldn't be "kosher" to leave until the services were over. Then a blathering, bumptious Yenta came up to Ruth, trying to console her.

"Now, Mrs. Mintz, I know it's difficult for you, but it's time to pay your respects to your husband. The widow *must* view the body."

Resignedly, with my help, Ruth struggled to her feet, as Martha and I walked her to the coffin. Again, I felt that Sol was not in that coffin, but standing behind us, pleading. The Yenta followed us and spoke, "Didn't the undertaker do a beautiful job? Why, you can't even see the bullet hole."

With that, Ruth fainted and collapsed to the floor. Her brother-in-law, Alan, snapped smelling salts under her nose, to revive her. Now, Ruth was mad. "Keep that God damned schmuck away from me," she ordered. We did. Alan apologized and swept the schmuck away.

The religious services were done beautifully and in very good taste. The Rabbi gave an inspiring eulogy that ended with, ". . . After all, what is life? Life is but a dream that ends when we awake."

That impressed me so much, that it inspired me to write a one act play about the funeral called, "When We Awake." It was presented at Emerson the following year. Barbara Dow played the mourning wife, and was marvelous.

After we returned to Minnie's house, it was required for all family members to "sit shiva:" that's seven days of mourning, where family members are required to sit on low stools, and not work, not bathe, nor shave. Of course, Minnie sat on the sofa, but Ruth insisted on the wooden stool. She followed all the rules, and proved to be a good Jew.

Bobby was just learning to walk and kept everyone entertained by scampering all over the downstairs, going from one person to the next, happily smiling at everyone. Even Minnie was amused. She declared, "Thank God, he's here. I don't know what we'd do without him." He *was* cute and funny.

After returning to Emerson, I had to buckle down and commence my studies. My favorite teacher was June Mitchell who taught P.O.E. (Principles of Oral Expression). She really brought out the "ham" in me. I was a Broadcasting Major, figuring that's really where my talent lay. June encouraged me to "act," and to join her Choric Speech Choir, where she gave me featured parts to play. As a result of her encouragement, I got to be in many theatrical productions at Emerson.

Because I was a friend of Perk's, Gertrude Binley Kay, the head of the Drama department, gave me a few small parts, throughout the year. Leo Nickole, was her assistant who just got out of the service, too. He would be directing the big musical at the end of the year, which we were all looking forward to auditioning for.

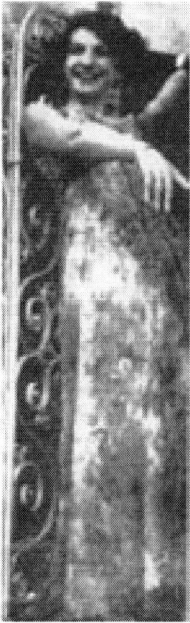

There was a phantasmagoria of new students to meet and befriend. Halfway through the year, I was "accosted" by Toby Seymour, a tall, lanky, exuberant Sophomore, who just "latched onto" me, one day, and started talking non-stop. Initially, she irritated the Hell out of me, but after a while, I got used to her, and she proved to be quite interesting.

Toward the end of the second semester, Toby wanted to audition for the part of the sexy sharecropper, who sings "Necessity," in the Musical Comedy, "Finian's Rainbow." She was very insecure about doing it, but I worked with her to get the number down pat.

At her audition, she brought the house down. That tall, lanky lassie loomed over the audience, as she slinked, and slithered, and slid all over that stage, her long arms extended and undulating. Boy, could she move! The part was hers.

She lived in a small mansion in Newtonville, about two miles from Barbara Dow. I was invited there for a nice Armenian dinner of stuffed grape leaves. Her charming mother was a delightful hostess, preparing and serving the tasty, exotic morsels. Mr. Seymour was a quiet man, who owned the Seymour Ice Cream Company. A good supply of all their flavors was kept in the cellar freezer.

Toby dragged me to the theatre to see "The World of Suzie Wong," with France Nguyen. "I don't like the stage, I like the movies," I had told her. She insisted that I accompany her, and I was captivated by the amazing stagecraft of the production. Maybe, The Theatre wasn't so bad, after all.

Sitting in the second balcony, in the cheap seats, we saw many new shows before they opened on Broadway. Of all the shows we saw, my favorite was Frank Loesser's, "The Most Happy Fella," with Robert Weede.

The music was so impressive and memorable that I came out of the theatre able to sing every song from the show. That came in handy, several years later, when without any rehearsal, I replaced a chorus member in a production of the show at the El Capitan Theater, in Hollywood.

One semester of living in the dorm was enough for me. When it was over, I moved down the street to the fifth floor of 137 Beacon Street, to share a room with a brooding Mike Bruder. He looked like a bigger, huskier version of Marlon Brando, and he played that part to the hilt. The girls fawned all over him, but he was determined to stay a virgin until he got married.

"Jeanie" was enamored with him, and tried relentlessly to make him succumb to her charms. He fought her off like the plague, even though he was, really, smitten with her.

One weekend, when he went home to see his family, Jeanie came by to visit, bringing a gallon of red wine. We started drinking and lost the entire weekend. After several weekends like that, the two of us started feeling a little guilty, so she stopped coming around. She went away and stayed away. I missed her, Mike didn't.

That first year at Emerson was an eventful one. It started out with me becoming a member if June Mitchell's Choric Speech Group, with Barbara Dow, Nannette Hellegers and Helen Teitelbaum.

We were a regular choir except that we spoke the words, rather than singing them. Nan played the mother in "Amahl and the Night Visitors," and Helen played "Gerald McBoing-Boing," while I played the bass/base parts.

Later in the year, I managed to become a Disc Jockey, with a classical music show, on WERS-FM, because I could pronounce the names of the composers.

Acting-wise, for the Hillel Club, at Boston University, I played a Rumanian Count of no account, in their production of "Watch on the Rhine;" for Easter, I played Judas Iscariot in "The Christus," Boston's annual Passion Play; at Emerson, I appeared in "Romeo and Juliet" and "Finian's Rainbow," with Don Perkins, plus a few other things. Not bad for a novice actor.

THE RETURN TO RICHMOND AVENUE

The winter in Atlantic City had been difficult. When spring came around, Ruth was still not quite over the tragedy. The Season was approaching, so it was time for her to get her mind off her troubles and go back to work. Fascination needed a good cleaning, and the new merchandise had to be ordered, unpacked, and "flashed" in the showcases. Ruth was always happiest when she was working.

Knowing she would need help for the summer rat race, she hired a Hungarian lady named Mrs. Csere to take care of the boys, and to do light house cleaning and cooking. Brucie intimidated her and gave her a hard time. Bobby was no problem.

On March 22, 1955 Daniel Schotter was born. Once he was old enough to travel, Kay,

Clarence, Linna and he came to Atlantic City for a visit. Bobby enjoyed having a new cousin to play with.

Because Smitty had been at Fascination for so long, Herman Rapp made him "The Manager." Joe really had no idea what that entailed, so Ruth "took over." He was a complacent follower, and didn't mind Ruth running the place, so long as he had the title of Manager.

They worked the night shift, and I was made the day manager, opening the place at ten in the morning, pitching, checking, and running the joint. That only lasted one season because Smitty, who was not a night person, preferred working days. So the following year, we switched. That actually suited me better, because I became the main Mike-Man, working the busy evening shift. Bigger audience!

Smitty stopped by each evening, to strut around, "acting" the part of the Manager and keeping an "eye" on the place. He was very conscientious, felt fatherly toward Ruth, and wanted to be there if she needed him. After a while, she ordered him to "stay the "Hell home," she didn't need him there. He acquiesced.

Pearl didn't return to Atlantic City that summer of 1955. She stayed in California where she and Larry began settling into their new life in La La Land. Virginia never returned to sell blouses, either.

There were new fields to conquer! Barking on the microphone became old hat, and easier and easier to do. My mouth operated on a kind of auto-pilot.

Connie continued bringing me sandwiches, and would drag me out on the Boardwalk to visit during my breaks. She got fatter and fatter, but that never got in her way of having many boyfriends.

Sam Segal, one of our steady players, started pursuing her, and soon asked her to marry him. She was tired of running around, and figured, why not?

He was fat, and she was fat. When they stood facing each other, it reminded me of the cartoon where an Indian Brave, with a sizable pot gut, faces his big bellied Squaw, and says, "How!" I kidded the two of them, mercilessly. Their marriage didn't last long.

Once a suitable time passed, Ruth began to stop by at the Virginia Bar for a drink, after work, and soon started dating John Heaton, one of the owners. She kind of liked his partner, Paul Swetkoff, as well, but he was married, and too interested in all the other lady customers, flirting with them outrageously.

The following summer, Martha allowed Marilyn to come to work in Atlantic City. She had just turned sixteen, and Ruth thought it was time for her to get away from her sheltered life in Pittsburgh. Ruth got her a job at Irene's Gift Shop, on the Boardwalk, selling *chachkas*. Because she had read so many books, Marilyn thought that she was smarter than everyone, and was quite condescending to most people whom she considered her inferior. Boy, did she have a lot to learn! Ruth and I, both, gave her a figurative kick in the butt to knock her off her high horse.

After working a few weeks selling junky souvenirs, and having to be courteous to customers, she soon descended from her lofty cloud, and came down to earth. Even though she was learning how to be polite to the public, in general, she was still a little snooty, and snotty, with me. It was difficult for her to "warm up."

One evening, however, she surprised me. Brucie, Bobby and I were sitting on the sofa, watching television, when elatedly and excitedly, she burst through the front door.

"Oh, Uncle William, Uncle William. You'll never guess what just happened. Some man tried to pick me up."

You would have thought she won the Miss America Pageant. Never before had I ever seen her so animated. She was actually thrilled that some schmuck followed her through the neighborhood, in his car, trying to entice her inside. Fortunately, she reached the house before he could entrap her.

At the end of the 1956 season, the politicians began a crackdown on all gambling. No one was aloud to "win" anything, in Atlantic City. Thus, we had to play the game "for amusement only." Customers didn't like that, but those were the rules we had to abide by. The thrill of "winning" was gone, so business was terrible.

As a result, I didn't return in the summer of 1957, Fascination couldn't afford me. So, I went to Los Angeles where I stayed with Pearl and Larry, instead. They were living in East Los Angeles, several miles from downtown.

The breweries added extra employees in the summer, and by going to work for any of them, I could make good money bottling beer. I got a job at 102 Brewery, where I became a temporary member of the bottlers' union. The hourly wage was exorbitant, but that suited me fine. I needed to make enough money for my tuition.

The Bottler's Union dictated that you worked seven and a half hours a day, and be paid for eight, got a half hour off for lunch, and received a ten minute "beer break," every hour. On this break, you were permitted to drink as much free beer as you wanted. What a summer! I put on twenty pounds.

Business at Liberty Motors was thriving and Ed loaned me one of his junker cars for the duration of my Hollywood sojourn. With it, I toured the city of Los Angeles, learning my way around. When I graduated in 1958, that's where I was planning to return, to make my big splash in the Movies. Ha!

EMERSON
The Final Years and the First Degree
Chapter Lucky Thirteen

For my Sophomore year, I got a room at 103 Beacon Street, in the servants' quarters, on the fifth floor. Where else? We called it the Starlight Roof.

Dorothea Leboff, a Senior at Emerson, lived at one end of the hall and I at the other. There was a room next to her, and another one next to me. Over the year, various weirdos came, stayed, and went.

Our floor had its own kitchen and bathroom. Dottie and I, occasionally, made meals for each other when we weren't eating at the Riverside Cafeteria, on Charles Street. She would be graduating in June, ready to "go out into the world," but was quite apprehensive about it. My job became instilling confidence in her.

She was naïve and innocent, yet, wore a leopard skin bathrobe, to and from her room. I kidded her mercilessly about wearing that "sexy" robe, and how well she would fit in at a bordello. She blushed, but enjoyed the teasing.

Her major was English Literature, so she didn't appear in any plays at school, although she would have liked to. One day, the playwriting class was auditioning actors for their productions, and I talked her into trying out. She wanted a glamorous part, but got the role of a slovenly landlady. That didn't please her, but we had great fun working on the role. It was a big stretch for her to play that part, but with exaggerated, sluttish makeup, she did it well. Her acting chops were whetted.

For their Platform Reading Class, Nan Hellegers had put together an hour version of "The King and I," in which she played, and sang, all the characters. She was the perfect Anna, and actually, not bad as the King. Platform Reading was an exciting course to take; you didn't need any other actors, you played all the parts by yourself. As a matter of fact, our teacher, June Mitchell, did a "reading" of "You Can't Take it With You," playing all eighteen characters. That was a feat!

Dottie could sing quite well, so the two of us edited an hour version of "South Pacific," for her class. That was a major undertaking. During rehearsals, she did a great job as Bloody Mary, singing "Bali H'ai," and as Nelly Forbush, singing "Cockeyed Optimist." It was performed in her class, and she got a very good grade.

After graduation, Dottie went to work for a P.R. firm in Boston, which led to her career in journalism.

For several years, our friend Toby Seymour studied acting with Stella Adler in New York City, but is now back in Boston, using her Armenian

name of Lorraine Seymourian. She writes for several publications and has her own radio and television shows. The three of us are still friends, today.

Dottie, along with her amiable husband, Harvey Snyder, always gives "Miss Lorraine" a helping hand, in all her endeavors.

Ed and Helen added to their family on November 15, 1956. That's when daughter Faye was born. Big sister Jayne was now nine years old, and loved having a little sister to care for. They were living in an up-and-coming, new town, called La Mirada, where they would reside until the girls grew up, and moved away.

Ed had finished building his boat, L'il Toot, and moored it in The Long Beach Marina, where it still floats.

A few doors down from our rooming house, at 111 Beacon street, stands The Butera School of Art. Always needing a few extra dollars, I applied there for a modeling job. After all, I had done some posing at Ringling. Of course, they only needed Life Models (that meant posing nude), so, naturally, I volunteered. If it was good enough for Charlton Heston, it was good enough for me.

The evening before my first job, I stopped by the nightclub at the Copley Square Hotel, which had the same ambiance as the John Ringling Hotel. Looking around at all the babes, I espied a good looking brunette sitting at a table with an older woman. Oh, my God! Could that be Wanda Barton? It looked like a mature version of the teenage girl I had known in Sarasota.

Excitedly, I walked up to her, expecting a happy reunion. She just gawked at me, and said she had no idea who I was. I reminded her of the many meals she had served me at the lunch counter, and of our "date" on the beach. Again, she denied knowing me. Boy, was my ego fractured.

In reality, she seemed a little intimidated by the older woman, who didn't say a word, not even hello, or goodbye. She just smirked. What kind of relationship was this? Sadly, I gathered up what was left of my self-esteem, and left.

The next morning, I was to report to Butera for my first modeling assignment. I had no embarrassment at all about posing in my jock strap. When it was time, I stood on my pedestal, dropped my robe, and struck a pose. Peggy, the nude model at Ringling, would have been proud.

After about ten minutes, standing there in all my glory, who should come into the classroom? Wanda. This time, she recognized me, but without saying a word, she walked up to the mantle piece, in the rear of this grand old Victorian living room, and put her purse on the ledge, staring at me, all the while.

Then, she took a pile of money out of her purse and laid it on the shelf. One by one, she straightened out the bills by putting them in nice piles, grinning lewdly at me, as she did it. That was the first time I felt naked. After class, she sped away, still not speaking to me. She never did. Ah, well. *C'est la vie!*

Nan Hellegers became very ill and was hospitalized with Multiple Schlerosis. Toby packed up two pints of ice cream in dry ice, and she and I went to visit her. Her body was so twisted, she could barely move, but she presented a valiant, smiling face, and was thrilled that we brought her the ice cream.

"Oh Toby, you've saved my life! You've saved my life!" Nan did tend to over dramatize her appreciation. She loved to eat, but this time, she wasn't able. So Toby and I fed the ice cream to her. Again, she sighed, "You saved my life."

After finishing the ice cream, she confided to us that the doctor told her she would never walk again. What a terrible thing to say to a patient.

"That doctor doesn't know what the Hell he's talking about," I chided. "You know damned well, you'll be walking in no time at all."

She agreed. Nan was and is, a very spiritual person, and *knew,* that through prayer, she would be well, again. This stately, voluptuous girl looked so tiny, and helpless in her hospital bed, as we left. But, cheerfully, she said her goodbyes.

Several days later, Toby, Dottie, and I went to see her, again, bringing more ice cream, of course. Determined to look her best, she wore a sheer, pink nightgown, that barely stayed on her shoulders. As hard as she tried, Nanny did not look well.

With the use of a walker, she attempted to show us that she could walk. Her two feet were turned inward, so that the sides dragged on the floor. Only the strength of her arms kept her from falling. Holding onto the walker, and with all her might, she managed to, painfully, slide two or three steps.

"I'll show them. They're not going to keep Nan Hellegers down."

She was right. Within a year, in high heeled shoes, wearing a sexy out-fit, and with the aid of an ornate cane, she was, again, strutting her stuff down Beacon Street and Commonwealth Avenue. When the men whistled at her, she was happy. Adoration was a very good medicine for Nan. After she ditched the cane, she was back to her old self, never looking back, and was as glamorous as ever.

In our final year at Emerson, I moved into her building on Commonwealth Avenue. Bob Gillespie, a friend of hers, lived in the same apartment house and was looking for a roommate. So, she introduced us. Compared to the other places I had lived over the previous three years, his was a palace. No way could I afford it!

Bob was making good money at I.B.M., so he made me an offer I couldn't refuse. It had a big convertible sofa-bed in the living room for me to sleep on, and of all things, a television, to watch. I was in heaven. The only problem, it was a good fifteen minute walk to the school — freezing cold in the winter.

After graduation, in 1958, she and Bob were the first to go to Los

Angeles, blazing the way for me to arrive after my summer session at Fascination ended.

Nan got a job as a coat model, while Bob worked at an employment agency. He was a good bullshit artist, so before long, he got a job at a top Theatrical Agency. Surely he would be able to help me to break into the "business." He didn't.

Nan was engaged to a minister, who jilted her for someone else. She was devastated, but nothing ever kept Nanny down, for long. After no time, she fell in love again, and got married, again, and again.

Over the years, we've been through many difficult times together, but have always managed to keep our senses of humor. I've seen her through three husbands, and all kinds of adversity.

Now, in 2010 she is living, very contentedly, in Las Vegas, with husband number four, Nestor Landeira.

Even though she's had several major operations, and Chemo-therapy, she is recuperating beautifully, and is as gorgeous as ever, still looking like a young girl. She doesn't believe in getting old. She never will.

Timothy J. Kelly was a very talented student, who not only was a versatile actor, playing such roles as The Wolf Boy in "Dark of the Moon," and the Soda Jerk in "Wonderful Town, but was a prolific writer.

He went on to become "The World's Most Published Playwright," with over three hundred plays in print with Samuel French, Pioneer Drama Service, Contemporary Drama Service, and others.

For his Master's Thesis, he wrote, and directed "Bright Boy," a drama about a fading movie star who falls in love with, and marries, an Italian actress. Lucrezia was a cross between Sophia Loren and Gina Lollobrigida. Italian actresses were all the rage, then.

The leading character was a Tony Curtis-type leading man, who had worked in the Yiddish Theatre. He changes his name to Toddy MacLean, the antithesis of Bernie Rosenblatt. Because the character's name was MacLean, I was sure that, one of Emerson's better actors, Peter MacLean, would get the part. Fortunately for me, he was a little too "Shakespearian," so the role went to me.

The production opened on March 21, 1956, and was very successful. I was ecstatic to play a movie star in this hyper-dramatic, original play. I emulated Curtis, by twisting some hair down on my forehead, into a curl.

Years later, in Hollywood, when I was actually old enough to play the part, I tried to get Tim to do a production, but the idea didn't appeal to him; he had too many other new plays he wanted to present. "Bright Boy" was a thing of his past.

The set was beautifully executed by scenic designer/costumer

Anne De Coursey. A portrait of my character was needed, so I painted it myself, and it was hung over the fireplace, by Anne. The lighting was done by upcoming lighting designer Lincoln Stulik, which set the mood of the scenes, beautifully. He went on to become one of the top lighting designers in New York City.

Two of our cast members in "Bright Boy," became big successes in the Movies and Television: Dick Dysart and Ramon Bieri. And, of course, Don Perkins, sporting a moustache and hat in this production, had a big career in Musicals, on and off Broadway. I could never get him to come to Hollywood to ply his wares.

Richard "Doc" Dysart played in the original Broadway Production of "That Championship Season," as well as countless character parts in films and television. His big breakthrough came when he played Leland McKenzie, the primary partner in "L.A. Law."

He and Don Perkins had been good friends, at Emerson, before going into the service. When they got out, each resumed his studies, and they became roommates.

They had a basement appartment on Charles Street, almost next to the 77 Club, where the two of them guzzled beer, almost daily.

The entrance to their flat was only four steps down from the very busy, Charles Street. Any passer-by could look right into their living room. As a result, their door was always open to any friend who happened to pass by, either before or after their visit to the "Sevens." How they ever learned their lines, and gave the remarkable performances they did, is astonishing.

In "Bright Boy," Dick played my "friend" and agent. He was wonderful to work with because he gave so much of himself when he performed. From the beginning, he was a superior actor, playing mostly character parts, such as King Claudius to Perk's Hamlet. He could get in and out of character in a trice.

209

During rehearsals of "Hamlet," he had a very dramatic scene where he was on his knees, praying. Gertrude Binley Kay, the director, told him to stop at a certain point in the speech, and to pause for three beats. When that pause came, he turned his head upstage, and, with a big grin, he sang, "One o'clock, two o'clock, three o'clock, Rock." Then, soberly, he returned to his dramatic rants and raves. Everyone backstage would break up, but he always managed to get back into character.

Barbara Dow was working as Stage Manager during this show and would run to gather anyone, and everyone, to see this display of devious discipline.

"Doc" always played older, character types, and never considering himself a leading man. One summer, however, at Martha's Vineyard, "Maggie" Kay insisted he play the role of Hal, the muscle guy, in William Inge's "Picnic." Even though he was chunky, and not muscular, he dieted like crazy, worked out a little, and somehow created the illusion that he was a "hunk." It's amazing what good acting can achieve. This was *not* one of his favorite roles.

Even though he and Don played the lead in many of the major productions at Emerson, neither was averse to playing smaller roles. Doc had a bit part, playing a sharecropper, in "Finian"s Rainbow," while Perk and I pranced around in the chorus.

His best performance, at Emerson, was that of the doomed John Proctor in Arthur Miller's play about the Salem witch trials, "The Crucible."

At the same time, Boston University was producing its own version with famed Broadway director, Jose Quintero. Those who saw both, liked our production better. The nuance and range of Dick's performance was incredible. I can still hear him saying, "I have given you my life. Leave me my *soul!*"

Tim Kelly played The Reverend Hale, Ray Bieri played Giles Corey, and I played John Willard, the jailer.

Ramon "Ray" Bieri was Emerson's leading man, and got to play most of those kinds of parts. He was my competition all through college. For a time, I resented him, because every part I went after, he got. The first part he got was Woody, the lead in "Finian's Rainbow," though I did manage to understudy the role.

Ray was a versatile actor, and followed direction perfectly. That's probably why he got so many good parts. I was more curious, and asked too many questions of the directors, and probably made a nuisance of myself.

We both went after the lead role of Bob Baker, in "Wonderful Town." Neither of us got it. Some new kid dropped in, from out of the blue, and sang "My Boy Bill," from "Carousel," so beautifully, that he got the part. Ray did play Wreck, the dopey football player, though, and was quite funny. I was the lead chorus member, playing several parts, and opening the show as the Greenwich Village guide. I did understudy The Lead, again. Ah well, always the bridesmaid!

When Leo Nickole was casting "Guys and Dolls," I thought for sure I would play the part of Sky Masterson. You guessed it, Ray got the part, but I did manage to grab the character lead of Nathan Detroit. Actually, I liked my part better. It got all the laughs.

Vivian Blaine, the original Adelaide on Broadway, was in town playing in "A Hatful of Rain." Our director, Leo Nickole, invited her to come to one of our rehearsals. With a tear in her eye, she quietly observed, from the back of the theatre, while Elaine Zimmerman sang, "Adelaide's Lament." Neither Ray nor I had a chance to strut our stuff in front of Miss Blaine; this was Elaine's show.

In our final year, the two of us had the opportunity to do our best work. He played Lennie to my George in John Steinbeck's, "Of Mice and Men." Lincoln Stulik, the lighting nut, was our director. With his lighting, he was able to create the most marvelous moods for the production.

Even though Ray and I were the same height, by my slouching, and him looming like a bear, we created the illusion that he was much bigger than I. After doing that show, I was no longer envious of Ray. We became friends.

This gentle, soft spoken guy played many rednecks, and rabble rousers, in the movies, and television. In his first film, "The Grasshopper," he played the hood who beat the Hell out of Jacqueline Bisset. In "Reds," he played the villainous police captain. On television, he co-starred, with James Garner, in the short-lived, 1981 series, "Bret Maverick," and was the lead in Norman Lear's, "Joe's World."

He didn't become the star that Dick Dysart became, but he never stopped working as an actor, appearing in hundreds of T.V. shows, making a very good living. He was one of our "gang" of Emersonians, who lived in Los Angeles. Over the years, we all got together, often. Of that group, Tim Kelly, Peter MacLean, and Ray have all died.

Peter MacLean was the youngest of our group of thespians, and an

amazing Shakes-pearian actor. He played Tybalt to Don Perkin's Romeo, and Laertes to his Hamlet.

During the run of "Hamlet," at one performance, they "dropped" an entire scene. No problem, the two of them ad-libbed, in iambic pentameter no less, and worked it back into a later scene, while Dick Dysart,

as the King, and I looked on.

He excelled in playing the classics, and at that time, that is all he wanted to do. He was big and bold on the stage, but very shy around girls, that is until he met his nemesis, Dorothy Geotis. She set her eye on him, and got him.

He was the most powerful, classical actor at Emerson, so, I cast him to play Jason, in Jean Anouilh's, "Medea," which I directed. It was quite a dramatic production, giving him the opportunity to "strut and fret his hour upon the stage." No one could have done it better.

The part of Medea was played by Nancy Newman, another of our versatile actors, who also played my housekeeper, in "Bright Boy." Barbara Dow was very effective playing the ancient Nurse; she was always best when playing drama. "Suffering" came easy to her.

Once he got out of college, and married Dotty, he and she had a fairly good career in the theatre. He made a few good movies, his first being a priest in "The Cardinal," in 1963. He also played the bank president, whose family is held hostage, in "The Friends of Eddy Coyle." Yes, he did learn to do other things besides Shakespeare.

On television, he guest starred in many Series, and was a regular on "General Hospital," "Days of Our Lives," "The Secret Storm," and "Where the Heart is," as well as appearing in the pilot of "Fantasy Island."

Dotty is quite an actress in her own right. She was never the "leading Lady" type, so she specialized in zany character parts. At Emerson, she played the kooky General in "Guys and Dolls." Drama was her forte, as well.

In "A View From the Bridge," she portrayed the long suffering wife of a longshoreman, while I played Rodolfo, an illegal alien. In Eugene O'Neill's "Great God Brown," she played Margaret. After I graduated, she got the lead in "Bloomer Girl," and many other shows, after that.

n his later years, Peter played Buffalo Bill at Euro-Disney, outside Paris, France, and Dotty played "Diamond Lil." His likeness is still used in all the advertising.

Dotty hasn't had the successes Peter had; she was busy raising two girls and a boy. In Hollywood, she was frenetically funny in a short, French Farce film, I produced, called, *"Une Soiree Elegante."* She played my wife, singing the campiest version of *La Habanera* you would ever want to see.

Under her stage name of Dorothy Constantine, she has made many guest appearances in movies and television. She is still, out there in Hollywood, working every chance she gets.

Rochelle (Shelley) Kaplan was a gawky Freshman who had a crush on me. She followed me everywhere, awkwardly trying to flirt, but usually giggled instead.

I was cast in Arthur Miller's, "A View From the Bridge," as the gentle, blond Italian boy. When Shelley found out, she approached me immediately. It seemed that her mother owned a beauty salon, and they would be able to turn my hair blond. No charge. Of course, I agreed.

Her mother was the nicest person in the world. She knew I would be embarrassed to sit in a women's beauty parlor, so she scheduled me for after the shop closed. The two Kaplans did an amazing job on my hair. It was quite a sight to see.

I thought that blond hair would make me look too pretty, but it didn't. I looked more like a hood, instead. When I went into a store, I seemed to intimidate people. They looked at me very suspiciously, and seemed to cower. I loved it!

Mama Kaplan invited me to Sunday brunch. Her table had, perhaps, ten or twelve people stuffing their faces. People came and went, and Mrs. Kaplan happily made each one what he or she wanted to eat, and she did it joyously.

She offered to make me a steak. My eyes lit up, but I declined. That didn't stop her. She grilled me the most delicious steak I ever had. It had been a long time since I had eaten one. She invited me to stop by, any Sunday, for a steak. She really meant it. What a delightful, giving lady!

Shelley had a high, giggly voice, and was naturally funny. Of course, she wanted to play serious parts. She asked me if I would do a scene with her for her acting class. Why not? She chose Eugene O'Neill's, "Mourning Becomes Electra," where she would play the beautiful, sensual Kristine, and I was to play her incestuous son, Orrin, who had to hug and kiss her. She was in Heaven.

Actually, the scene didn't go badly. The teacher, Leo Nickole, was quite impressed. Unfortunately, he still didn't cast her in any parts; she usually worked on the stage crew.

In her pursuit, she came to visit me, one summer, in Atlantic City. She wanted to meet my Jewish family and friends. Ruth was, as always, a gracious hostess, treating

her like a daughter. She and Connie hit it off, too. To see my two Yentas, gabbing a mile a minute, was a sight to see.

Shelley is responsible for my going into the newspaper business. In March of 1968, when she and her future husband, Allan Abrams, came to Los Angeles, they introduced me to Allan's uncle, Lee Ross. Through him, I got the idea to publish my very successful theatrical publication, the *Drama-Logue*, which I sold to *Billboard* Publications in 1998. But that's another story.

Shelley and Alan stayed in Los Angeles, and over the years, along with all the other ex-Emersonians, we have remained good friends.

The head of the English Department at Suffolk University, Dr. Ella Murphy, was looking for someone to restart their Drama Club. June Mitchell recommended me, and I got the job. Suffolk is a Law School and had a wonderful assortment of conscientious students wanting to hone their "performance" skills, by acting in the productions.

The first year we opened with four one act plays. The "Contessa," Helen Teitelbaum, was sweet enough to do the makeup. Yvonne Kalman assisted her. She was the daughter of Emmerich Kalman, the famous Hungarian composer of operettas. Yes, another blonde Hungarian girl!

Some of the cast members included Annie Young, Candy Kreutel, Celia Letorney, Kathy Flower, Maureen Sugrue, and Jeanne McCarthy.

One of my students was a tall, skinny kid, named Paul Benedict, who desperately wanted to act. I cast him as one of the four guys in, "If Men Played Cards as Women Do," and later that year, as Donald, the "on relief" boyfriend of the maid, in "You Can't Take it With You."

In the second year, he played the bumbling Detective Blore in "Ten Little Indians." Unfortunately, there was no part for him in "Picnic," so he became the stage manager. For all of the productions, he oversaw the set construction and, conscientiously, worked behind the scenes.

What he lacked in acting talent, he made up for in exuberance. He was diligent and determined. Nothing was going to hold him back. And nothing did.

Years later, he played Bentley, the British neighbor, on "The Jeffersons" television series. His career lasted many years. He appeared in numerous films and stage productions, playing mostly loony characters. On December 1, 2008, he was found dead in his apartment, in Martha's Vineyard.

After my two years of teaching at Suffolk, I turned over the reins to Peter MacLean. He stayed on for an additional two years, until it was time for him to graduate. Then, he and Dotty got married, and went to New York to tread the boards, and seek their fortune.

Two thirteen week radio series, for WEEI Radio Station, was produced in 1957/58, by a fellow student, Gerald Lennick. The first series was "Famous Short Stories;" the second was "A Yankee Homecoming," a series about famous New Englanders. Performing Poe, O'Henry and the like, was great fun for us. I was the announcer/narrator of all the shows, as well as, an actor playing many roles.

Helen Teitelbaum was remarkable and versatile, playing a host of parts in all the dramatizations, often two or three characters in the same production. This nice Jewish girl played Mary Baker Eddy, the founder of the Christian Science Church (in a low-cut cocktail dress, no less), and Clara Barton, the founder of the Red Cross, in another sexy frock. She not only played these women as adults, she played some of them as babies, gurgling and cooing in their cribs. That was a sight to see!

During those last two years at school, we were seeing each other *almost* exclusively. One day, she and I were nearly entrapped into eloping. Her close friend, Kay Wishengrad, tried to make it happen by borrowing a convertible to drive us to Connecticut. Again, I said no, just as I did with Joan Erbig, in Florida.

By the end of our final year together, she got tired of waiting for me. She met a drummer in a nightclub, where she and her best friend, June August, went to work as waitresses. His name was Saul Weisman, and they married the final week of the 1958 school semester.

Even though they were engaged, we still saw each other. I couldn't believe that she was actually going to go through with the wedding. She giggled about it, and said to me, as she dashed away to her ceremony, "Don't worry, we'll get married the next time."

Well, they're still married, and have a son, Craig, and a daughter, Robin, plus several grandchildren. Despite everything, we're still friends.

The Fraternities produced Comedy Revues each year. They were usually written by Tim Kelly. Even then, he was quite prolific. My fraternity, Phi Alpha Tau, produced a Musical Comedy Farce called "Bring 'em Back Alive," a mishmash of acts, skits, songs and dances.

Naturally, I reprieved my Apache Dance, to "Blue Violins." This time, I had a professional dancer, Miss Connecticut, as a partner. It went over well, but I must say, I enjoyed my two previous amateurs more.

Barbara Dow is the last person on earth you would expect to play a *femme*

fatale, she was just too wholesome. The part of a Western Dance Hall hostess, who sings the Eva Tanguay song, "I Don't Care," was available for one of the shows. Barbara is definitely not a singer, but I figured she could "talk" the song through, so I worked with her on the routine.

She wore a tight, emerald green corset-like costume, all covered with spangles, and fringes, and feathers. Her long legs were covered with fish net stockings, and she wore a jeweled garter above her left knee.

I did her makeup, giving her big red lips, and turquoise blue eye shadow. She was embarrassed, but brought the house down, sexily strutting across the stage, with a long cigarette holder. Boys began seeing her in a new light.

Helen Teitelbaum brought the house down, too, with her impression of Marilyn Monroe, and with black hair, no less. Standing center stage, without leaving her spot, she heaved, and shimmied, and purred, in an enticing display of sensuality.

She was beautiful, and a natural born comedienne, and should have played many other parts at Emerson, but she hated to rehearse. She loved to come in at the last minute, and fill in for somebody; that excitement is what she craved.

For the part of Violet, the "Lady of the Night," in "Wonderful Town," she did have to rehearse, but only minimally. There were so many other things that kept her busy; what they were, I couldn't tell you, but she was always in perpetual motion.

My four years at Emerson College was the best time of my life. I learned, and did, so much there, as well as making so many life-long friends, too many to write about here. I hope that those not mentioned will forgive me. I still think of them, often, and love them all.

On June 15, 1958, I graduated with a Bachelor of Arts degree in English, and Theatre Arts. The ceremony was held in the Old South Church, in Copley Square. Like high school, I can't remember a thing about it. It must have happened though, because I still have my diploma, and tassel from my cap.

The final week was hectic. We performed the Sophocles Greek Tragedy, "Antigone," at the Hatch Shell of the Boston Esplanade. Dick Dysart played King Creon, Don Perkins played his tragic son, Haeman, while I was part of the Greek Chorus.

Done as a Platform Reading, Ray Bieri and I effectively reprised the first and last scenes from "Of Mice and Men," for the Alumni.

216

After the 1958 summer season at Fascination, I was off to Holly-wood, to become a movie star. That's another book!

2010:

WHERE ARE THEY NOW?

EPILOGUE

PAPA: After living quietly with Margit for twelve years, Papa Died April 12, 1961, two weeks before his seventy-second birthday. They were visiting Sam and Betty in Florida, when he had an apparent heart attack.

He had been a health nut all his life, watching everything he ate, and exercising fairly frequently, including standing on his head "to get everyting moving goot." Still, for some reason, he died earlier than he should have.

The examining physician wrote, "Acute Myocardial Insufficiency" on his death certificate. I guess it was an educated guess, we'll never know for sure what it was.

Sam shipped the body back to Pittsburgh, where he was buried next to Mama, at Jefferson Memorial Park, in Jefferson Township.

MARIE: When her three boys grew up, Marie sold her house on Hendricks Island, and moved to an apartment in Coral Ridge. For years she improved, managed, and sold various apartment buildings, before finally retiring to a condominium in Pompano Beach. Here, her portrait did not overwhelm the room; it was hung over her sofa.

To keep her head above water, for many seasons, she would sublet her condo, and move in with Sam and Betty.

Duane got a government scholarship to medical school, and became a doctor. He studied at Johns Hopkins Hospital, in Baltimore, and interned at the V.A. Hospital, in Los Angeles.

Butch went into the Marine Corps, right out of High School, and later became a Medical Occupational Therapist, specializing in geriatrics. Jim became a top salesman for the Saint Grobain Corporation, a construction supply corporation.

Shortly, after his graduation, Duane married another doctor, named Jan. So,

218

for a while, there were two Doctor Carmalts roaming around. They divorced, and I believe she is still using the name of Carmalt.

Years later, Duane married Patti, a psychoanalyst, who had a sixteen year old son by a previous marriage. She and Duane had a son of their own, called Zachary, born September 2, 1988, the day after Marie's death.

Butch married a Pittsburgh girl named Kathryn Blacker, on April 17, 1968, in North Miami Beach. He handled venomous snakes, and wrestled alligators, from 1969 to 1974, at Flamingo Gardens in Davie, Florida. The two of them, with a thirteen foot alligator, went to Atlantic City to stay with Ruth, and to perform at The Million Dollar Pier, the summers of '73 and '74.

They had two sons, Michael, who was born on February 18, 1969, and Brian, December 11, 1974. Michael married Dianna Beighle on August 10, 1996, in West Palm Beach. Their son, Alexander Ley, was born December 2, 1998, and their daughter, Lillian Elizabeth, was born June 17, 2002.

Brian moved to Germany, and married Julia Schimmann, from Bremen, on July 5, 2002. They have two daughters: Ava Elizabeth, born on July 26, 2002; and Thea Marie, born September 19, 2009.

Jim Straker married and divorced, then married Marcy Elliott in Charlottesville, Virginia, on September 8, 1979. Christopher James was born to them on August 19, 1981, and Erin Marie was born July 1, 1985. Erin Marie married Christopher Robinson on April 17, 2010.

Marie often visited Duane in California, who lived way out in the toolies; so, half the time, she stayed with me at my house. She brought Michael for a visit in the early '70s, and Brian in the mid to late '70s. They both reminded me so much of their dad, when he was little, that I called them both, Little Butch.

On her last visit with Brian, she tripped over a telephone wire and fell. Like Mama, she had had cancer, and probably, this fall started it up, again. Duane did his best to comfort her, but you could see the panic on her face.

She died on September, 1, 1988, two weeks before her seventy-fifth birthday. Memorial services were held on September 14th, at the Coral Ridge Presbyterian Church. Her best friend, Nellie Starr, and her three beautiful daughters, along with Marie's three boys, attended.

MARTHA: The first big obstacle Martha had to overcome was in the mid-'60s.

Marilyn went to work for a Senator with seven children, in Washington, D.C. She had an affair with him, and became pregnant. The baby boy only lived for a few months.

The next man in her life was Raji, an Indian student, who lived next door to her. On one of her visits to Atlantic City, while sipping Chevez Regal Scotch, she related their story to me.

There had been a huge book-case in her room, that separated their two apartments. Raji had been in some sort of an altercation, and when his "guest" left,

he got so angry that he banged on the back of the bookcase, pushing it over into Mame's apartment. The boom scared the Hell out of her.

Then, seeing "this great Indian Raja" standing before her, alongside her heap of scattered books, she took it as some kind of an omen. When those "Walls of Jericho" tumbled down, their relationship began.

A year or two after her baby died, she fell in her shower, hitting the tender spot on her head, and died of a brain hemorrhage. She had lain there, in that shower, for several days, before she was found by her landlady.

Martha and Joe had a terrible time coping with the untimely death. Ruth immediately went to D.C. to help them through their crisis. Marie had come as well. It was Ruth who went to identify the body at the Mortuary.

After much deliberation, they decided to donate Marilyn's eyes, and other organs, to the medical center before her cremation. Her ashes were placed over the grave of her dead baby.

The Jogeeses' troubles were not over. They lost their Lewis-Sheppard franchise, lost all their investment in the business, and were flat broke. Joe was nearing sixty, not the best time to search for employment. Somehow, he got a job selling batteries for a company in Houston, Texas.

Lizabeth adapted to her new surroundings well, and after graduating from high school, she went to work as an assistant editor for an Oil Trade Magazine. Later, I tried to get her to come and work for me, at my publication, in Hollywood, but she preferred staying in Texas, with her pot smoking boy friend.

Martha kept busy by working as a rental agent for a major shopping center. After Joe retired, he made model ships and trains in the bedroom. His eyesight was failing, but it gave him something to do, and it was a respite from Martha's chattering.

Each year, Martha went to Florida, or came to California, for a visit. We always had a great time together. So long as she had her vodka and fresh orange juice, she was happy. At the stroke of 5 p.m., she had her little drinky-poo.

All my friends, in California, loved her, and enjoyed listening to her far-fetched, entertaining stories. Of course, she was always so "lady-like," puffing on a cigarette, sipping her drink, and never speaking over a whisper.

After Joe died, she lost her job. This was too difficult for her to handle. She was accustomed to getting up every morning and walking to the real estate office. After she was fired, she just stopped doing anything, except her crossword puzzles, watching T.V., and sipping cocktails. She slowly deteriorated, losing most of her vitality and excitement.

Liz became a drug addict, and really wasn't in the best shape, herself, to take care of her mother, so she put Martha in a nursing home. She hated it there, and to spite everybody, she stopped eating, stopped answering her phone, and just wasted away.

When she became hospitalized, Sam and Betty drove in from Florida, while Pearl and I flew in from L.A., to see her. She was not conscious. Betty held her hand, trying to get her to talk, but no luck. A few days later, on July 10, 1999, she died at the age of eighty-three. We still don't know what she died of. One can only suppose that this funny, fascinating woman died because she no longer wanted to live.

KATY AND CLARENCE: The Schotters sold their Wexford home and moved to Phoenix. They lived there for many years near Danny and his bride Donna, who were married on June 23, 1979. They had twin girls, Summer and Taya, on May 28, 1985.

After a while, those Schotters relocated in Tucson. Later, Kay and Clarence moved to California for quite a few years, where we, jointly, had many family reunions.

In late 1960, Linna went to California, and visited with Pearl and Larry. She liked California and decided to stay.

Before long, she met Ken Ainslie and they married in an outdoor chapel, on a beautiful bluff, overlooking the Pacific Ocean, on June 8, 1974. Their delightful daughter, Jenifer, was born on October 14, 1977.

Jen came to Sarasota for her girlfriend's wedding in 2003. We had lunch together, and I could swear that I was talking to Linna; they both had that same sweet face, and were so much alike.

The following year, she married Mitch Daugherty on November 20, 2004, and had a daughter, Keara Lin, on September 20, 2008.

Linna divorced Ken, and became a Medical Technician in a major Los Angeles hospital where she met her future husband, John Ritums. They married on November 22, 1980. Their son Paul was born on September 29, 1982, and their daughter Krista, on September 11, 1984.

They moved to Lake Oswego, Oregon, and all three kids graduated from the University of Washington. Linna is still a medical technician, Ken sells Real Estate.

While living in California, Kay had major surgery in 1994, when she had her esophagus removed. No one has ever survived that surgery for more than a year, except, of course, Katy.

As of this writing, in 2010, Kay and Clarence are still "alive and kicking" in King City, Oregon, where they go for walks almost every day, holding each other up, and amazing all their friends and family, with their dexterity.

SAM AND BETTY: They stayed in Ft. Lauderdale, for many years, at 1514 N. W. 11th Street. Betty drove a Broward County school bus for thirty-three years, and Sam ran the laundry facility at the Broward General Hospital, until his retirement.

Denise married Larry Wheeler on October 14, 1972. She told me, she picked him up at a Drive-in restaurant because he "looked so cute, sitting in his Corvette Convertible."

They dated four or five years, until Sam told him to "shit or get off the pot!" Then, they set the date. They have no children.

Sam, III, married Terri Polley on July 1, 1978. They have three sons: Jonathan, born on December 13, 1982; David, on March 13, 1985; and Benjamin, on April 10, 1992.

After Denise and Sammy grew up, and got married, Sam and Betty bought a new house, and moved to 4601 N.W. 41st Place. Sammy and Terri moved nearby to 4345 N.W. 41st Terrace. Denise and Larry bought a house and moved to Pompano.

In the early '90s, Larry discovered a wooded fairyland in Lily, Florida. They purchased several acres, built their own home, and are living there today. Sam and Betty purchased the adjoining property, installed a double-wide trailer, and proceeded to spend several week-ends a month there, until Sam officially retired. Then they sold their Lauderdale home, and moved into the double wide, way out in the boondocks.

Many of our family reunions took place in their jungle paradise, as well as my California home, in Toluca Lake. One year, Betty thought it would be a good idea to go on a family cruise. Many of them commenced in Florida.

So, for a while, we took several family cruises, together. They were great fun. We'd get several rooms across from each other, sneak our own booze aboard ship, and party. The women, especially, preferred these reunions; they didn't have to cook or cater.

After sixty years of marriage, and several years of fighting cancer, Betty died on March 24, 2009. She is buried in the nearby Lily Cemetery, only about a quarter of a mile from her home. Sam stops by, most days, to visit with her.

ED: After many year of marriage to Helen, they divorced. When the girls grew up, Ed was ready for a new adventure.

He met, and married, a German girl named Margot. She had been married to an old boating buddy of his, named Gerhardt. She, Gerhardt, Ed, and Ed's boat L'il Toot, all appeared in one of my movies.

Ed played a "dirty old man," (typecasting if there ever was one), Margot was the "sugar mama" to a young guy, and Gerhardt was the accordion playing Captain of L'il Toot.

Margot was the love of his life. She adored him, and doted on his every wish, calling him *schatze*, the same term of endearment Mama used to call him. The two of them had so much fun together, drinking and partying, perhaps a little too much. Margot had liver problems and wasn't suppose to drink. She tried to stop, but just couldn't. At the age of fifty-two, she died of cirrhosis of the liver.

She was cremated, and Faye picked up the ashes, bringing them to the Long Beach Marina, where L'il Toot was moored. All their boating friends followed L'il Toot, out into the bay. The Reverend said a few words, and Margot's ashes were poured into the water.

There were about twenty boats attending the services, and all aboard threw flowers into the water. It was quite a sight, seeing all the beautiful flowers floating over, what had once been, Margot.

Faye came with her husband, David Frears, who she had married in 1979. In 1985, she came to work for me at *Drama-Logue*, and worked her way up to Editor-in-Chief. There, she stayed, until I sold the paper to *Billboard*

Publication in 1998.

Their daughter, Adelyn Jayne, was born on August 30, 1990. At the age of fifty-one, Faye died, unexpectedly, of complications following surgery, on April 28, 2008. Ed was heartbroken, and went into a deep funk. He, perhaps, mourned, and drank, a bit too much, leading to a stroke on Christmas Eve, of that year.

Jayne came to work at *Drama-Logue*, several years after Faye. She had been working for Paramount Pictures and 20th Century Fox in the personnel department. Both jobs were only temporary. So, when she was laid off, she joined us at the paper selling advertising, along with Pearl.

For many years, she was engaged to Dennis, her high school sweetheart. They never married.

She is now teaching grade school, and living happily in Eagle Rock with her two dogs and cats.

After a year and two months in a nursing home, Ed is recuperating nicely, and is back home living in his trailer park, in Seal Beach.

RUTH: For several more summers, I had returned to work for Ruth at Fascination. She was a widow, and Bruce and Bobby needed a man's influence around them.

Once Paul Swetkoff, the co-owner of the Virginia Bar and Hotel, got a divorce, and was available, he and she started dating. The boys, especially Bobby, liked him, and soon they were married, on April 14, 1960. Now, Ruth had two businesses to "run," Fascination and the Virginia Hotel.

Initially, Paul and John Heaton only owned the Virginia Bar, but then they bought the adjoining hotel/motel. Pre-season, Ruth not only scoured and "flashed" Fascination, she now had an old, dilapidated hotel to get in shape. She cleaned and scrubbed, while Paul painted and mended.

During the season, the Virginia Bar was open all night. Many of the jazz musicians in town, as well as those from the bands that played the Steel Pier, started "jamming" in the bar. Once the hotel was in shape, almost all the bands that played The Steel Pier, began staying at their hotel, including the Stan Kenton Band.

Bruce couldn't wait to grow up. He got married to Jayne Taylor on June 21, 1968, a school teacher, several years his senior. That didn't last long, so he remained a bachelor for many years, until he met Barbara Kennedy. They married on April 1, 1988, and have no children. She and her family are in the automobile business, the same as Bruce.

Bobby married Danne Leest in 1978. The two of them worked as "dealers," in Las Vegas, preparing themselves to work in Atlantic City, when gambling would become legal. When that happened, he went to work at Caesar's Palace for three years. Their daughter Sabrina was born on May 13, 1979.

After his divorce from Danne, he married another casino "dealer," Dawn Parry, on June 26, 1993. She had twin daughters, Veronica and Marie, from a previous marriage. Bobby worked as a Pit Boss for twenty-four years at The

Sands Hotel, until it was torn down. He is, now, back at Caesar's Palace.

Paul and Ruth's daughter Sue was born on February 22, 1961. She met John Peterson, and married him on April 26, 1984 in Somers Point. Their son John, Jr. was born on March 2, 1986, and their daughter, Ashley, was born on April 1, 1993.

On April 22, 2006, Sabrina Mintz married Ryan Leavengood. They had a son, Jonah, who was born on November 18, 2008.

In June of 2000, Bruce and Barbara had a surprise seventh-fifth birthday party for Ruth. Sam, Betty, Pearl and I flew in for it, and had a great time.

PEARL: For several years, Larry worked as a bartender, and Pearl as a waitress, until they could afford to buy a cute little beer bar, in San Gabriel, called The Skip Inn. The two of them did all the work, and pulled all the shifts. The only time off they got was when, once in a while, I would pull a shift for them.

They stashed away every penny they could, until they saved enough to buy "The Roman Candle," a nice cocktail bar, in Culver City. Pearl, who hates to cook, not only waited on customers and served drinks, but she did all the cooking in the kitchen, as well.

She was quite a whiz, dashing around the bar, and back into the kitchen, serving everyone, quickly and efficiently. Of course, she didn't forget to "hustle" the drinks, too; that's where the money was made. Very little was made on the food.

When they sold the bar, Larry went to work for Wham-o, the toy company that created the hula-hoop. He worked himself up into a top position. On his watch the Frisbee was created. He stayed there until he retired.

His only desire seemed to be, going from a small boat, to a bigger one, and then to a bigger one. Pearl didn't like spending so much money on boats; it irked her, too, that there was no way of writing any of the expenses off on their tax forms. She would have preferred saving the money, for their retirement.

Pearl kept working at bookkeeping jobs, and waiting tables during the lunch hour. She could not sit at home, doing nothing. Eventually, she came to work for me at *Drama-Logue*, selling advertising and doing my books. She loved the job, even if it was a long commute from her home in Arcadia.

Larry was a little resentful of Pearl's success at *Drama-Logue* and wanted her to stay at home, and be a good little housewife. After all, he was making very good money at Wham-o! She was not willing to be a full time housewife. After twenty-five years of marriage, they divorced.

In 2000, Pearl moved to Port Charlotte, Florida, about forty miles from Sam and Betty. A year or so later I moved to Sarasota, where I had so much fun as a kid at Ringling Art School. I had always planned on retiring there.

SAM, PEARL, BILL, RUTH, KAY, ED AND MARTHA, CHRISTMAS 1986

SUE BORDY: Little did we know that Sue would be dead, after only a few more years of living.

The following is the affidavit of Wilbert N. Swartz, Jr.: "I am the owner of the Swartz Café located . . . across from West View Park parking lot. I have known the above named deceased for the past 6 years. She resided around the corner from my place of business and often frequented the café.

"On Monday, April 22, 1963, she was in the café in the early evening and left about 8:00 p.m. At closing time about 1:00 a.m., Tuesday, April 23, 1963, when my bartender, Charles Salak, left the café to go home, he spotted her car in the West View Park parking lot across the street. He went over to see if he could be of any assistance figuring she may have car trouble or be sick.

"When he saw blood on her face, he came to the café and informed me of his findings. I went back over to the car with him and when I saw the situation, I told him this is a police matter and immediately phoned the West View Police. They arrived, made an investigation and summoned Dr. Logan who pronounced death on the scene. The County Detectives and the Coroner were called and she was removed to the County Morgue pending disposition."

The following is the written report of Officer William Braun, dated April 23, 1963: "I proceeded to the parking lot of West View Park and met West View Police Chief Clogan and Officers Buchelmeyer and Kirscher. They stated they had received a call at 1:10 a.m. from Wm. Schwartz, owner of a tavern opposite the parking lot on Perry Highway. Schwartz had stated his bartender, Chas. Salak, [from] Allison Park, had discovered the above deceased in her car when he, Salak, had gone to get his car in the same lot after finishing work.

"The West View Police called Dr. Kenneth Logan, Ross Twp., who pronounced Miss Bordy dead at 1:30 a.m. Miss Bordy was seated in her car - 1957 Dodge - Penna. #867-472 - behind the steering wheel leaning to the left against the door jamb. She had a gunshot wound in her right temple. Her right hand was in her lap, also the gun used. The gun is a 32 cal. U.S. revolver #37289. It contained three loaded and one discharged shell.

"Dr. Logan stated she had been dead about 3-4 hrs. Miss Bordy left a suicide note. Chief Clogan talked with Mrs. Alice Teffel, Glenmore Ave., West View, a drinking companion of Miss Bordy, who stated that at 10:20 p.m. last evening Miss Bordy called her and said, 'Come on out, Alice, I have $3.00 and I'll buy our last drink together.'

"Alice told Miss Bordy that she was in bed and would not go out. Miss Bordy on a previous occasion told Alice that she was pregnant and that she had a gun and was going to kill herself. In addition, Mrs. Teffel had told Chief Clogan that Miss Bordy also told two other drinking companions that she had contemplated suicide.

"Dep. Coroners Charles and Calloway removed the body of Miss Bordy to the County Morgue, also the suicide note, gun and shells and her purse. Car was towed from the lot by the West View Police."

BILL BORDY: Hollywood was not easy. After arriving there, it took me quite a while to accustom myself to the strange environment. As I said, that's another book. But, I will gloss over some of the highlights.

For the first few years, it was very difficult trying to be a "star." I did manage to work a season of stock at the Laguna Playhouse. I acted with Bob Crane, who was making his stage debut, in "Send Me No Flowers," and with Karen Kupcinet, the daughter of Irv Kupcinet, the Chicago columnist, in "The

Miracle Worker." Ironically, both stars were mysteriously murdered, and neither murder has ever been solved.

In September of 1964, I got fed up with the Rat Race, and "retired" to Europe, for two years, spending a year in Paris, where I studied French at the Sorbonne, and tutored students in English. In London, I worked as a chef in The Chicken Inn. It was an awkward time for me, because the Hippies and the Mods were taking over the culture. I was in my early thirties, and too old for the young crowd, and two young for the older crowd, but I managed.

After returning to Hollwood, I had to start all over. In 1968, with the aid of Shelley Kaplan's "uncle-in-law," I started *Drama-Logue*. It took a while to get it off the ground, but eventually it made me a good living, and I became a minor celebrity.

During this time, I did manage to get a few acting and hosting jobs, but most of my time was taken by the growth of the paper. Once it got established, I did produce several minor movies, directing some, acting in all, and co-writing most.

My first endeavor was a short, French Farce called *"Une Soiree Elegante,"* written by Senta Smith. I, and Dotty MacLean, played husband and wife. It won a silver medal at The International Film and Television Festival in 1982.

When I first got to Los Angeles, I met, and got "involved" with, Barbara James. We had a very stormy, and erratic relationship. Except for about a ten year "gap," we are still "together."

In 1960, when Roger Corman was making all those horror movies based on the works of Edgar Allan Poe, Barbara and I wrote a script called "Annabel Lee." In it, I was to play the young artist. Low-budget producer, Mikel Conrad, was to produce and direct it, but he became Ill and died. It never got made.

I met Michael Rissi, and his wife Maria Lydia, on a trip to Europe. He is a young film maker who had one of his films distributed by the Corman Company. And, he knew who I was. Aha!

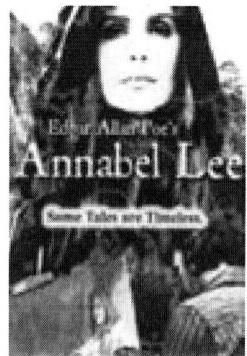

We decided, now was the time, to produce "Annabel." He did a rewrite of the script, and we shot the project in Santa Barbara. Instead of playing the young, leading man, I played the villain, the part that was intended for Vincent Price.

"Edgar Allan Poe's Annabel Lee" played to sold out performances at the Santa Barbara Film Festival of 2010. It has played several other film festivals, and we are still looking for distribution. Hopefully, by the time you read this book, you will be able to see the movie as well.